I Know Now

A WOMAN'S
HEALING

Violence to Victory

Trauma to Truth

Cinda Stevens Lonsway

To My Detective and To My Roommate

For your gentleness following the violence,
For your acknowledgement of my victory over it,
For your compassion through the trauma,
For your support while I discovered my truth.

Forever—thank you.

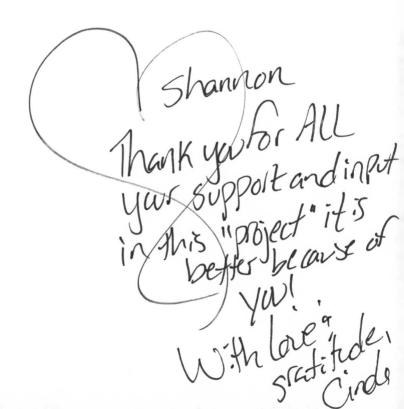

Shannon
Thank you for ALL
your support and input
in this "project" it is
better because of
you!.
With love &
gratitude,
Cindy

CONTENTS

INTRODUCTION

This is more than the story of a naive, vulnerable girl surviving a violent attack and the two horrific months that followed—*Part One*.

This is more than the story of a suffering, shattered mother trying to hold it together for her family and finally finding peace—*Part Two*.

This is more than the story of a wiser, healthier woman who now knows what it means to awaken to her own inner spirit and inner strength—*Part Three*.

This is a story of a girl's survival, a mother's healing and a woman's sacred insight.

This is an exploration, an expedition of a lifetime...from violence to victory, from trauma to truth.

I was that girl, the mother, this woman.

This is my story.

Part One

THE ATTACK

Now

There is a time in everyone's life when we wonder...*if I knew then what I know now, would I have done things differently?*

Looking back now...to 1981, when I was attacked by an intruder at the age of 19...I can't help but ask: *If I knew then what I know now...could I have responded in a more mature and reasonable way? Could I have been braver and acted with more awareness? And if I had...could I have done more to protect my roommate and myself?*

Asking these questions is cruel and unfair. They imply that I did something wrong or mishandled the situation. Even if I had done things differently... there is nothing that could have changed what happened.

Yet, there is a gift in hindsight: *insight*. Hindsight and insight—both are sacred. It is this sacredness that allows a person to see...*to see*...and understand the why and the how things happened the way they did.

Chapter 1

THE MOTHERS

The sound of the squeaking front door makes me turn. Katie walks out of the house with a tray of cheese, crackers, glasses and a pitcher of iced tea. I reach behind her to pull the door shut but the latch doesn't connect and the door pops back open. I leave it. It's a mild October evening in Portland. There are no insects or pests to worry about getting inside, just Katie's pest of an indoor cat, Buffett, who might try to escape.

I'll keep an eye out.

"Any sign of them yet?" Katie asks.

"Nope, not yet," I answer.

We're standing on the covered front porch of our newly rented 1940s bungalow style home. The house is beige with its large windows framed in now-faded brown trim work. The porch is just wide enough for two small chairs and a tray table that is still folded and leaning against the side of the house. I unfold the wooden table so Katie can place the tray on top of it. She pours herself a glass of iced tea, ignoring me. She's fully aware that I don't like her iced tea. I reach for a piece of cheese.

"What do you think they'll say?" she asks over the top of her glass.

In the soft porch light, I watch a spot of condensation run down and fall from Katie's glass. The water drop balances for a moment in the center of a small section of peeling brown paint. It slides down the paint's curling side and onto the dry exposed wood. It disappears. Another drop follows. This time it hits wood and vanishes the second it lands. There is more exposed dried wood than paint on this old porch.

"Does it matter?" I ask, reaching for another slice of cheese and a cracker.

I hope I sound nonchalant, but really, I'm not. I'm a ball of nerves. Katie and I are waiting for our mothers to arrive. We've just moved into this house, and after a few days of sprucing it up, we are eager to show it off. Katie had a great idea to have an "open house" for them. Even though we would never admit it to each other, we're each hoping for both mothers' approval.

A car comes around the corner and drives up the steep hill in front of our house. Another car follows. A delivery truck comes around the corner following too closely, shifts down and coughs up a puff of black smoke. Katie and I wave our hands over our noses as the smell reaches us.

It's five o'clock in the evening, rush hour. Steady streams of commuters come off the interstate, around our block, to cross one of Portland's many bridges and head east over the Willamette River. Our house sits on the corner, on the boundary of the Lair Hill neighborhood. Some call this area charming.

I hope our moms do too.

The loud ocean-like sound of interstate traffic and the scent of exhaust from the truck fill the air. The cheese in my mouth tastes sour. I contemplate pouring a glass of Katie's iced tea, but think again. I don't need anything else adding to the acid already accumulating in my nervous stomach.

"I wish they'd get here already. I'm starting to worry. It's getting dark. They won't be able to see anything," I say just as another delivery truck comes around the corner, shifts down and spews exhaust our way. "On second thought…maybe it's better. I'm going in and taking the food with me. Are you done with your glass?"

I pick up the tray as Katie places her glass on it. Pushing the door open with my foot, I enter the house, then close the door with my hip. It pops back open. Buffett comes running up and I shoo him away from the door.

After placing the tray on the coffee table, I step back to view the surroundings through our parents' eyes. The old house, once charming in its day, has plaster walls, picture molding, and wood floors in the living room and bedrooms. White painted moldings trim the paned windows in all the rooms.

In the center of the living room is our oversized brass and glass coffee table. We have six different shaped candles, all lit. They give the room a welcoming glow and wonderful scent. Next to the tray is a pile of magazines that are fanned out. Copies of *Glamour* and *Seventeen* are on top; hidden underneath is *Cosmopolitan*. Against the front wall, under the large window, is a beat-up sofa that we've slipcovered with a white bedspread.

The TV, with two antennas stretching out toward the ceiling, is on top of the teak stereo cabinet in the opposite corner. It was a high school graduation gift from my father and is the best piece of furniture in the house. Katie has her favorite album, "A White Sport Coat and Pink Crustacean," playing on the stereo inside the cabinet. Jimmy Buffett's voice is singing "The Great Filling Station Holdup" to us through the two large speakers. The melody carries the longing in his words—he's wishing he were somewhere else, drinking a beer. That holdup cost him two good years. The lyrics are hysterical and seem appropriate to my nervousness. I giggle and it makes me feel better.

Along the far wall, a bookshelf of wood planks and cinder blocks is filled with knick-knacks, plants and some of our favorite books. A slight draft of cool air finds its way to me. I shiver. The draft is coming from the round hole in the wall on the opposite corner. I walk over and move the large potted ficus tree a few more inches over to hide the obvious flaw.

This will be an issue for the moms, I just know it.

"They're here!" Katie calls to me. "Oh, how perfect; they're arriving at the same time! It's like they coordinated it."

I hear a loud series of honks and laugh. I don't need Katie to tell me my mom is here. She's doing her usual rhythmic honking to announce her arrival.

Katie's yelling continues, this time at one of the moms, "Park anywhere on the side of the street. Don't stop, keep moving. Keep moving!"

I hear another car honk followed by another set of gears grinding down. This time it isn't my mom who's honking. I rush back outside to join Katie on the front porch. I wave at Katie's mother who is just driving by in her small silver Ford Granada. My mom has already found a parking spot midway up the block. I watch as she pulls herself out of the car. She stands, stretches her long, thin limbs and closes her car door with fluid elegance.

"Helloooo," my mom sings loudly, waving both arms at us. "I'm here!"

I get my height, six feet of it, from my mother, *but not her gracefulness.* I do a soft shake to loosen my own long, thin limbs and wave back.

"We hear that you're here, mom," I say under my breath and Katie giggles with me.

Katie's mom finds a spot on the other side of the one-way street, parallel parks, turns her wheels toward the curb and sets her emergency brake. When she gets out, she slams the car door with authority and waves at us. Like her daughter, she is not tall, yet her posture gives her the presence of importance.

Katie sighs and I watch as she straightens her back, standing at attention, ready to greet her mom. I do the same, but it makes me even taller and feels awkward, so I let my back muscles relax.

"Hi, Sweetie!" my mom squeals.

"Hi, Mom," we both say at the same time as they approach the house.

"Careful, that first step is a bit rough around the edges," Katie says and points to the crumbling bottom one.

Despite the warning, Katie's mother steps on the damaged cement and stumbles. My mother catches her by the elbow.

"Well goodness, that's dangerous!" Katie's mother says as she realigns her sweater and dusts off her slacks.

"Sorry. I tried to warn you," says Katie.

Katie elbows me in the ribs. I elbow her in her shoulder. Katie snorts, but she keeps looking straight ahead. When her mother reaches us, Katie gives her a hug and I do the same with mine.

"Let's see this place of yours," says Katie's mother, rubbing her hands together in what appears to be forced anticipation.

"I'm so excited," says mine, but with no enthusiasm to back up her word choice.

I can tell already that the moms are as apprehensive as we are.

OK, let's get this over with.

Chapter 2

THE HOUSE

This all feels so strange. But I get it. This is a moment of truth telling and showing. Both 19, we have a lot to prove to our parents since Katie and I dropped out of Oregon State University. Our goal today is to show our parents that we're serious, smart and taking charge of our lives.

We just need to convince our moms of it.

I think back to when Katie and I first met. It was a year ago, our freshman year, during the college's sorority rush orientation. When I walked into the room, shy and awkward, I noticed a girl sitting at one of the tables. She looked confidant—her back straight, her chin high. She was wearing a brown corduroy sports coat over a cream turtleneck and jeans tucked into leather boots. An umbrella with a curved wooden handle lay next to her feet and a huge handbag hung from her chair. She reminded me of a modern-day Mary Poppins. She had a notebook out, pen in her hand, ready to take notes. It hadn't occurred to me to bring anything to take notes with. I chose to sit next to her.

She smiled. I nodded. She stuck out her hand.

"Hi there, I'm Katie."

"Hi, I'm Cinda. I didn't think to bring anything to write on…stupid of me."

"Oh, no problem, I have plenty." She reached into her large handbag and found another notebook and a pen.

A few days later, after rushing sororities, we both decided that the Greek life wasn't for us and dropped out. By the end of the year, we dropped out of school too.

School frustrated me. I knew exactly what I wanted to do with my life. My passion was in retail merchandising and school wasn't supplying me with what I felt I needed to make my dreams happen. I wanted to start working in my field right away. I wanted to move to Portland and get my career rolling.

Katie needed to work to earn extra money. She was planning on going back to school once she saved enough to help her parents pay for her tuition. It was her idea to move to Portland and I jumped at the opportunity to join her.

Dropping out of school did not sit well with my parents, but I knew it was the right move and did it anyway. I got a full-time job as a salesperson in the girls' junior department at the elegant and historic downtown Meier & Frank department store. Katie worked as a receptionist in a high-end business office.

The squeaking door brings me back to the moment. Katie and the moms are heading inside. I follow behind.

"Come in…we have some iced tea and snacks," Katie says pointing to the coffee table.

I lean against the door to push it closed and turn the deadbolt to hold it shut.

The moms look around the small, cozy room. Their smiles are subtle, but I think they are smiling.

I hope they're smiling.

"Why is there a hole in the wall?" asks Katie's mom.

"Well, that didn't take long," Katie says under her breath. Then to her mother, "I think there used to be a wood stove there. See the platform below it? I think that hole was where the stove pipe went."

"Are they replacing the wood stove?" my mother asks.

"I don't think so," I reply.

The tiled platform is approximately three inches high. It protrudes out from the corner of the living room. To its left is the arched entry to our two bedrooms and bathroom. To the right is another arch, an entrance to the kitchen and eating area.

"There's a draft coming through this!" says Katie's mom as she walks closer to inspect the hole through the limbs of the ficus. "Your heat bill will be outrageous if you don't cover it up!"

Katie answers, "Not to worry, I have a call in to the landlord. You've met the hole-in-the-wall; now meet the rest of the house. This is our living room," she raises her arms, palms up.

"Cheese anyone? Katie's iced tea?" I swing my arm at the tray of cheese and crackers.

My mom reaches for a cracker and cheese combo. She chews, makes a strange face and pours herself a glass of iced tea. After a swig of the dark liquid, she sets the glass back onto the tray. Katie's mother ignores the offer and walks into the kitchen.

"It sure is dark in here," she says as she reaches for the light switch, which is already turned on.

The single domed light on the ceiling does little to brighten the dullness of the room. The linoleum is faded and torn. Before the mothers arrived we super-glued the rip to make it look less noticeable.

"Is that a rip in the linoleum?" Katie's mother asks.

This lady, she misses nothing....

I follow my mother in the opposite direction, toward the bedrooms and bathroom. Buffett, the young grey tabby, named after the man who is now singing "Why Don't We Get Drunk and Screw" on the record player, runs out of the kitchen toward us. My mother, who is not a cat person, gasps in surprise as he runs ahead and spins off toward the right. We hear a crash. My mother startles at the sound.

"Not to worry, that's just Buffett playing with his reflection in the mirror. He's such a spazz. He runs around that corner too fast, slides on the wooden mat, then jumps at his reflection in the full-length mirror outside my bedroom."

Buffett comes running back toward us and then into the kitchen.

My mother shakes her head and then heads to the bathroom. It's a direct shot from the archway in the living room. I adore our bathroom because it still has some of its original fixtures. Everything is white porcelain. The pedestal sink is on the right, just inside the door; the toilet is next to it in the corner. A small, narrow window is in the center of the far wall. Along the left is a cast-iron claw-foot tub that runs the length of the wall. A large metal hoop holds up the white shower curtain. Two people can't easily fit into the small space, so we both peek in through the door.

"Oh, Cinda, this is cute!" I'm relieved that she agrees with me. "Which room is yours?"

I point to the right. Katie's room is to the left. Our doors face each other in this small hallway. The wooden mat Buffett skidded on earlier runs between our two doors. To the right of my bedroom door, the full-length mirror leans against the wall. Just then, as if on cue, the cat runs between our feet, hisses at his reflection in the mirror, arches his back, jumps sideways and in a very ninja-like move kicks at himself and runs away.

"Cute," my mom says again, but this time sarcastic.

"He's a gigantic pest for sure. The strangest thing is that he hates men. I'm not kidding!"

My mom gives me a look like she doesn't believe me.

"Honest! He pounces on every man that walks in this door. He scratches and bites at their ankles. He turns all ninja on them."

"Men?" she asks.

Of all the words for my mom to get stuck on, it's that one.

"Here's my room," I say, trying to change the direction of *that* subject.

To the immediate left is the foot of my bed. I have no bed frame. The box spring and mattress lay on the floor, covered with a pink-and-white flowered polyester bedspread. Next to it, the white nightstand with oversized red knobs holds a small, flimsy lamp with a red lampshade, and an electric clock. The matching dresser stands against the far wall between the window and the closet.

This is my childhood bedroom set. I can tell by my mom's expression that seeing the furniture again is making her feel sentimental. She painted the knobs and the lampshade for me when I was 12...when red was my favorite color.

"Well, perhaps we should get you a bed frame? Oh, and I like what you did with your window treatments," her sarcastic tone is not missed.

The two large corner windows are covered in bed sheets. When I moved in, I cut an old white sheet in half and used thumbtacks to secure each half to the top moldings of each window frame.

"Well, no one will see them but you," she says and pats my upper arm. "It'll work in the meantime."

I'm not saying anything about my boyfriend. He's seen these curtains a few times already.

Seeing my room through my mother's eyes is a bit defeating. Childhood furniture, sheets for curtains, no bed frame—*all seems rather immature.*

We turn and walk into Katie's room. Katie and her mother are already in there, so we peek through the door. Unlike me, Katie has an entire bedroom set: bed frame with headboard, and a matching dresser and nightstand with a large, sturdy reading lamp. Her bed is covered with a flowered chintz comforter and matching pillow shams. It's a glorious bedroom. She wasn't tacky enough to hang old sheets on her windows—there's nothing hanging over them.

The two women are sitting on Katie's bed, leaning into each other and laughing over a framed picture of the two of them.

Oh...smart...framed photos of family. Great idea. Wish I would have thought of that.

"Well, enough of this. I'm hungry. Let us take you girls out to dinner," says Katie's mom. She turns on her heels like a soldier and exits the bedroom. My mom and I move aside to let her pass and follow her.

"Thank God they didn't go into our basement," Katie whispers to me as she walks by. "The landlord still hasn't taken those clothes away."

I agree. The basement is awful. I hate it. I'm sure my mom would too. Not only is it dark, damp smelling and dangerous feeling...there's a pile of clothes down there. These clothes aren't ours...they were here when we moved in. I haven't looked at them because for some reason they freak me out...they're creepy. Katie has snooped through the pile and says they look like they belong to a man...maybe the past tenant... maybe the landlord. Either way, I wish they were gone.

As we gather our purses and put on our coats, I overhear my mother whisper to Katie's mom, *"I don't like this. Not one bit, I don't. I just don't like the feeling of this place at all."*

As we drive to dinner, I can't help but be bothered. Something about my mother's concern doesn't sit well with me. I try my best to push it away, but I can't.

"I just don't like the feeling of this place."

Chapter 3

THE PROWLER

A week goes by and Katie and I get used to certain habits. With such a small bathroom, our nightly routines are like a dance as we take turns at the sink. I brush my teeth in front of the full-length mirror in the hall, giving Katie the sink to wash her face. We trade so I can wash my face and she uses the hall mirror to brush her teeth.

On this night, she's showering while I'm sitting stretched out on the couch in the living room. I'm using the oversized pillow I just bought as a back support against the armrest. While I'm talking on the portable phone to Scott, my boyfriend since high school, I watch my reflection over my feet in the house's side window. It's cold inside and seems extra dark outside.

Katie comes out of the bathroom and stands under the archway to the living room. She's brushing her teeth and waves at me to tell Scott hello. I laugh. Her hair is wrapped up in a towel and she's naked.

Oh, how I admire her confidence. I wish I could be more like that.

"Katie says hi," I tell Scott.

"Is she naked?" he asks.

I laugh. "Yes, she is!"

Scott laughs with me. Although he hasn't been witness to it, it blows his mind that Katie parades around the house naked in front of me.

"Tell her to put a robe on it," he yells into the phone hoping Katie will hear him. I hold the phone out to her.

She sticks her foamy tongue out at him—fully aware of what he's saying. This isn't the first time he's said it. She turns back into the bathroom.

I see my reflection in the window and watch myself smile and laugh. I love living with Katie. I grew up sheltered, so being around such a confident spirit is inspiring. I don't think I'd ever be able to walk around naked, but I'm learning to adapt to her nakedness.

I start to tell Scott about a customer at work that day when, over my left shoulder, a movement outside catches my eye. I peer out the front window, which runs behind the couch, but all I see is my own face. I continue with my story. Then, I catch a movement outside the side window, over the top of my feet. My reflection becomes distorted. It's as if my reflection changes to a different person. A person with crazy, frizzed out hair. Then it returns to my face. I scream.

"What! What is it?" Scott shouts.

"What! What's wrong?" Katie rushes into the room forgetting the lotion she's rubbing on her arms.

"Oh my God, I think someone was looking at me through that window!" I point to the window.

Katie shakes the towel off her head and wraps it around her body. She runs to the window to look out. She needs to cup her free hand around her face to be able to see outside.

"Is everything all right?" Scott yells.

I forgot that I was holding the phone with him on the other end.

"Oh, my God! I think someone was looking in our window!" I tell him.

"Your blinds are open? What the hell? Cinda! You should always close your blinds at night. Katie parades around naked all hours of the day and night, and it isn't safe. Of course, someone is spying on you!"

I'm not going to remind him that we don't have any blinds.

"Fine, OK already, you're right," I assure him. "I'm sure it was nothing. I'm tired and I'm going to go to bed. I'll talk to you tomorrow."

I hang up the phone and go to Katie's side.

"See anything?" I ask.

She shakes her head "no" and turns to go back into the bathroom. She removes the towel from around her body and hangs it on the bar.

"Maybe we should get some blinds?" I mention as I head into my own room.

"We can't hang up anything permanent unless we plan to leave it when we move out," she responds.

"But that's like...creepy, don't you think? That there might be like...a prowler out there, peeking in at us. I mean...aren't you freaked? You really didn't like...see anything?"

"There's nothing out there. I would've seen him running away," she says as she applies more lotion to her body. "There's no place to hide out there."

"Katie, I saw something move outside the front window and then the side window. Maybe you should at least put something over your bedroom windows."

"Cinda, don't be silly. There's nothing out there but a large empty lot. Keyword: *empty*. There's no one out there to see in."

I'm sure I saw someone looking in the windows at me. I'm positive I did.

I'm totally freaked, but Katie isn't. So, I try to talk myself into believing and behaving like Katie, but it isn't easy. Instead, I go into my bedroom and get two thumbtacks out of the top drawer of my nightstand and tack down the bottom of my sheets. I want to create a barrier to the outside. I shiver as I feel the coldness through the glass, but also because...*I'm afraid.*

I go into the bathroom to thumbtack a hand towel over the window. When we moved in, the bathroom window had opaque contact paper stuck to it for privacy, but I feel better with a towel up too. The window is lifted open a crack to let out the steam from the shower, and the cold breeze feels nice on my flustered body.

I head back into the living room and shut off all the lights. I carefully peek out the side window, hiding my body behind the wall. It's dark out there, but the streetlights offer enough light to make out the empty lot next to us. It's the size of a small field. Katie's right. Why would a prowler hang out in such a spot to spy on us?

I remember the movement out the front window—the motions that first caught my eye. The porch would make it difficult to see inside the house from the sidewalk. Someone would have had to climb the steps onto the porch.

Oh God, could someone really be that intrusive?

Chapter 4

THE INTRUDER

A couple days go by and we haven't put up blinds or any other kind of window coverings. There haven't been any more occurrences of anyone looking in on us, so we've relaxed. I use the excuse that I've been busy with work, which is true. Katie's barely home either and when she is, she reassures me: "There's no reason to be concerned. There's no way anyone could see inside. We're too high up from ground. There's nothing out there but an empty lot. Besides, who would care anyway? What is there to actually see?"

For the last few days, I've been working the night shift. Tonight, I get off the bus around ten o'clock in the evening and walk the three blocks to the house. It's the middle of October and the spirit of Halloween is unmistakable. A cold, thick haze hangs in the air, fallen leaves blow around me, tree branches shake and sputter. With only porch lights and random street lights lighting my way, I hurry home, dodging natural shadows in the near darkness. The chill I feel seems to be coming from something more than just the weather.

It feels different tonight…creepy, eerie…like ghosts are haunting the neighborhood.

I climb the steps and unlock the front door. On the coffee table are Katie's purse and the day's mail. *She's home.* I push the door shut, set the deadbolt and turn the lights off.

"Hi, how was your day?" Katie calls from her bedroom.

"Non-eventful," I call back.

I walk into her room and pet Buffett who is lying at the foot of her bed. He stretches toward me and purrs. I really like when he's calm like this, which is rare and precious. His fur is warm to the touch and I wish I could pick him up and hold him, but think better of it. If I stir him up right now, we'll not get any rest.

I bend down to take off my flat-heeled black shoes. Relief sets in.

"We're already stocking up for the holidays at the store. There's so much stuff coming in daily. It's a lot of work to get the clothing hung and onto the floor. Ugh, I've got to go to bed. I'm exhausted."

29

I stand up to leave, "'Night…sleep tight! Don't let the Buffett bite. 'Night, Buffett, you sleep tight too."

I shut her bedroom door to keep Buffett contained during the night and head into my room.

Katie shouts, "I'm doing laundry in the morning. Leave a pile for me. Oh, and your mom left a message on the phone. She said your stepdad isn't feeling well and had to come home early from work, so they're going to bed early. She'll call you in the morning. 'Night, Cinda."

Best friend ever. She does my laundry and acts as my secretary.

I smile, relieved that Katie doesn't mind doing the laundry in that god-awful basement. I'm not comfortable being down there. I hate the rotten, moldy smell. Plus, the landlord still hasn't taken care of that pile of clothes.

Those clothes…totally creep me out.

I have yet to meet our landlord. Katie made the arrangements with him when we moved in and has continued to be our lead contact. She's called about the hole in the wall, the tear in the linoleum and those creepy clothes. He doesn't seem to be very attentive. He doesn't seem to be in much of a hurry to help.

In my room, I check the sheets covering the windows then strip off all my clothes. It's cold inside my room, so I debate on what I want to wear to bed. Usually I wear pajama pants and a T-shirt but this time I choose my floor-length red bathrobe. It looks and feels like a giant, soft sweatshirt with a partial zipper in the front and a hood in the back. I pull it on over my head. As it slides over my bare skin, it brings instant warmth. I zip it up to my chin.

Perfect! Warm and cozy.

I go into the bathroom and brush my teeth. I pay close attention to cleaning around the braces on my back teeth. At my last visit, the orthodontist put brackets on my back molars to close the gap in my bite. I attach three small rubber bands to the brackets, connecting the top teeth to the lower ones on each side of my mouth. It's hard to open my jaw now. I go back into my room, leaving the door open for extra warmth and crawl into bed. I feel my body relax.

I'm so tired…I'll sleep well tonight.

Hours later, somewhere in the deep recess of my sleeping mind, a noise finds its way to my ears. I'm not fully awake, and refuse to wake up any more, but I can I hear the wooden mat slide on the floor outside my room and the full-length mirror rattle.

Ugh, Buffett. Why did Katie let you out of her room?

Sure enough, I hear Buffett hiss. Then growl. Is he hunting something? Is he chasing a mouse?

Ugh! Please don't let it be a mouse.

I'm trying hard to not wake up, but my mind is consumed with mice now. I hear Buffett growl and hiss again. I can hear his padded paws spinning out on the wood floor near my bed.

He's chased the mouse into my room!

With difficulty, I open my eyes and squint across my bedroom floor. My room is too dark to see anything. The green glow from my clock gives the room an eerie feeling. The numbers flip over to 3:05. I hear Buffett hiss again.

He seems intent on catching that mouse?

The sound is now at the foot of my bed, next to the door. I turn over and prop myself up on my elbows. I squint into the darkness, trying to get a better look at that annoying cat or perhaps his prey. Standing at the foot of my bed is a silhouette—*a silhouette that is not Buffett's.*

Not of a cat.

Not of a mouse.

Not of Katie.

It's the silhouette of a man.

Chapter 5

THE SCREAM

My mind tries to register what it is seeing. My eyes try to focus in the darkness. I sit up a bit more, squinting, trying to understand if a man is really in my room.

What is a man doing in my room?

I ask the only logical question that comes into my foggy brain.

"Are you the fix-it guy? Are you here to fix the hole in the wall?" My voice is dry, sleepy. I look again at the clock. The green glowing numbers flip over and read 3:06. "Maybe you can come back in a few hours?"

"Shut up!" commands a masculine voice in a strained whisper.

This makes no sense. Why would the landlord tell the fix-it guy to come so early? Did he let this guy into our house?

"Who are you? How did you get in here?"

"Shut UP!" he demands again, his low voice stern and clear. Then he says, "Shit! You're not who I thought you were."

He's still standing at the end of my bed. I hear Buffett hiss and growl again. It wasn't a mouse Buffett was hunting—*it was this guy.* The man's silhouette seems to be kicking...the cat. I hear Buffett meow. The man's foot must have made contact. It occurs to me that this isn't a very friendly fix-it guy.

"Damn cat," the man's voice growls.

I hear the door to my room shut.

I'm now fully awake.

I'm now fully aware that I'm alone.

I'm alone...with a strange man...in my room...in the middle, in the dead, in the *dread*...of night.

If this guy isn't here to fix the hole in the wall...why is he here?

Without warning, he lunges toward me.

I scream.

The sound that comes out of me is unrecognizable. It's like nothing I've ever heard come from me before. It's animalistic, guttural, a sound from somewhere so deep inside of me that I don't recognize it as my own.

It's an awful sound.

It's the sound of pure terror.

Oh, my God! I'm being attacked!

Chapter 6

THE OFFENSE

He lunges toward me, hitting me in the center of my chest, knocking me back against the mattress. His hands struggle to find my arms. I try to avoid his grip. I kick. I attempt to scream again but he covers my mouth with one of his hands.

In the struggle, the blankets get wrapped tighter and tighter around my body. I'm trapped by both the bedding and the man on top of me. Both of his hands are now covering my mouth and nose. With my bed this low to the ground, he's positioned himself above me, using force to keep me still. All his weight is pressed on my face. I'm pinned. I can't move. I can't breathe.

Oh, my God! Oh, my God, this man is trying to kill me!

I can feel his breath on my face as he whispers warnings to me. The pounding of my heart is so loud in my ears that I can't make out his words. The sound of the scream still echoes in my skull.

I can't breathe. Oh, my God, I can't breathe.

In a panic to take in air, I try to get out from under his weight. The more I fight to get him off, the more force he applies and the more I can't move…or breathe.

What do I do? Oh, God please help me!

I taste blood. Blood! The taste of blood distracts me from my panic.

Why am I bleeding?

My nose…it hurts. Is it bleeding? My mouth…it hurts more. I remember the brackets on my back teeth, the rubber bands. How could I have screamed with my mouth rubber-banded shut? Could a rubber band have pulled a tooth out?

Did I lose a tooth when I screamed?

With my tongue, I feel for a missing tooth but the pressure of his hands makes it difficult. Blood pools inside my mouth. I can't swallow. I still can't breathe. The lack of air makes me dizzy. My panic returns.

I need to get his hands off my face! I need to breathe.

The taste of blood and perhaps my light headedness changes the focus of my panic. There must be a way out of this! I need to figure out how to get out of this. I need to calm down.

I need to calm HIM down.

I manage to pull my left arm out from under the blankets, from underneath him. He doesn't seem to notice. I grab at his hands, hit them, scratch them, try to pull them off my face. He thinks I'm fighting him and applies even more pressure. Pain shoots across my face. I take note… the more I fight the more violent he becomes.

My lungs are empty. I'm afraid I might pass out. I can't have that happen. I don't know what he's planning on doing. I don't want to find out.

With my free hand, I do the strangest thing. I tap the top his hands. I tap again and again.

Tap, tap, tap.

I feel him freeze. Perhaps my action has confused him. He seems distracted. His pressure and grip ease but I need to get him to remove his hands. I need to keep tapping.

Tap, tap, tap.

I motion for him to take his hands off my face by sweeping my hand across the top of his.

Tap, tap, tap, swipe. Tap, tap, swipe.

He seems to understand and removes his hands long enough for me to take in a deep breath. I choke on the blood and start to cough. He immediately puts his hands back over my nose and mouth.

"Don't you scream again," he hisses.

I take note…I need to convince him I won't yell again. I cautiously put my left hand around his right wrist and firmly pull it off my mouth. He lets me.

He lets me!

I take another deep breath and swallow the pool of blood. It's disgusting. He lunges for my mouth again, perhaps, thinking I'm going to scream. I put my arm in front of my face to block him. He grabs my wrist and pins it on the bed. I pull my other arm free from under the covers to protect my face. He grabs that one too. He crosses my arms over my chest and kneels on them. His weight is crushing. All the air I just took in is pushed out of my lungs.

"Wait," I gasp. I force the words to come out: "I promise I won't scream. I promise you. Let me sit up."

My determination to survive is paramount. I refuse to let him smother me again.

I lean to one side, throwing him off balance and freeing my arms. He stumbles but only for a moment. In the darkness, his hands grab at me again. I connect with one of his arms and use it to pull myself up. I'm now sitting, facing him, holding onto his arm. He appears to be sitting on his knees. He twists his arm out of my hand, swirls it around my arm and grabs my wrist. He leans forward on his knees and tries to wrap my arm around my back. His other hand comes up to my mouth. I block it with my free hand. He grabs that hand and with force, he tries to push me back down and pin me again. I resist being pushed over.

"Wait," I wheeze, trying to fight. Then with more force, "Wait. You can't do that. You're hurting my mouth."

He freezes.

Keep talking...keep talking.

"You're hurting my mouth when you push on it. I'm bleeding. I won't scream. Just stop hurting me."

He sits there...not moving...still frozen in place. Perhaps he's trying to figure out what I'm saying or why I'm talking.

I use this free second to do a quick inventory of the inside of my mouth with my tongue. I feel for any damage, for any lost teeth. My teeth are all there. Cut flesh dangles from the inside of my cheeks and pain shoots through my body as my tongue makes contact. I swallow more blood.

He still hasn't moved. He must be confused...or shocked.... I use this as a chance to pull one of my hands free.

Before he can grab at it again, I say, "Wait, see, you hurt my mouth," I swipe the inside of my cheek with my finger. When I pull it out, I can see the contrast the dark blood makes on my pale skin. I show him, not caring that he can't see it. "See, there's blood. When you do that...you cause my braces to cut into my cheeks...they're getting ripped up... they're bleeding. It hurts. I'm not going to scream again. So just stop it."

He *still* hasn't moved.

Keep talking!

I open my mouth and pull my cheek back to show him. It hurts like hell to do this. I assume he can't see me—I can't see him, but this continues to distract him enough to give me a chance to pull my other arm free from his grasp. He fumbles, trying to find it.

I keep talking…it's worked so far.…

"I have rubber bands, stuck now on my brackets. I need to take them out…so I don't choke on them. Hold on while I find them."

I move my hands to my mouth. He lets me—he lets me, but I notice, when I move…I sense his body stiffen. I take note. Every movement I make is a potential threat to him. If I'm to prevent him from lunging at me again, I need to keep him calm. I need him to believe that I'm not a threat.

I need to believe that I am.

"Don't worry. I just want to get the rubber bands out of my mouth. That's all I'm doing. I'm not going to scream. I'm not going to fight. I'm just getting my rubber bands."

I exaggerate my movements so he can make out what I'm up to in the darkness. I open my mouth larger than necessary. With my fingers, I search my back teeth for the rubber bands. Of the six, four of them snapped off and are dangling from either the top or bottom brackets. I struggle to unhook them. The other two are broken. I spit them all into my hand.

"See, six rubber bands." I hold out my hand to show him. Even though he can't see them, I know he's watching me closely. I drop them onto my bedspread. I rub my hands together to dry them off from the spit and blood.

In the darkness, my eyes fight to see, to adjust, to grasp their surroundings. I focus in on his silhouette…it shows that he is on alert, tense, ready to pounce. I glance at the clock. It glows a green 3:34. It's only been half of an hour. The adrenaline, the taste of blood, the panic…it's overwhelming my insides, my brain, my senses.

It's as if this is happening to someone else. But it's not. It's happening to me, right now.

God, help me.

Chapter 7

THE DEFENSE

I've got to keep stalling…talking…until I can find or think of a way to escape this hell, his grip—*him*. I settle on distraction. Distraction has worked—confusing him with the unexpected worked. I have no idea what I should do next or how I'm going to distract him again. My cheeks hurt. My nose is tender. My lungs burn. This guy—*whoever he is*—is mean, he's serious, he knows what he's doing. Whatever I decide to do…I need to do it with caution.

I take a chance. I start up another conversation.

"Funny, I thought you were the fix-it guy here to fix the hole in the wall," I attempt a laugh, but it comes out like a frog's croak. "If you aren't the fix-it guy, who are you? Why are you here?"

He doesn't reply.

Crap. Tread carefully, Cinda, c a r e f u l.

I can feel his tension increase with his silence. I swallow the terror that is stuck inside my throat. I want to scream, yell, cuss. I want to push, shove, run. I want to get him out of here, out of my room, out of my house. But if I do that, if I make him mad, he might kill me.

If I don't think of something quick…he's going to strike again.

"How did you get into the house?" I'm trying to sound calm but my panic is right on the surface.

Stay calm, Cinda. Stay c a l m.

"Through the bathroom window," his voice is stern and sends a shiver down my spine.

He's talking. He can't lunge if he's talking.

"You broke into our house? Through the bathroom window?"

It's a stupid question. I'm being repetitive. But…nothing makes sense to me. I can't wrap my mind around what's happening.

If this is a dream, it's a nightmare…one I wish I'd fucking wake up from already!

"What do you think?" his sarcasm validates my concern that his tension is real.

"Are you planning on leaving that way too?" I ask.

I wish he'd leave now.

"No, that wouldn't make sense. I'm going to leave through the backdoor. I already have it unlocked." I hear a touch of pride.

He has a plan. He's thought this out. This isn't just a random visit.

"Smart," I say, totally freaked out that he pre-planned this. "Do you make a habit of this? Breaking into people's homes in the middle of the night?"

"Maybe!" Now he sounds snide.

Oh God, is he planning on raping me? Why me?

"Of all the houses, why did you choose our house?"

"I've been watching your house. I've. Been. Watching. You." There's a surge of power behind each word.

I remember that night when I thought someone was looking at me through the window. I was right. Someone was—*he was!*

I am frozen in fear. His words are registering: He's pre-planned this. He's done this kind of thing before. He knows what he's doing...*I don't.* I don't know how to protect myself. This gives him the advantage—it makes him even more dangerous.

I need to monitor him...monitor every one of his actions.

If he's done this before then he's expecting me to behave like the others. I need to do the unexpected. I need a strategy.

Oh God...how did it end...for the others? How will THIS end...for me?

Thinking of the others he may have hurt makes me think about Katie.

Oh God, Katie!

What if he already got to Katie? Did he kill her? My panic rises to the point that my head may explode with it. Colors begin to flash across my eyes. My chest tightens with the horror of the possibility.

Then, as quickly as I have that thought another comes. I remember something he said when he first woke me up. He said he thought I was someone else. Did he think I was Katie? Was he after Katie? Did he mean to go into her room instead?

Wait! If he thought I was Katie...then that means Katie is safe.

I glance at the clock, 3:45. If Katie's safe, she isn't waking up anytime soon.

Keep talking. Keep him talking.

"So...you live around here?" I ask, hoping to stall, so I can strategize a getaway plan.

"What business is that of yours?" he growls; his frustration is growing. I hear it in his tone.

Crap, crap, crap! I got too personal.

"You said you were watching us. So…I was just assuming you lived around here." I'm doing my best to act and sound nonchalant, nonthreatening, *non-frightened.*

"I live under a bridge," he snaps, he's irritated now…angry.

If I don't recover and calm him down, I'm doomed.

"Under a bridge?" I ask, but it's too late. I feel the bed move under me.

I'm doomed.

Chapter 8

THE UNTRUTHS

The bed moves. He lunges. He pushes me backwards then climbs on top of me. Before I can do anything to protect myself, he grabs a pillow and covers my face. I can feel both of his hands pushing down on the pillow.

"I'm done talking!" His voice is hard. Mean. Determined.

I squirm and twist my body, trying to get out from under him. He repositions himself, straddling my stomach. His weight makes it hard to move. My hands are still free. I grab at the pillow, then at his arms. They don't budge. I tap his hands, *it worked before*, but this time there's no response. I hit his hands, his arms. I scratch them. It's getting more difficult to breathe and the panic is consuming my oxygen.

If I pass out, I might not wake up.

I'm not aware of how much time is passing. All I am aware of is that I am dying. Things are growing dark, darker…darker. I feel a slight release of pressure on the pillow as one of his hands struggles with the blankets covering my body. I use it to my advantage and turn my head to the side. This allows me to take in needed air. He raises his body off mine to pull the blankets out from under him and off me. Without his weight pinning me, I quickly turn my body to its side. I connect with his inner thigh and push against it with my hips. This throws him off balance and he falls sideways. I pull the pillow off my face.

I roll my body away from him and out from under his left leg. I sit up, gasping for air. He lunges again. I put a hand up to stop him. He barges into it. I connect with his bare chest. It's a very personal and repulsive connection. I hold strong, keeping him at an arm's distance. I can feel his heart beating fast under my palm.

Hold steady! Cinda, you can do this. Think, think, think.

My lungs hurt. My body aches. I'm exhausted, but I'm alive.

I glance at the clock. It glows 4:46. *Time...what a weird concept.* Is it moving fast or slow? Either way, time is all I have right now. I need to keep it in my favor.

I need him to leave...leave me alone...leave my house.

"Are you hungry?" I ask, forcing the air out and surprising myself with my own question. "You've got to be hungry!"

"What?" he asks, sounding confused, annoyed.

"Are you hungry?" I choke out the words.

He pushes against my hand with his chest. I keep it planted against him.

"I was just wondering.... I mean...you said you lived under a bridge.... So...I'm wondering...maybe you're hungry? I have a steak. I can cook you a steak."

I'm trying to sound calm and in control, but I cannot believe what I'm saying. I have no idea where this question came from. I have no idea if we have any steak. Worse, I have no idea how to cook one if we do. I try to think about what's in our pantry but I am too freaked out to see it clearly.

Please don't say yes.

"I don't want any fucking steak!"

He pushes his chest against my hand again. I hold my arm firm and push back, holding him in place. He doesn't resist. I wish I had the superpower strength to shove him off my bed, through my window, all the way across the highway...*onto the highway.*

I ask a different question.

"How about a cup of coffee? Are you thirsty? I also have tea. But I don't recommend my roommate's iced tea. It's way too bitter."

For whatever reason, I'm attempting to make it appear as if I'm sharing an inside joke. So I force a fake laugh. I don't get this strategy of mine. I'm totally winging it. But maybe...being friendly will work?

He laughs back, but it's a mean, vicious laugh.

"I don't want any fucking coffee! Are you fucking serious?"

Thank God, he didn't say yes....

We have coffee, but since I don't drink coffee, I don't have a clue how to make that either. I am shooting ideas out of my mouth like bullets through sludge. They're not reaching their target.

Think, think, think. Keep him talking. He liked talking about his getaway plan.

"You said you're planning on leaving through the back door? It's like you're familiar with this house?"

"Yes, I know this house." He pauses, laughs. I can hear a sneer in his voice. He then says, "Is the pile of clothes still in the basement?"

An instant chill shoots down my spine. I'm frozen in fear. I'm sure he can feel it through my hand. Out of reflex, I pull my hand away, breaking contact with his body.

My mind is racing with what this might mean.

He knows about the clothes. He's been inside my house before.

The thought is horrifying. Then another thought occurs to me. Maybe he's just trying to scare me. He's acting like he's superior, like I'm stupid. So much so, that he's just sitting there, gloating. He's not moving, not lunging. It's like he's enjoying this...like he's getting pleasure in me freaking out.

If he thinks I'm an idiot, let him think it. *Perhaps I am.* But if acting strange and stupid and asking bizarre questions keeps him from attacking, then I need to keep doing it. When I behave in ways he can't predict or anticipate; it keeps me safe.

I feel the bed move under me. I can hear him breathing. I still can't see him, but his silhouette is just inches away. I take a deep breath to calm my trembling body. But instead of fresh air filling my aching lungs, I inhale the sickening smell of his foul breath. It is an appalling mixture of stale alcohol and musty cigarette smoke. It's followed by the rank smell of his body odor, his unbathed skin. It's nauseating.

I reach out my hand again, hoping to use it like I did earlier. He hits it away, but doesn't move any closer. I keep talking, rambling, distracting.

"So...you say you live under a bridge," I say while choking down bile. "Which one?"

"I'm not going to tell you that!"

"Well...? I've offered you steak and coffee. You've been in my house. I think you should tell me *something* about yourself."

He doesn't answer. But he doesn't move either. I wonder if he's thinking about answering me. The silence feels...*deadly.*

I keep rambling.

"OK, how about you tell me your name?" The question comes out too fast. I regret it instantly, but can't stop myself. "What's your name?"

"Are you fucking serious? I'm not going to fucking tell you my name!" His laugh is that of a choked lion ready to spit out a giant hairball.

"Well..." I hesitate.

Think, think, think...you're pissing him off.

I force myself to laugh with him as if I were trying to be funny.

"If you aren't going to tell me your name, then I'll call you Bob. Is that OK? Bob?"

I'm taking a real risk here, and I know it.

Oh, my God! Cinda, what are you doing?

It's obvious that he's not enjoying my questions. I need to keep it friendly. I try to sound sincere with my questions so he won't feel like I'm snooping for information.

"Bob?" I ask again, "Will that work for you?"

"What? Will what work for me? What are you saying?" He's annoyed.

He's irritated, but at least he's talking and when he's talking he's not attacking.

I also note that every time I move, I can feel his body tense. Since it's still dark, we are both on high alert to each other's movements. So, I decide to wave my hands around as I talk. My idea is that he will be intent on watching my hands—not trusting them. If he's concentrating on my hands, my hope is that it will keep him from lunging again. If I keep asking personal questions and stay in constant motion, maybe I can distract him long enough to find a way out of this.

"Can I call you Bob?" I ask again, "I need to call you by a name, so Bob it is? I'll call you Bob."

"Sure, you can call me Bob. You can call me whatever you want." I notice the air of superiority in his tone. He then chuckles and in a thick voice says, "So, what's your name?"

Something deep inside cautions me not to tell him my name, but I need to tell him something. If he's really been watching us, he may already have our names. If so, I don't want to anger him by lying. Yet, at the same time, if he doesn't, I don't want to give him any personal information.

"My name is Cindy."

Cindy's close enough to Cinda. I was called Cindy growing up so it doesn't feel like a lie when I tell him. This should satisfy him if he's aware of my name already, and it will prevent him from getting my real name if he doesn't.

I take my hand and reach it out to shake his. I surprise myself with this gesture. I think it surprises him too when he responds.

We shake hands.

"Nice to meet you, Bob, I'm Cindy."

The second we connect, I can feel his tension. This gesture is more disturbing to me than when I had my hand on his chest. I almost pull my hand away, but don't. I can feel the coarseness and calluses of his hand.

A choked chuckle escapes him—*the lion and his hairball.* I take it to mean he's amused. I imagine that no one has ever carried on like this with him before. This is working. Having a conversation, exchanging names...*albeit untruths*...is working.

I'm stalling for more time.

More time is safe time.

I look at the clock and watch in slow motion as the eight flips to a nine. The numbers seem to be mocking me. I may be stalling for time, but time seems to be speeding up. The numbers read 4:59.

"What do you do, Bob, besides break into people's houses in the middle of the night? Do you make a habit of this?" I laugh so he doesn't think I'm serious, *but I am.*

"I'm a Vietnam vet," he replies, ignoring the rest of my question.

"You're a Vietnam vet? Wow, really?" I try to sound impressed.

"I don't want to talk about it! What do you do?"

I need to answer this question with care. Just like with my name, if he's been watching us, he has seen me catch the bus to go downtown. I can't be caught in a lie, but there's no way I'm going to tell him I work at Meier & Frank. I think of another store nearby.

"I work at The Galleria downtown."

The Galleria Mall is on the same bus route. It has multiple stores inside. If he comes looking for me there, he'll have no idea which store I work in.

"What do you do there?" he asks with no emotion. He even sounds curious.

Is he having a conversation with me?

"I'm a salesperson." I'm not going to tell him anything else.

"Humph," he suddenly sounds tired.

A noise outside the bedroom door startles him. Buffett is scratching to come inside. I feel Bob's tension rise between us. I feel the bed move under me.

Not a good thing. He's tense and he's tired. Not a good combo.

"It's only the cat. It's only the cat," I reassure him, in a desperate attempt to calm him back down.

He isn't reassured.

Instead…he lunges.

Chapter 9

THE UNTHINKABLE

I have no time to respond. No chance to protect myself. He grabs me by my shoulders and twists my body. I'm facing the mattress, lying on my stomach. One of my arms is stuck underneath me. He grabs my other arm and holds it behind my back. He climbs on top of me. I can feel a knee in the middle of my back and his other knee pinning my wrist at my waist. He is pushing my face down with one hand and with the other grabbing at the blankets around my legs. I squirm. I kick. I try to scream. Nothing is heard. The movement doesn't faze him.

He moves his knee onto the back of my neck; the other is still on my arm and waist. I feel him pulling up my bathrobe—*he'll soon have me naked if I let this happen.* I'm in a panic, a full-blown panic. I try to wiggle my hips to throw him off, but his weight is too much. I kick my legs, but they make no contact.

His hand replaces his knee on the back of my neck, but the pressure is still the same. He changes positions. He seems to be straddling my hips now, sitting on my lower back. There is more pressure on the back of my head. He's using both hands to push my face deeper into the mattress.

It's obvious now. His intention is to suffocate me, to get me to pass out. Then to rape me. Breathing is becoming difficult, if not impossible.

Oh, my God! I can't breathe. I can't breathe.

I can feel his determination. He's using more brute force. He's going to do what he came here to do. He's going to take this to the end.

This is it. This is where he rapes me. This is where he kills me.

I think of Katie finding me dead. I think about my parents. I think of Scott. I begin to feel light headed. My body is going weak…limp. Through a nearly unconscious haze, I can feel him struggle to pull my bathrobe up my back, up to my shoulders. But I still can't move. Somehow, he has kept me pinned while attempting to remove my clothing.

I feel the pressure on the back of my head release. I instinctively lift my face off the mattress to catch a needed breath. I gasp for air. But this is a big mistake.

He pulls the entire back of my bathrobe over the top of my head and around my face. The zipper, which is zipped up to my chin, prevents him from being able to remove it. My arms are still inside of the robe. He shoves my head back down onto the bed.

My head and arms are wrapped up inside my robe. I am tied up, trapped, pinned by my own clothing—*and I'm naked.*

I can feel the robe tightening around my face…around my neck. He's twisting it—tighter and tighter. I'm being strangled. A gurgling noise escapes my throat. It's an awful noise. I hear it again. My eyes flutter. Tears escape. Everything around me grows quiet. I start to black out.

I give up.

I give up the fight to breathe.

This is how I die.

But I'm not dead yet….

Through my dulled senses, I feel him shift his position. As he maneuvers his body above me, the stranglehold of the robe loosens. It loosens just enough for me to take in needed air through the fabric.

He's no longer sitting on me, but I still feel his knees on both sides of my hips. He grabs my shoulders and starts to twist my body. He's trying to turn me over. I'm too dazed to respond. I'm too weak to struggle. I'm too afraid to fight. He uses his full strength to roll me over and my body follows his lead. Perhaps he expects me to resist, but since I don't, the ease in which I roll causes him to lose balance. He releases his grip on me.

Inside the fog of my brain, it occurs to me that he is no longer in control. I quickly sit up and smash into his body causing him to fall backwards on my lap. My head and arms are still trapped inside the robe. I'm naked from the neck down. Breathing through the fabric is difficult. I panic, desperate to free my face. I feel him sit back up on my legs. Despite being bound by the fabric, I manage to push him away, this time with force. He is no longer on me. I know I only have seconds before he's back. I struggle to untangle from the noose-like grip of the bathrobe. I pull my arms out then reach behind and pull it off my head and face.

I'm free.

I gulp for air. I gasp, over, and over again. My lungs scream out in pain with each intake of oxygen. I search out Bob in the darkness—desperate to find him. I can see him at the end of the bed. He's sitting at my feet, appearing stunned, confused, disoriented.

How do I get rid of him? God help me, I can't let him do that to me again.

My lungs are in agony. My throat hurts. My bare skin is cold.

Yet I'm more alive than I've ever been. And I'm pissed. He almost succeeded in killing me. I will not allow that again!

The bathrobe is still in my hands. I gather it into a ball and throw it at him. He catches it.

"Bob, you didn't need to manhandle me! If you wanted me naked all you had to do was ask." My voice is hoarse and cracks with pain and emotion.

As my eyes continue to adjust to the darkness, I can make out Bob's body. I can read his body language. It occurs to me, if I can see him…he can see me. I'm naked. He's not. We're staring at each other.

I glance at the clock. Its green glow seems brighter to me now. It reads 5:20. He's been here for over two hours—*two fucking hours.*

I need to think of something before he attacks me again. He isn't going to back down. He just tried to kill me. If he lunges again…I'm dead.

Think Cinda, think. Distract him. Distract him!

"Are you hungry yet?" I ask him, my throat burning, "How about some cheese and crackers?"

We do have those.

As I talk, I make a point of exaggerating my hand motions. I can see how he's distracted by watching my moving hands, still not trusting them. This gives me a chance to look at him. I'm going to remember everything about this guy.

His face is oval. His skin is light colored. He's white. His lips are thin. His eyes are not dark. His nose is broad or flat, like maybe it was broken before.

"I don't want any of your fucking food!" he growls at me. He is tired of this. I hear a difference in the tone of his voice.

"Maybe you'd like some coffee now? It's getting to be morning."

He has light colored hair curling out from under his gray knit cap. I can see that there's a bump in the back of his hat. He must have a ponytail tucked up in there. He's wearing worn out, light blue jeans with holes in them. He doesn't have a shirt on, but I'm sure he did when he first got here. His body is thin. He's about my size.

I hear him sigh. I wish his exhaustion meant he'd leave, but it only means we're running out of time. If I'm not careful, things could get out of control and violent again. To prevent another onslaught, I need to give him the impression that I'm cooperating, not fighting with him.

"You must be tired," I say with false empathy.

Maybe I can convince him he IS tired...suggest he go home...back under the bridge he crawled out from.

I feel powerless in my nakedness, a sitting target, but I must pretend I don't notice or care. I need to buy more time, but I don't want any more of it. I'm exhausted too. I have to figure out how to get him to leave. I watch as he slowly crawls over the bed toward me. He looks like a panther approaching its doomed prey.

I refuse to be his prey.

I refuse to be raped by this man.

I refuse to give him that power over me.

I came close to dying before.

I will not let that happen again.

"Bob, you don't need to get rough with me," I tell him quickly, my voice stern. Then as he gets closer, "Don't do that again. Just tell me what you want."

I know full well what he wants, but I sure as hell won't give *it* to him willingly.

Think, Cinda, think...God, help me.

Then, out of nowhere, comes an idea. It disgusts me to think of it. But it might be my last chance.

Could this really work? It's a gamble, a huge risk, but I have to try.

I find the bedspread next to me and as Bob crawls closer, I lie down. When he reaches me, I lift the covers and invite him in. We're now lying under the covers together, inches away, our faces almost touching. It's intimate and it's awful. I can smell him. I can smell his stench, his body odor, his breath.... It's too much to bear.

"See, isn't this better? No need to be rough."

He slides toward me and tries to kiss me. I turn my head. He nuzzles up to my neck and begins to kiss my ear. He sucks on my earlobe. The rapidness of his breath increases and is hot on the side of my face. The smell of his stale breath is overwhelming, still reeking of alcohol and cigarettes, combined with his sour body odor. His hands find the rest of my body, rubbing up my legs, my stomach and on my breasts.

I bite down on my lip so I don't scream.

His hands feel like sandpaper against my skin and it hurts. Every nerve ending is alert and on fire. Even though his touch is making my skin crawl, I can't let him sense how repelled I am.

Keep cool, Cinda. You're stalling for time...stalling for the perfect time...the perfect excuse to stop this madness. Stay alert and look for it, something will come. Please, God, help me.

His movements are erratic and hard to follow. He moves even closer. His body is now pressed up along the side of mine. He's almost gentle, yet still forceful.

Oh, my God, he thinks I want this. He assumes I'm enjoying it. I want to throw up. I want to scream.

Another idea comes to me.

Either this works...or...I'm toast.

"Bob, wait," I say, pressing a hand on his chest. "Slow down for a minute."

I push against him.

"Why?" He asks between heavy breaths.

Here goes. Please let this work. Please believe me.

"We're friends now, Bob. Right?" I try to make my voice sound light and whimsical, "We're friends. Right? Friends."

"Sure, whatever," he says as he leans in for a kiss on my lips.

I turn my head slightly and his lips land on my cheek. I shudder at the intimate repulsiveness of it all. I push my hand harder against his chest. Attempting to push him away, without making him angry.

"Bob. Stop!" I say firmly, pushing even harder against him, forcing him to move away, to stop touching me, kissing me. "If we're friends..., if we're friends, we can't make love. Right? Friends don't make love. It ruins their friendship."

I keep my hand pressed up against him, keeping him at a safer distance. I hold my breath.

Does he buy it? Does he believe me? Will it work?

He stops. He rolls onto his back and lets out a heavy sigh. Is he really considering what I've just said? I took a huge gamble.

Did it pay off?

I watch him closely. As the room is getting lighter, I can see that he's looking up at the ceiling, probably considering his next move. He seems exhausted—*shit, what if he falls asleep?* Beyond his head, the clock reads 5:55. I don't understand how three hours could have gone by already. It scares me to my core to think that the lost time could have been when I was being smothered or strangled. Lost time. Time I'll never get back. Time where I was almost lost entirely.

I've got to figure out a way to get him out of my bed, out of my room, out of my house...my life. I don't want to ever EVER lose time again.

We hear a crash. It startles both of us. Bob sits up in a panic. I'm not panicked though—I know this sound. I know it well. It's Buffett—doing his ninja move at his reflection in the mirror.

Thank God, thank God, thank God!

"Bob, quick, that's my roommate waking up!" I attempt to sound worried for him, "She wakes up about this time. You need to get out of here. I don't want you to get caught," I lie.

In seconds, Bob grabs his shirt, is out of my bed and gone.

He's gone.

Gone!

Chapter 10

THE BLUE KNIGHTS

I lie in bed waiting...waiting. My heart is racing, pounding so loud I can't hear to make sure if Bob has left the building. I hold my breath and strain my ears, listening. I don't hear anything. I didn't hear him run away, or a door slamming, or Buffett hissing, or Katie screaming, or windows breaking.

Is he really gone? Or is he hiding?

Slow and quiet, I get out of bed. My legs are barely able to hold me up. I find my bathrobe on the floor near the end of my bed—where Bob tossed it. I pull it over my head and thread my shaking arms through the sleeves. The rest of it falls over my trembling body. I try not to remember that this same bathrobe was just used as a weapon to strangle me...a weapon that didn't succeed at killing me...*I'm all right.*

I'm all right. I'm alive. I'm here and Bob is gone.

I tiptoe out of my room and peer into the bathroom. The window is open and the towel I had tacked up the night before is on the floor. He said he had come in that way—*it looks like he did.* I walk up to Katie's door, debating whether I should open it or not. I'm fearful of what I might find on the other side. I slowly turn the knob and peek inside. She's in her bed, still sleeping. I close her door.

Buffett comes running up to me, hissing. He's probably freaked by Bob's sudden exit. I bend down to pick him up but he hisses again and jumps away from my reach. I'm a bit heartbroken by his refusal. I was seeking his comfort, the feeling of his soft fur, but he's having none of it.

I walk into the living room and look around. I see nothing unusual. Buffett then runs past me and into the kitchen. I'm grateful. If Bob is still here, Buffett will alert me. I can see that the front door is still locked with its deadbolt.

Bob didn't go out through that door.

I walk into the kitchen. The back door, which Bob claimed to be his escape route, is shut but unlocked. I lock it. I turn to the basement door. It's still shut and locked.

Buffett is now purring at my feet. I pick him up. When I hold him to my chest, I notice that my bathrobe is on backwards, the hood hanging in the front. I leave it. It's too much effort to fix.

Bob is gone. He's really gone. Oh God, did that really...really...just happen?

I can't wrap my brain around it. I can't understand or grasp it. How could something like this happen...*to me*. I can't fathom, comprehend, make sense of it. How? How is it possible that I just spent three hours—*three hours*—fighting for my life?

Three fucking, terrifying hours!

"Buffet," I whisper to the cat; my voice comes out in spurts of raw, painful emotion. "You saw it, right? It really did happen, right?"

Using my free hand, I reach for my throat. With my fingertips, I gently massage where the robe strangled me. It is tender to the touch. I swallow and wince. I clear my throat, causing pain to shoot in all directions. I take a deep breath. My lungs burn. My eyes water in response to both the agony and the memory. With my tongue, I feel the inside of my cheeks. Strands of torn tissue hang loose. The bleeding has stopped, but it stings. My nose is still sensitive from being crushed, but it isn't broken. My body is sore all over.

My legs are suddenly weak. They're shaking to the point that they can't hold me up. I need to call the police.

It's what you're supposed to do when something like this happens, right? Call the police?

I'm not sure my voice will support me, but I must force it. Buffett squirms to get away, but I hold him tight to me.

"Buffet," I whisper in his ear as I rub my face up to his. "Please, stay with me."

I reach for the portable phone, open a drawer and take out our phonebook. I struggle to carry the cat, the phone and the phonebook back into my room. I shut the door with my foot. Morning's light, coming through the white sheet curtains, casts the appearance of a gloomy fog throughout the room. It matches the way I am feeling.

I'm stuck...stuck inside a fog of numbness and shock.

I turn the light on and sit down at the end of my bed. Buffett escapes from my arms and sniffs at my sheets. His hair is raised, his tail pointing straight up. I don't have to imagine what he smells. *I won't ever forget it.* I open the phonebook to the front page where the emergency numbers are listed.

This isn't an emergency—anymore. I am not under attack—anymore. Bob is gone. He's not here—anymore. This isn't an emergency.

I turn past the emergency numbers and flip through to the government blue pages. I run my finger down the pages, looking for the Portland Police Bureau non-emergency number and call.

"Portland Police, how can I direct your call?" a woman's voice answers.

I start to shake. I'm not sure I can talk clearly.

"Umm," I swallow hard. "I'm not sure if this is an emergency or not... umm...my name is Cinda Stevens. A man just broke into my house and tried to rape me."

As I speak these words out loud, the reality of what just happened—or nearly happened—sinks in.

A man just tried to rape me. Bob tried to rape me. Oh, my God. Oh, my God. Hold it together Cinda. Hold it together.

"Are you all right?"

"Yes, I am." But my body is telling me otherwise.

What the hell? What the hell? What the hell?

Suddenly, I want to vomit. I want to run away. I want to cry and scream. Reality is setting in. My mind is going wild. My body is going into shock. I can feel the truth welling up inside of me.

"Is he still in your house?"

"No, he just left." I want to cry. I fight off the emotion.

"Do you have a description?"

Oh God...what did he look like? What did Bob look like? I don't want to remember. I don't want to think about him again.

I feel my stomach lurch upwards and I swallow down the bitterness that wants to escape. I close my eyes and try to be brave enough to tell her everything I remember. I tell her his build, his skin color, his knit hat, his ripped jeans, his denim shirt...everything.

I hear her relay the information into the system. As I wait for her to come back to me, I watch the phonebook bounce on my lap because of my shaking legs. I toss it onto the ground and reach for Buffett.

"A police officer will be at your door shortly. Are you hurt?"

I'm a wreck. I'm scared. My body is so tense that it hurts. But I'm not *that* kind of hurt.

"No, just really freaked out. Do you need my address?"

She tells me she's sending the police based on the phone line I called in on. "Stay on the line with me," she instructs. A moment later, I hear a knock at my front door. I nearly jump out of my skin.

"Someone's at my door," I whisper into the phone.

My heart is racing so fast I'm afraid I might faint.

Oh God…what if it's Bob coming back…coming back to finish?

"That will be the police, honey," she assures me. "Can you take the phone with you to the door?"

"Yes."

I take a deep breath, swallow hard and will my body to relax. It doesn't work.

"You can let me go when the police are inside the house with you," she says.

I somehow manage to walk across the living room to the door. A large man dressed in police blues is standing on the porch. He's as large as the doorframe. *He's huge.* On his shoulder, his walkie-talkie is giving out the description of Bob between bouts of static.

"Yes, it's the police. They're here," I tell the woman on the phone.

"OK, honey. You're safe now. They'll take care of you."

Safe.

Safe…a word I never gave much thought to…before now. Now, it's the most beautiful word I can think of.

S A F E.

I want to cry because of her kindness and for using the word safe. I can feel the emotions well up and constrict my throat. I don't want to hang up and stop talking to her. We've been talking for only a few minutes, but she's become my lifeline, my safety line, my line to sanity—I'm afraid to let her go. But she hangs up before I can plead with her to stay with me.

I move aside for the giant policeman to enter my small home. I lock my knees so they don't buckle beneath me. The safety I feel with him in my house is palpable. As he enters, he seems to shrink down to a more reasonable size. My mind may be playing tricks on me, or perhaps it's my heart needing a gigantic man dressed in blue to be my savior.

I need him to be larger than life, or at least larger than Bob.

"Miss," he says with a nod. He pinches the button on the walkie-talkie pinned to his shoulder and talks into it. "I'm in the house with the victim."

I'm not sure what he says next because my mind is stuck on the word "victim."

Victim?

Am I really a victim? I wasn't officially raped. I wasn't beat up, or murdered. I'm alive and well enough to stand here with this giant man, with my sweatshirt bathrobe on backwards.

Victim?

"Mind if I take a look around?" he asks. The crackle coming from his walkie-talkie is interrupted because other officers are telling him that they are searching the area outside.

"Sure. Yes. Do. Umm…I'm sorry that my bathrobe is on backwards. I…umm…had to get dressed in a hurry." I can feel my face flush—*I am so embarrassed.*

I can't believe that just moments ago, I was naked, on my bed, with a violent man. Can this policeman see it on me? What does a victim look like?

Do I look different now?

"It's OK, miss. I don't mind," he gently says, glancing my way with concern. "Are you all right? Do you need to sit down?"

"I'm OK," I tell him, worried that I might look worse than I feel—*which is crappy.*

What does a victim look like? How is she supposed to behave?

"I need to tell my roommate what's going on. I don't want her to wake up to all this and be frightened."

The officer searches the house as I head over to Katie's room. His presence offers me a level of courage and confidence I need right now. The static noise from his walkie-talkie, and the voices traveling through it, echo around the house. Although it is jarring, it's also reassuring.

It's the sound of safety, of his strength, of his power over Bob.

I knock lightly on Katie's door and open it. Buffett runs to be let into his master's room, away from the giant man and all the noise. He jumps on her bed.

"Katie. Wake up," I whisper.

"Huh," Katie says turning over in her covers.

"Katie, wake up," I whisper again but a little louder. I can't believe how calm my voice sounds. "I don't want you to panic, but a man broke into our house tonight and tried to rape me. The police are here, so you might want to get up."

Katie bolts upright in bed. Her eyes go wild as she tries to focus on me and register what I just said.

"What? What? What did you say?"

Katie dissolves into tears as I stand at the door, not having a clue what to do. I had hoped not to frighten her but it didn't work. She is scared. I scared her and I feel responsible.

"Katie, I'm OK. The police are here, so you might want to get dressed."

I can hear the crackle of the walkie-talkie getting louder. The policeman must be walking toward us.

The noise startles Katie even more. Her panicked eyes search out the noise behind me.

"Oh, my God! Oh, my God! Oh, my God!" she screams in panic, on the verge of becoming hysterical. "Cinda! Cinda! Oh, my God!"

I hear loud static in my right ear. I turn and see the policeman looking over my shoulder. Katie screams at the sight of him. Her eyes are wild as her brain tries to catch up to what she's heard me say and what she is seeing.

"Everything OK in here?" he asks.

Katie is sitting up in bed. Her blankets have slid onto her lap. She's naked from the waist up. The policeman turns around and walks the few feet back into the living room.

"Cinda, I heard voices last night! I thought it was Scott! Oh, my God!"

"Katie, I'm all right. I'm just so relieved that you're OK. I was afraid that…. Well, he's gone. The police are here. We're safe."

I do my best to remain calm, hoping if I remain calm she will too.

"Miss," the police officer is calling me from the other room.

Katie gets out of bed and stumbles around, looking for something to put on. She hasn't stopped crying. I close the bedroom door and walk into the living room. I feel sorry for her. She's usually so cool, calm and collected. It isn't that her reaction is wrong. It means that something awful *did* happen and she knows enough to be upset.

Something really…really…awful did happen…and it happened to…me.

My savior in blue is standing at attention like the soldier he is, like the superhero he is, like the knight in shining armor he is. It's not just his stance and stature…it's his presence that makes me feel safe, truly and unbelievably safe, that maybe everything will be all right.

"Miss, they've captured a suspect. Are you willing to go with me to identify him?"

Bob? Could they have captured Bob?

"Sure…umm…I need to change. Is that OK?" I ask, almost in tears because of the gentle way he is talking to me…and because…I may be seeing Bob again.

"Of course; I'll tell them we'll be on our way in a few minutes."

He leans into his shoulder, punches the button on his walkie-talkie and informs the officer on the other end.

I rush into my bedroom and shut the door. I have trouble taking off my bathrobe because my arms feel weak and useless. I struggle to pull it over my head. A flash of Bob having just done the same sends me into a panic. I hold my breath as I quickly pull it off. I grab my underwear and step into them with shaking legs. I almost fall over. As I connect the bra hooks behind my back, I feel a strange sense of security. I slip a T-shirt on with ease but need to sit down on my bed to pull on my jeans. I grab a sweatshirt out of a drawer, slip my arms in and zip it up to my neck. I slide my tennis shoes onto my feet without bothering to hook the back of the shoe over my heel. I'm wearing them like slippers.

As I leave my bedroom, Katie is coming out of hers wearing sweatpants and an oversized shirt. She's hunched over with her arms curled around her chest. She sees me, hesitates for a second, straightens her back and looks right at me. I can tell she's measuring my emotions. I walk up to her and put an arm around her shoulders. She's shaking— or perhaps it's me.

"I'm all right. I didn't mean to scare you. Katie, he didn't get to do what he came to do. I kept him from doing it."

"Miss, they're waiting," the police officer's voice echoes through the house and makes both Katie and me jump.

"They caught a guy. I need to go identify him," I tell her.

Katie looks panicked.

"Can you call into work for me? Let them know I'll be late coming in. But don't tell them what happened. I don't want to freak them out."

"Cinda, are you serious? You are *not* going into work today!"

Katie places her hands on both of my shoulders and looks up at me, directly into my eyes. She takes a few seconds before she speaks.

"Cinda, you are not, I repeat...NOT going into work today. Don't be silly. It's obvious that what's happened hasn't sunk in yet. I'll call and tell them you're *not* coming in." She is speaking with her familiar authority.

I'm grateful to be told what to do. I appreciate Katie taking charge and begin to feel things getting back into their proper place. I realize how dependent I am on her steadiness.

Of course, she's right...work is a stupid idea.

"Should my roommate go with us?" I break eye contact with Katie and focus on the officer. "It might not be safe for her to be alone in this house right now."

"There's an officer outside. He'll stand guard while we're gone. There are others policing the neighborhood. She'll be safe. I assure you."

I follow the officer outside. The early morning sky is lit with red and blue lights coming from two police cars parked in the street. As we walk down the front steps, another officer walks toward us. They nod in some unspoken and understood language. He leads me to his car.

Morning commuters slow down to stare at us in curiosity. A wave of self-consciousness comes over me. I wonder what these people are thinking when they see me with this policeman. I feel guilty, as if I've done something wrong. I feel awkward and exposed, as if I'm the criminal.

Is this what it feels like to be a victim?

Guilty?

Chapter 11

THE SUSPECT

The officer opens the front door to the passenger seat of his car and I slide in. He walks around and gets into his seat, locks his seatbelt and turns on his siren to warn traffic we have the right-of-way. As we dodge through rush hour traffic with lights and siren blaring, cars pull over and make room for us. I can't shake this feeling that I've done something wrong, that others are looking at me wondering what crime I've committed.

We drive a few blocks until we get to a gravel parking lot. I don't recognize this part of my neighborhood. In the middle of the empty lot is a police car with its lights on. An officer exits the car and waits as we pull up. My officer positions his car nearby. The standing officer opens the door to the back seat of his car. A man fitting my description of Bob is sitting in the back seat, handcuffed and looking frightened.

The officer asks me, "Is this the man?"

Through the window, I look at the man with hands tied behind his back and see similarities to Bob, but I'm not sure. I hesitate to roll down my window because it's acting as a protective shield. I roll it down anyway to get a clearer view.

"Take your time," the officer says.

The guilt I felt on the way over here is still hanging over my head. It's exaggerated now...because what I say will determine the potential fate of this person. As much as I want to capture Bob, I'm worried that this man isn't Bob. I am more worried that I might send the wrong man to prison.

This is too much. This man's...future. This...responsibility. It's too much.

I can't bear the thought of looking at Bob again. I don't want to see him again, *ever*. But, to be sure, I need to get a closer look.

"I can't tell from here. It was really dark in my room."

"Take your time," he responds with a gentleness and patience that I appreciate.

His tenderness, though, doesn't help my overwhelming concern of making a mistake. Over the radio, I hear that they've caught a couple other suspects. I need to identify this man now.

"Is it possible for me to get a closer look?" I ask timidly.

"Are you really up for that?"

"I don't have a choice, do I?"

I open the door to let myself out. The police officer standing outside the other car immediately stiffens and stands at attention. I see his right-hand rest on his gun. It's a subtle move, but it makes me feel safe. I suppose he wasn't expecting me to get out and wants to make sure that the guy stays put in his car. My officer comes around the car and stands with me. I see him nod at the other officer.

Together my officer and I walk toward the car. I feel the gravel under my shoes. The flashing lights are blinding me, and at the same time giving off beautiful colors of security. The policeman whose car we are approaching leans over the door. I hear him tell the man not to move. I see the man freeze in understanding.

When I approach the vehicle, I take in the man's appearance. He is wearing a knit cap. His shirt is similar to Bob's, lightweight denim. His jeans have holes. I stand there looking down at him. The thought of being this close to Bob again sends a shiver of terror down my spine.

Is this Bob? I am not sure...I am not sure.

An unbearable thought occurs to me.

"I need to smell him," I whisper, my emotions deepening my voice, followed by instant regret at the suggestion.

"I'm sorry?" asks my police officer, stunned. "What did you say?"

"The guy that...well...you know...I mean...he had a really strong smell," I tell him, almost embarrassed and dreading the thought of smelling it again.

With the police officers on either side of me, I feel somewhat safe. My knight in blue nods as the other officer leans in before me and threatens the man not to move. I think of Bob's awful, nauseating, foul body odor. The smell still lines the hairs inside my nostrils. I have no desire to do this, but it's the only way I can be sure.

I cannot believe this. What the hell? This is awful.

Despite my inner freak out, I lean into the car and sniff. I smell toothpaste. I smell maybe some aftershave. I don't smell much of anything else.

I don't smell Bob.

"I'm not sure…he looks like him…maybe," I whisper to my police officer as I straighten up. "But he doesn't smell like the guy that broke into my house."

"What else do you remember about him? Qualities that stand out… that were unusual."

"I remember his hands being really, really rough." I shudder as I remember Bob's sandpaper hands on my body.

"You want to feel his hands?" the other officer asks, surprised.

I nod yes. But everything inside of me is screaming, *NO!*

The other officer is already leaning in and undoing the man's handcuffs. He is whispering something to him and I can see that the man is planning on following the orders. The officer positions the man sideways so his feet are outside of the car. I look at my policeman and he nods for me go forward.

"You'll be safe. Or we'll kill him."

I try to smile. I hope it's a joke.

I pray that it isn't.

The officer is holding the man's wrists out to me. As I reach down and touch his hands, I avoid looking at his face. If it is Bob, I don't want him to see my fear. If it isn't Bob, I don't want him to see my guilt. His hands are rough.

But not Bob-rough.

"It's not him," I tell the officers with disappointment and with a touch of relief.

Oh God, this poor man.

As I get back into the car, I look back at the man. I empathize with him. I can't possibly imagine what it must have been like for him—to have been on his way to work or wherever and get arrested.

This man…this innocent man…got put into cuffs because of me.

"Are you willing to look at another suspect?"

I nod in agreement. I lean back against the seat, exhausted.

He turns his siren on and again cars make room for us. We drive a few minutes to our destination. We pull up next to a police car parked outside a convenience store. The officer gets out and opens the back door. In the back is a handcuffed man looking confused and frightened. This man is wearing a knit cap and jeans with holes in them but he isn't Bob.

This man is black.

I remain in the car and tell my officer that this isn't Bob.

"The guy that assaulted me is white."

He radios out that information. The other officers, who apprehended other men, now tell him that they then have nothing.

As we drive back to my house he asks, "How are you holding up? You did incredibly well back there. I'm just sorry that it wasn't the guy. We're going to catch him. I promise you. We will."

My emotions hang all over my body like a wet blanket. They aren't offering any warmth or support, *they just feel heavy.* The feeling of disappointment that it wasn't Bob conflicts with the sense of relief that I didn't have to see him again. They mix with the feeling of guilt I have about that poor man who got detained because of me. And then there's the overpowering emotion of feeling unworthy of this officer's support and kindness.

I'm just a 19-year-old girl, and it seems like the entire Portland Police department has come to my rescue.

I'm beyond tired. I want to get back to the house. I need to be back with Katie. I have a deep yearning to go home—home to my parents.

I need my mom and dad.

Chapter 12

THE TRIP HOME

My knight in blue drives me back to the house. As he walks me up the front stairs, he speaks into his walkie-talkie, informs the police officer inside we are back. The door opens and Katie springs from the couch, runs toward me and gives me a hug. I tell her that the guy wasn't my guy and she groans.

The other officer says, "I've thoroughly searched the house, its windows and doors. Everything is secure and safe. Officers are monitoring your neighborhood today and we've increased patrols in the area around the clock. We're doing our best to protect the two of you."

"Thank you," I tell him, and I mean it.

"You really should get some blinds up on your windows," my officer says, pointing to us and then at the windows. He looks at Katie and says, "Especially in your bedroom, young lady."

We both nod, embarrassed. He saw Katie naked this morning,

Oh God, Bob saw ME naked this morning!

"Stan, we need to…" the other officer signals toward the door. My officer nods back.

"Like I said, we'll be patrolling your neighborhood today. That guy won't make a move while we're around."

We walk them to the door. Despite his words of encouragement, I don't like the idea of being in this house without them.

"A detective will be contacting you today or tomorrow. Lock up behind us," my officer says over his shoulder.

I lean into the door and turn the deadbolt. Katie's standing right next to me. She's looking directly at me, trying to take a reading of how I'm holding up. I wonder what she sees when she looks at me. Do I look different? Does being a victim make someone look different?

Do I have that look now?

I haven't looked in the mirror since I brushed my teeth last night.

"What do you want to do now?" she asks.

"I'm not sure I can work today," I mention, avoiding her eyes.

"Ya think?" she says sarcastically and tries to laugh. "I called your work and told them you weren't coming in. I called in sick too. I don't think you should be alone."

"Thank you, Katie." I'm grateful. She may have been freaked out earlier, but now she's solid and strong. "I think I should call my parents and tell them what happened."

I find the phone on the couch where Katie was sitting earlier. As I start to punch in my mom's phone number, I feel Katie's hand on mine, stopping me.

"Cinda, I don't think this is something you say to a parent over the phone. I think they need to see you—to see that you're all right. I think you should tell them in person."

"I suppose you're right. Will you go with me?"

"Of course, and I'll drive. I'm going to brush my teeth, change my clothes and then we can head out. How are you holding up?"

"I'm OK…I think…I'm just confused and tired."

I follow her into the bathroom and grab my toothbrush. We both squeeze into the bathroom around the pedestal sink. It feels nice to be close. I glimpse at us in the mirror. Katie looks bright and awake, but worried. She smiles at my reflection. I turn my attention to look at mine.

I don't even recognize myself. Something IS different…behind my eyes…it's written on my face…an invisible sign that reads: "I've been assaulted, almost raped, almost killed."

Is this the mask of a victim?

I haven't touched my hair since I went to bed last night. It's ratted and knotted and the ponytail sits cockeyed on the side of my head. I can't believe I left the house looking like this. I want to cry when I think of why, and what did this to my hair…*to me*. I look away from my reflection. The memory is too much to accept. I don't like what my eyes do when I see them remembering.

Stop, stop, stop remembering, Cinda…stop thinking of it.

Avoiding eye contact with myself, I turn and look at the window. Bob said he came in this way. I shudder as I pull the ponytail scrunchie out of my hair and brush out the knots. It hurts, but the pain doesn't bother me because other parts of me hurt more…*like my heart*.

It's time to tell my parents.

What will they say? What will they think…of me?

I brush my teeth without looking in the mirror. My hands are shaking and I hope Katie won't notice. After I spit out the toothpaste, I splash some cold water on my splotchy face. Katie hands me a towel. I don't plan on changing my clothes or even attempting to put on makeup.

We get into Katie's sky-blue Ford Torino. As we drive around the block to take Interstate 5 southbound, I think about taking a nap. I lean on the door and close my eyes. On the back of my eyelids an entire movie plays out. Screen after screen of Bob lunging, grabbing, and trying to suffocate me. It replays over and over again: attack, retreat, attack, retreat.

Napping isn't going to work. I lean my back against the door and curl my legs up on the bench seat. Katie watches me through the corners of her eyes. As she maneuvers the long car in and out of traffic, we remain quiet. Once we get south of the Portland city limits, traffic thins and she looks over at me. I smile.

"You want to talk about it?"

"Yeah, I probably should. Dad always said, 'Keeping things inside will eat you up. It's best to talk about it.' So, maybe I should try."

I tell her the story from the beginning—with Buffett growling and hissing at what I thought was a mouse. As I tell the story, I feel a rush of adrenaline shoot through me. Instead of being afraid of my story, I become alive with it.

"Oh, my God, Katie!" I say with animation in my voice. "It was the craziest thing. I'm lying there in bed, still asleep, all pissed off at your stupid cat for waking me up. Instead, Buffett knew this guy was NOT supposed to be there. He was attacking Bob! He was trying to protect me!"

"Bob? Oh, my God, Cinda. Did you know him?"

She's trying to drive and look at me at the same time. Her long car seems to glide where her eyes look and I hear the bumps of the lane markers telling us that the tires are over the line. She looks back to the roadway to get the car back to center. She looks at me again, still with an expression of shock.

"You knew him?" she asks again.

"What? Oh. No! No! I didn't know him. I needed to call him a name and he wouldn't give it to me, so I decided to call him Bob."

"So, you decided to call him Bob?"

Bump bump bumpbumpbump go the tires over the lane markers. She looks back at the road, centering her car. Silence follows. I say nothing about her driving. I am too busy remembering how it was that I came about deciding to give the creep a name. My blood is pulsating rapidly through my body. It almost tickles. It is the kind of tickle that hurts. I want to laugh at being tickled. I want to laugh about calling the guy "Bob."

What the hell?

"Katie, when he first lunged at me, I screamed. I didn't realize I could make a noise like that! Didn't it wake you up? I can't believe it didn't wake you up. It seemed to echo in my ears for at least an hour."

"I heard something…but it didn't register. I listened for a bit and heard whispering, so I thought Scott came up to visit. Cinda, I'm so sorry."

She looks over at me. I can see the anguish on her face.

Bump bump bumpbumpbump.

Silence as she looks at the road. She's blaming herself.

"Katie, it is not your fault. God, please don't blame yourself."

She doesn't respond and that moment hangs between us for a few seconds.

I continue, "Katie, I knew I had to distract him. I offered to cook him steak!" A laugh escapes. The adrenaline is still pumping through my veins. I exhale and shift in the seat to avoid more laughter that seems to want to come.

She takes her eyes off the road yet again to look at me. I can tell what she's thinking; it's written all over her face. She's shocked that I laughed. There is nothing funny about this…but that laugh must have struck a chord in her because when she looks back to the road, I see that she's smiling.

She decides to see the humor because she laughs as she asks more questions. "Steak? You offered to cook him steak? Cinda, have you ever even cooked a steak? I don't think we even have any steak in the refrigerator or the freezer! Do we? And why steak, of all the things you could have offered?"

"No, I haven't ever cooked a freaking steak, and no, we don't have any. Isn't that just crazy? Oh, oh, and I even offered to make him some coffee. Coffee! I don't drink coffee! And I don't have a clue how to make that either!"

A laugh escapes. I attempt to control it, but it's hard. The pent-up emotions don't want to be silenced. Deep-seated hysteria begins to bubble its way to the surface. It sounds a bit like a crazy laugh.

Katie responds, her laughter awkward, "Let me see if I understand this. A man breaks into your bedroom in the middle of the night, attacks you, and you offer to cook him dinner?"

She's probably laughing because I am, but unlike my hysteria, her laugh is backed by confusion, laced with concern, rooted in caution. But I also know…we're laughing because this is just too crazy to be real. This shared moment is taking away the sting.

"It's crazy, but it just came out. I panicked and I just started saying anything I could think of to keep him distracted!"

This is just too freakin' CRAYZEE!

It is so unbelievable. This is so unbelievable…as if it's another person's life we're talking about.

"Did he take you up on it?" Katie wonders. "Wait, he obviously didn't. What would you have done if he said yes? Shit, Cinda!"

"Oh! I also offered him some of your iced tea. But then I unoffered it. I warned him not to accept the offer because your tea is so bitter!"

Hysteria is setting in. I can feel the shock and emotions mixing. It's a frightening cocktail. I'm afraid that if they completely mesh, I might lose myself inside the insanity.

Hold on, steady, Cinda. Hold it together.

Katie gives me a quick look of worry and then turns back to the road. She asks another question, pulling me back from the edge.

"So…get to the part about naming him Bob!"

"He said he had been watching us. Remember when I saw that reflection? I was right! It was Bob watching us!"

I stop laughing. I see Katie's face tighten. She's not laughing anymore either.

"Well…I thought that if he had been watching us, that he might know stuff about us already. So, I didn't want to piss him off by getting caught in a lie. Yet, if he didn't know stuff, I didn't want to give him any information."

I see Katie's hands tighten on the steering wheel. She doesn't look at me.

"I also wanted to seem friendly enough to be able to get information out of him. I knew he wouldn't open up to me if I didn't give the impression I was opening up to him," I pause for a second, remembering. "So…when he refused to give me his name, I told him I would call him Bob. When he asked me my name I told him Cindy, instead of Cinda. I thought that was close enough to the truth!"

For the hour-long drive, I tell Katie bits of the story and answer her questions. Hearing my own story being told through my own voice and words doesn't make it any more believable or bearable. It doesn't make it any easier to accept that this happened. It doesn't help me understand why it had to happen.

As we approach the Albany exit, the one that will take us to my father's medical office, I can feel tension build up inside of me. I have no idea how I'll tell my dad. I have no idea how he'll respond to this kind of news. My father and I have a very close relationship, especially after my parents' divorce. I'm concerned that this news will break his heart. I need to find some way to tell him so he won't be too upset. And...so he won't be upset that I interrupted his work and time with his patients.

I'm fearful he might blame me.

Or worse...think less of me.

Chapter 13

THE DAD'S CONCERN

We pull up into the parking lot at my dad's office. I get out of the car and shut the door with care. I try to do it silently, in hopes that I don't alert anyone that we've arrived. Now that I'm here, I'm even more nervous about telling him.

Crap, crap, crap…what is Dad going to say? How will he take this kind of news?

"Do you want me to go in with you?" asks Katie.

"Of course, yes. Please. Do. Come. I couldn't bear it in there without you."

I catch a glance of my reflection in the car's window and wish I had put on a touch of makeup. I look pale and tired and stressed. He'll see that something is wrong. I wear it now. I wear the mask, the sign of a victim.

Shit.

Katie follows me through the door. I see Jackie, his receptionist, at her desk. I must behave in a way that won't startle her. I don't want her to alert my dad that something's wrong.

"Hi, Jackie. If Dad isn't with any patients, can I see him? We won't be long," I say, standing tall and trying to appear stronger than I feel.

Her face lights up when she sees me, "Cinda! Sure, hold on just a minute."

She disappears from behind the desk and walks down the back hallway. I couldn't tell from her face, but it seems like she isn't worried.

I hope I can do the same for my dad.

The anxiety of seeing him builds up in the pit of my stomach and causes it to cramp. My desire to run away is real. I think about changing my mind. My eyes come to a rest on the exit sign across the room. I debate if I should take it.

"Maybe I should just call him later," I whisper to Katie. She grabs my arm, willing me to stay put…it works.

I notice the plaque on the wall with my father's name on it. It reads: *Dr. Kenneth McAlpine Stevens, M.D.* ◈ *Otolaryngologist* ◈ *Head & Neck Surgery.*

"I love saying that word: otolaryngologist," I say with pride.

Katie giggles.

I glance around the waiting room and see children and adults, each with some sort of breathing, swallowing or hearing issue—each needing a piece of my dad's time and expertise. The guilt for disturbing him increases.

"Cindy? What brings you down?" My father says behind me. Hearing him use my childhood name warms my heart and makes me feel young.

I do feel young…vulnerable…afraid. I wish I were 10 years old again and he could hold me and make it all better.

I shake it off. I'm an adult now. *I can do this.*

I turn to see my tall, fit, handsome father walking toward us. His dark hair and black-rimmed glasses add to his regalness. He is wearing a white lab coat over a blue shirt, with a black tie, and black slacks. A black and silver stethoscope is draped over the back of his neck. He's smiling.

But then a look of concern flashes across his face.

Shit, he sees it, that victim thing I'm wearing.

"Jackie, please hold my calls," he says without looking at her. His eyes haven't left mine. "Tell my patients I'll be with them as soon as I can."

He leads us down the hall, into his office and shuts the door. He sits down behind his wooden desk and motions us to sit in the two leather chairs opposite him. I take in a deep breath. An awkward chuckle escapes. I quickly cough to cover it up. I look at Katie for support. She nods at me.

"Sometimes it helps to just spit it out," he says, leaning forward on his desk.

"Well…umm…so sorry to interrupt you at your work. I can see you're really busy."

"Cindy, you're always welcome here. You always have priority. What is it? What's up?"

"Well…Dad…this is a little weird to tell you. But I thought that you'd want me to be the one…umm…well…it's so strange to say out loud," I pause, I swallow, I take in a deep breath. Then as I exhale, I tell him in a rush of words, "A man broke into our house this morning and tried to rape me but I'm OK and he didn't get away with it and the police have been called and I even had to identify a guy but it wasn't him."

I stop talking and bite my lower lip waiting for his reaction. He's silent, sitting there, handsome and impressive, in that white lab coat. He leans forward in his chair. He looks at me, then at Katie, and then back at me.

I hold my breath. I can't read his face. I can't tell what he's thinking. *Did he hear me? Did he understand me? Does he believe me?*

After a moment, he asks, "Are you, all right? Cindy. What the hell? Are you really, all right? Are you OK?"

He looks at Katie and asks her, "Is she, is she, all right? Is she OK?"

"Well…" Katie hesitates, looks at me and then back at my dad. "To be honest…I'm still waiting for her to break down. I don't think it's hit her yet."

She looks at me. They both look at me.

I look back at them. I don't get how they want me to respond. I don't get how I'm supposed to respond.

How do other women in my situation respond?

I don't respond. I shrug my shoulders and stare back at them.

"Guys, I'm OK! I'm more than OK. I kept the guy from doing anything to me! I beat him at his own game! It took me three hours, but I did it. Seriously, I'm OK!"

"Three hours?" they both say at the same time.

"He was in our house—in your room—for three hours?" Katie asks; her eyes giant.

"Yeah, it sucked," I answer.

"You beat him at his own game? What does that mean? What are you saying?" My father asks confused.

"Dr. Stevens, it's a crazy story…your daughter…she's amazing," Katie says, encouraging me to pick up the story.

I take a deep breath and start to talk. I decide to tell him a lighter, softer, easier version of the story. I choose to be careful, not to share everything— especially not the more frightening parts…or the naked parts. Instead, I focus on the strange and bizarre parts—offering food and drink and giving that violent man a name. I tell the story fast as I look at the top of his desk or at the stethoscope hanging on his chest. I tell the story fast so he can't interrupt or ask questions.

The more I talk, the less real…the less believable…it seems. I worry that he might not believe me.

"And now I'm here—alive and here to tell you about it."

Dad sits in stunned silence. I worry that I've said too much. I worry that I've scared him. I had hoped to avoid it. I take in a breath, chew on my lower lip and wait.

"Well, here's what I have to say," my dad's voice is stern, angry, and I feel my body tense in habit to his tone. "I've made it perfectly clear that I don't believe in guns. But right now…I wish I had one, because I'd use it to kill that son of bitch."

His sternness isn't directed at me. It's directed at the guy that assaulted me. My dad is serious. He's serious and he's mad and I love him for it. He wants to shoot Bob.

He'd kill Bob for me.

I hadn't realized how much I needed my dad to be mad—mad enough to kill someone—because that someone hurt me. In the middle of all this, my dad threatening to shoot Bob makes everything feel better.

Well…almost better.

"What do you need from me? How can I help you? What can I do for you?" He walks around his desk and sits on its edge. He appears to be pissed, afraid and confused all at the same time. I don't know how to help make him feel better. I don't know how to make me feel better, either. Reality is setting in and I don't know if I can keep it from coming.

"I just thought you should know," I tell him awkwardly. I avoid making eye contact since he is staring at me, concern pasted all over his face.

He reaches out to me, grabs my shoulders and pulls me to him. He gives me a long, tight hug. I melt in his embrace and feel some of my tension ease.

"Sometimes these things take a while to set in. You're in shock right now, so be patient with yourself. I love you and I'm here for you. I'm just so damn glad you're safe."

As I turn to leave, he gives Katie a hug goodbye too. I hear him whisper, *"When she comes out of shock, she'll need someone nearby."* Katie nods.

"I'm really all right, you guys! Really. I am."

We head back to Katie's car. When I get inside, I sit down and relive the conversation I just had with my father. I entered afraid of what his reaction would be. Now, I feel a strange, yet wonderful sense of being loved and protected—*protected*…something I never needed from my dad before.

I realize something else too. Even though it was a man who harmed me, it *is* men who are making me feel safe again—the police officer who showed up at my house, the policeman with the guy in the back of his car, my dad.

Thank God for these men.

I'm so glad Katie made me come tell my dad in person.

Now, I can tell my mom.

Now, I can tell Scott.

Chapter 14

THE MOM'S WORRY

Thirty minutes later, we pull into my mother's gravel driveway. Mom's home is an old plantation-style house built in the 1880s. Nestled in an apple orchard, it's a charming two-story house, painted white with black shutters. A red bench on the front porch, which has followed my family wherever we moved, is a welcoming sight.

When we get out of the car, I can feel my guts gurgle with anxiety. I really don't want to have to tell my mom…this is my mom—*My mom.* This is going to be hard for her to hear. It's going to scare the crap out of her.

We walk in through the backdoor. I call out my mother's name so we don't startle her. She appears around the corner from the kitchen with a giant smile.

"Cindy! What a great surprise! Why are you here?" she squeals and gives me a giant hug. She does the same for Katie.

Then she looks at me.

"Cindy? What's happened?"

Ugh, this victim thing is like a flashing neon sign.

The look of worry on her face breaks my heart. It will break her heart if I tell her. I can't tell her…*I can't do it.*

I change my mind.

I'll just make up a different story and then we'll be on our way.

Katie sees my hesitation and says, "Can we sit down?"

Mom leads us into the living room. The furniture is so far apart that it doesn't seem intimate, but we sit anyway.

Both women look at me. I look at them. Nothing comes out.

Katie speaks up, "Ah…OK, then…. We came here to tell you something that happened to Cinda last night, well…actually this morning." She looks at me to see if I want to pick up the conversation. I don't say or do anything, so she continues. "A man broke into our house last night."

My mother gasps, and looks at both of us. "Oh, my gosh! What happened?"

Katie looks at me, encouraging me to continue with the story. I don't respond. "Well...he actually broke into Cinda's room."

My mother gasps again and looks right at me. I swallow hard.

I should tell her. I've already told Dad. I must tell her too.

"OK...here goes. Mom, first off, I'm fine," I pause to take in a breath and force myself to continue. "The guy who broke into our house, he came into my room and tried to...."

I get choked up with emotion and stall.... I try to fight off the tears, but I can't.... My mom has always been able to do this. It's a nasty trick of hers. Her look of sincere worry has always broken down my defensive emotional barriers.

I can't hide anything from her.

"I was wondering when the tears would come," Katie says looking at me, her voice soft and kind. "She's been trying to be brave, I think."

"Tell me what happened...honey," my mom's voice is shaking.

I know my mom...even though she's asking...she doesn't really want to know, she's too afraid of what I might say.... Her controlled emotions aren't helping my resolve. I swallow back my own emotions and gather courage.

"Mom, he jumped me and tried to rape me," my voice cracks.

I said it...It was awful to say, but I said it.

I tell the rest at a quick pace, "BUT, it didn't happen! It didn't happen! I tricked him! I distracted him! I offered him steak and coffee! I even asked his name! When he wouldn't tell me, I gave him a name! I called the police! They came to the house! I had to identify a suspect. It wasn't him. And now I'm here." I take a breath.

I force a laugh. Katie does too.

My mother isn't laughing. I don't expect her to be laughing. She stares at me looking shocked and silent. My dad did the same thing.

What are my parents thinking about after I tell them? What is going on in their heads? What is it like to have a daughter that was almost raped and killed? Are they afraid? Are they mad? Do they believe me? Do they blame me? What will Scott think?

Scott! Shit, I need to tell Scott!

"I need to tell Scott. He needs to hear this too."

I jump up, leaving my mother hanging and head into the small kitchen. I pick up the mustard yellow receiver off the wall-mounted phone and dial in Scott's parents' number. As the phone rings, I untangle its long spiral cord. Memories come flooding back of the long conversations he and I had on this very phone when we were in high school.

"Hello," he answers. His voice soothes me.

"Hey, Babe. It's me."

"Hey, Babe. What's up?"

"I'm at my mom's, with Katie. I have something I need to tell you. Can you come over right away?"

"Ah, sure. I'll be right there."

I pour myself a glass of water...stalling my return to the living room, where my mother is waiting. In just a few minutes his small black Toyota Hilux pickup pulls into the driveway. Scott has been part of my life for so long that he just walks into the house. I greet him at the back door.

"What's up?" he asks.

I give him a hug and a quick kiss. He smells wonderful and familiar and again I feel safe in the presence of a man.

"What's going on? What brings you down here? Babe, are you OK?" he asks looking at me.

I can't hide *it* from him either. Being with my mom has my emotions right on the surface, but I am determined that I will not scare him, either. He just needs to know the basics. Plus...what would he think of me if he really knew what I did?

Inviting Bob to lay with me...no! No! He can't know that!

"I've got something to tell you.…. Let's go sit in the living room. I'm in the middle of telling Mom."

We walk back and sit on the couch. I hesitate, swallow my emotions, take in a breath and force out the words, "Something happened to me last night."

With care, I choose my words. I tell both him and my mother what happened, leaving out anything and everything that might disturb them—*or me.*

When I'm done, Scott just stares at me. He looks at me with a puzzled, concerned expression. It's the same expression as my mom's. What is it? Why do they hesitate? Do I appear different to them now?

Am I different?

"I'm OK! It was a crazy night. But it's over now," I'm quick to assure them both, wanting them to change their expressions.

Silence.

Perhaps their brains are processing the information. I look at Katie for support. She shrugs her shoulders, not knowing what to say or do, either. The silence is killing me. I don't know how to take care of them. I can barely take care of myself.

I wish I could make it easier for them—easier for me.

"Oh, my God," Scott finally says. Worry is now written all over his face. "Are you sure you're OK? Are you staying here tonight?"

"I'm OK," I say for the umpteenth time. And then again for the sake of repetition, "He didn't get away with what he came to do. No, I'm not staying, I need to work tomorrow."

Two different expressions come from the women in the room. My mother likes the idea of me staying overnight and is nodding in agreement with Scott's suggestion. Katie's expression is that of disbelief; she can't believe I am thinking of work right now.

They are both right. I don't want to go back to that house and I don't want to go back to work, but I can't just hide from it either.

The sooner I get back to my normal, the better.

Mom interrupts, "Well…I'm hungry. Are you guys hungry? I'll fix some lunch."

"Yes, please," Katie and I say at the same time.

I'm so grateful for the interruption. Plus, it's already one o'clock and neither Katie nor I have eaten. It's not surprising that my mom wants to feed us; she nurtures that way, like most moms do. But really, I think she's trying to adjust the attention away from the subject of the attack, switch gears, get back to normal. It's her way. In any crisis, she tries to get things back to normal as quickly as possible.

It's where I got it from.

Scott speaks up, "Thanks, but I need to get to work. I was headed out the door when Cinda called. Walk me out, Cinda?"

He stands, takes my hand and leads me out to his car. Once alone, he gives me a warm and gentle hug. It's long and wonderful. Again, I breathe in his clean goodness.

"Cinda, I don't know what to say. Do you want me to stay here with you? I can call work and tell them I'm not coming in."

"No. Thanks though. I should get back. I guess a detective is coming to the house to get more information."

"I hate to leave you like this. I'll come up to Portland as soon as I can."

He grabs me again and holds me close. I can feel his heartbeat against mine. I feel his love for me and it acts like a vacuum sucking up my insecurities. I wish I could stay right here, like this forever.

As I wave goodbye, I feel the guilt rise up inside of me. My story... this thing that happened...isn't scaring just Katie and me...it's scaring everyone I tell.

Would it have been better, easier, less scary for them...if I had just kept it to myself?

Why didn't I just keep it to myself? Did they really need to know?

I don't want them to be afraid. No one should have to feel burdened by what happened to me. I need to figure this out on my own. I'm an adult now. But...*yet*...I really do need their support. I want them to know that something awful happened to me...they deserve to know. I can't imagine them not knowing.... It's all so confusing and conflicting. I'm not sure what is the proper way to behave in a situation like this.

I want to do the right thing...but I don't know what that is....

Still confused and consumed by my thoughts, I walk back inside. Katie is sitting at the kitchen table talking to my mother who is standing at the stove. They stop talking when I enter. The smell of grilled cheese sandwiches and tomato soup fills the room.

Mom asks, "We were just talking about what you'll do next?" She spreads mayonnaise on one side and butter on the other side of the bread slice then slops it on top of the cheese bread already in the heated pan. "I don't want you to go back to that house. I never liked that place."

Yes, Mom. I remember you not liking the house.

Right now, I agree with her. Katie and I look at each other. By the expression on her face, she can't imagine going back either. But...I need to deal with it. I need to get over it. I need to get past it. Who knows; perhaps they've caught Bob by now. Perhaps this is just a really, really bad day and tomorrow will be normal again.

I need to go back.

"The police said that a detective will contact me today. So, I need to get back. Plus, I have to work tomorrow."

Get things back to normal...as quickly as possible.

No one responds. Mom places the sandwiches on plates and pours the soup into bowls. The three of us sit down to eat. We talk of the weather, of my work, of my brother who is getting ready to graduate from high school and my other brother and sister who are both in middle school. We talk about my stepdad and his failing health. We talk about Katie's mom and her dad. But we don't venture again into the conversation about the attack.

My mother is good with not talking about upsetting things. I'm grateful to have this distracted and light-hearted moment. She isn't pretending that nothing happened...*she's trying to get us to stop thinking about it.*

After lunch, Katie and I say our goodbyes. My mom gives me a hug that's so tight my back pops, but it's backed by love...a love that only a mother can give.

I slide into Katie's car and we wave goodbye. It's hard to leave my mom. I can't imagine what's going through her mind. I lean against the car window and try to sleep as Katie drives us back to Portland, back to the house....

The house that Bob broke into.

Chapter 15

THE DETECTIVE

Katie and I have been home for an hour and have already seen two police cars drive around our block. Even though our neighborhood is being patrolled and our house is being monitored, we're feeling jittery, exposed and vulnerable. We can't help but wonder if Bob is watching us right now. This is a strange and frightening way to feel in a home, a home that just the day before felt safe. It's unsettling…it's scary to think that things might never go back to normal.

Until Bob is caught, I won't feel safe.

My nerves get the best of me and I start pacing around the living room.

Why hasn't the detective called yet?

"I can't stand this. I can't stand this. I wish he'd call already!" I voice my frustration as I walk back and forth in front of Katie.

"He'll call. He'll call. Shit! This IS crazy! Yesterday we were eating popcorn and laughing at a stupid TV show! Now, this creep changes everything! We won't feel safe until they put that asshole behind bars!" she chimes back, sharing my stress.

When the phone rings, we both jump. We giggle at each other's overreaction. I pick up the portable phone from the coffee table.

"Hello."

Please be the detective, please be the detective.

"Cinda Stevens, please," says a male voice on the other end.

"This is Cinda."

Please be the detective, please be the detective.

"Cinda, this is Detective Thom Redmond. I've been assigned to your case," his voice is gentle but all business. "I'd like to meet with you and talk about the incident that took place in your home this morning. When would be a good time for me to come to you?"

"Anytime," I tell him relieved. *Thank God, it's the detective.* "We just got home and would love someone here. We're really freaked out."

I wonder…*what does having a 'detective assigned to my case' mean?*

"I'll be coming with another detective to hook up an alarm system in your house. We'll be there within the hour."

"OK," I'm disappointed it isn't sooner.

I look at the clock: 4:45. I can't believe this day is almost over and yet it has felt like the longest day of my life. It's starting to get dark outside, and the weather has changed. The sound and smell of rain seeps into the house. Rainy nights once made me feel cozy and brought comfort. Tonight, though, the sensation is heavy and the dampness adds to my sinking feeling…of dread.

I am dreading—dreading, dreading, dreading—my first night after Bob.

An hour later, we hear a knock on our door. I rush to answer it. Katie catches Buffett so he won't escape. She stops me before I unlock the deadbolt.

"Who is it?" she calls out. She looks at me with the expression of disbelief. *She's right…things are different now.*

"Detective Thom Redmond. We spoke on the phone earlier."

I open the door. Standing on our small front porch are two men, both in khakis and Columbia Sportswear rain jackets, their hoods up. The first one removes the hood of his jacket. Drops splatter on the porch. His face is friendly, his smile sincere. He wears glasses under a head of thick brown hair. He greets us by showing his badge from his wallet. The other man holds his wallet open too. In his other hand is a toolbox.

I invite them in.

"Cinda?" the first man asks, looking at the two of us.

Katie points to me, as I point to myself. He shakes my hand. Katie, fighting to keep Buffett from attacking the men, nods.

"I'm Katie, her roommate. This is Buffett," she says and the cat hisses.

"I'm Detective Thom Redmond," he says, cautiously watching the cat. "This is Detective Cooper."

The second detective leans in for a handshake with me. He nods at Katie, who with a quick apology, runs to her room, deposits Buffett inside, shuts the door and returns.

Detective Redmond says, "I've been told some of the details of your case. If you don't mind, I'd like to ask you some questions?"

"Of course," I answer, but a huge wave of apprehension flows over me. *Oh, I really don't want to have to remember it again.*

"Would you like some coffee? Or some iced tea?" Katie asks.

I shake my head at her, but she ignores me.

"No. Thank you, though," Detective Redmond answers. He looks at the man who came in with him. "While we talk, Detective Cooper will install the alarm system. Would you mind showing him where you'd like it?"

"An alarm system?" I ask, curious.

"Well, it's more like a panic button," Detective Cooper tells me. "I understand that a man broke into your home in the middle of the night? I assume he attacked you in your bedroom?"

"Yes," I answer, trying not to think about *that man* in my bedroom. I shake off the cloud of dread hanging over me.

"Did he come into your room?" he asks, looking at Katie.

"No, I don't think so. Although…come to think of it…. Buffett was out this morning. He always sleeps with me and I sleep with my door closed. Somehow he got out…."

I look at Katie, surprised. She's right. Buffett always sleeps with her. He was with her when I said goodnight. Did she get up to go to the bathroom and the cat snuck out? Or, did Bob go into Katie's room first?

"Cinda, how did it play out? How did he make himself known?" Detective Redmond asks.

"At first, I heard the cat hissing and I thought he was chasing a mouse. But when I opened my eyes, I saw a man. I thought he was the fix-it guy our landlord sent to fix the hole in the wall. I asked him to come back later," I laugh. They don't. I continue, "I screamed, after he told me to shut up and then he attacked me."

I shudder. Detective Redmond takes notes. Katie turns pale. Detective Cooper observes. Buffett scratches at Katie's bedroom door. Life seems to be turning into short sound bites. I seem to be super focused on everything.

It's all so strange.

"Sorry about the cat," Katie apologizes. "He's locked up so he won't attack you. He doesn't seem to like men."

"She's right," I agree. "He wasn't chasing a mouse, he was attacking the guy who broke into my room. It's as if Buffett was trying to protect me."

Thank God for Buffett.

"Do you know how he got into your house?" Detective Redmond asks me, looking up from his small notebook.

"Yes, he actually told me! He told me he came in through the bathroom window," I feel my heart racing and notice that my hand is shaking as I point in that direction.

Detective Cooper walks toward the bathroom. We follow him. It's a tight squeeze with the four of us in the short hallway between our bedrooms. Detective Redmond maneuvers his way between us and enters the bathroom. He lifts off the thumb-tacked towel, unlocks the bathroom window, lifts it open and pokes his head outside. It's grown dark outside and a cold breeze blows around us. I shiver. So does Katie. We move closer together.

"Hmmm, this window is high off the ground. It wouldn't be easy to climb through. Was it left unlocked?"

Katie answers, "I'm not sure. We usually leave it open a crack to help vent out the steam from the shower. But last night, neither of us took a shower, so I'm not sure if it was open or not."

I nod in agreement. I don't remember.

Detective Redmond pulls his head back in. His brain must be ticking through possibilities because he's whispering to himself when he says, "He'd had to have opened the window first...which would have been difficult from the outside...he could have used a stick or broom handle to push it open, if it was unlocked, of course...but he'd have to have made a running jump to get up to it, or climbed on something.... Tomorrow, in daylight, I'll check to see if there are any scuffs on the outside wall."

He backs up a few feet and looks around the bathroom. He bends down looking at the floor, I assume for any markings Bob might have left behind.

He continues talking to himself, "There aren't any footprints in here... and it's muddy out there...."

He moves his hands like a mime, pantomiming what Bob might have done after he climbed through the window. He signals from the window to the toilet and then to the floor.

"If he did come in this way, he'd had to have made some sort of noise. You heard nothing of him entering?" he asks both Katie and me.

I answer first, "I didn't hear anything until Buffett woke me up."

Katie says, "I didn't hear any noise from the bathroom. But I did hear soft voices coming from Cinda's room. I thought Cinda's boyfriend was here, so I didn't do anything...I didn't do anything to help her." Her voice cracks with emotion.

Katie's visibly upset. I lean into her, pressing my side up to hers for support. As strange as it is to have detectives in the house, their presence is making me feel safe, but not her. Having them here, asking questions, requiring me to relive the night...seems to be causing her more anxiety.

Having them here is making what happened even more real…more real and more frightening.

Detective Redmond shuts and locks the window and reattaches the towel with the tacks.

To Detective Cooper he says, "Coming in this way, it doesn't make any sense." Then to us, "Girls, I have a feeling he came in another way. I'm going to look around. Cooper here will take care of things."

Detective Redmond squeezes between us and heads back into the living room and then the kitchen.

"Cinda? Which room is yours?" Detective Cooper asks.

I point. We walk the few steps into my room.

"Oh, my God, I'm so sorry, my room is a mess!" I gasp.

I haven't been inside my room since I called the police right after Bob left. My sheets and comforter are in shambles. My red sweatshirt bathrobe is lying on the floor. My dresser drawers are open from when I had to get dressed in a hurry. I walk to my dresser and shut the drawers. I pick up the bathrobe and then look at my messed-up bed.

I swear I can still smell Bob's body odor in my room. I walk around the detective and lean down over my bed. I grab all the sheets, blanket and comforter into a giant ball. I hold my breath so I won't smell any residual scents.

"There's no way I will sleep in those again."

Detective Redmond walks back into the room just as I throw the bedding on the floor in the corner.

"Cinda, the report stated that it was an attempted rape. Is that correct? I ask for clarification to make sure there is no semen on the sheets." Detective Redmond asks, his tone gentle, respectful.

His question throws me off balance. It shakes me to my core. I hear Katie moan next to me.

What would I be like right now if Bob had raped me?

"I kept him from doing what he came to do," I sound comfortable in my answer, although my intestines are tied in knots.

He nods. I can't read his expressions, but there it is again—that silent pause. A wave of uncertainty comes over me.

What if the detectives don't believe me?

My room seems extra small and I start to feel claustrophobic with the four of us standing in it. My anxiety increases and my breath comes in short spurts.

Detective Cooper breaks the silence by asking, "Where would you like me to install your panic button?"

A panic button? What the hell is a panic button?!

I don't know what a panic button is, or what I'm to do with one. I look at him for an answer.

Detective Redmond answers my silent question with a calm and empathetic tone, "Cinda, we're concerned that this man will come back. Since he wasn't *successful*, we fear that he may return to try to *finish* what he started. When pushed, this button will alert the police and all officers within a five-mile radius will be here within minutes."

What?

I'm not sure I hear him correctly? What did he just say?

Bob might be back?

Chapter 16

THE PANIC BUTTON

My intestines tighten. My stomach constricts. I want to vomit. Shock rises as blood drains from my head. I'm afraid I might faint. In an instant Katie comes to my side. She's watching me. We lock eyes and I feel some of the nausea leave, but as quickly as it leaves, it returns.

I look deep into Katie's eyes and plead for her to answer my telepathic questions: *What is going on here? What is happening? Is this even real?*

I try to make sense of it. I go through a mental list of what's taken place so far. *1. A man I don't know broke into my house. 2. He attacked me, nearly raped me and almost killed me. 3. Police are everywhere. 4. There are two detectives in my house... in my bedroom. 5. They want to install a panic button...because.... I swallow hard. 6. Because they think the man, the man I named Bob, might come back.*

What the hell is going on?

What the hell is going on!

Again, Detective Cooper asks, "Cinda. Cinda, where would you like me to install the panic button?"

I snap out of shock, just enough to catch the word "panic." This isn't the first time he's said the word, but it's the first time I hear it. *Panic!* It takes every ounce of personal willpower to not totally freak out and panic myself all over them.

The men look at me, waiting for an answer. I stare at them.

Do they have a clue how I feel right now?

They are intent on doing their job. They've done this before. This is routine to them, but it's all new to me. I wonder how many panic buttons they've had to install in Portland.

What I really want to know...is...how many have had to be pushed?

"If he attacked you while you were in your bed, then I suggest we install it next to your nightstand," Detective Cooper recommends.

I look around my room. Flashes of seeing Bob's silhouette at the end of my bed come in and out of focus. There is no way in hell I am ever,

EVER sleeping in this room again. But, I don't want to appear like a frightened child in front of these men. I must act in a mature way. I need to get control of myself, of my fear, of this situation—*but how?*

It occurs to me what I can do. It's what I used to do as a kid, to help make any situation feel better, feel different. As a child, I had a habit of rearranging my room often. I did this every time I felt I needed a fresh start or a new outlook. If there was ever a time to create that again, it's now.

I tell them, "OK, but I need to rearrange my room first. I need my room to feel completely different from the way it is now, or I will never stay in here again."

Since I have very few pieces of furniture, it's an easy and quick move. We move my dresser next to the door and the bed to the opposite wall. The foot of the bed now faces the door. If Bob enters, I'll see him instantly. I put my nightstand next to the bed in front of the large window and plug in the lamp. My room looks different. It feels better.

Detective Cooper asks me again where I want the button installed. I consider the options.

If Bob comes back, *oh God,* he'll be pissed. He won't fall for any distractions or attempts to carry on a conversation. If he sees me reach for anything, *oh God,* I'm dead. I'm certain.

Oh God, I need to get to it without him realizing what I'm doing.

"I need to be able to reach the button without him seeing me do it. Can it be close to my pillow? Maybe between my nightstand and my bed?"

Detective Cooper sets his toolbox on the floor. In a few moments, the button is up. It resembles a doorbell. He asks me to test it. I crawl onto my bed and lie down, feeling silly and vulnerable. I reach for the button and push it. There is no noise—*it doesn't seem to be working.* But, over Detective Cooper's walkie-talkie, I hear that the test was successful.

Thank God, it's a silent alarm and not a siren that would wake up the entire neighborhood.

It's getting late, and being on my bed is reminding me of how exhausted I am. I shudder as the memory returns of 3:01 this morning. The detectives must notice, because they decide it's time to leave. Detective Cooper gathers up his tools and clips shut his toolbox. Detective Redmond hands both of us his business card.

"Girls, please keep this on you at all times. Call me for any reason. If I'm not on duty, someone will pick up. Someone will always pick up, I promise. They'll get the message to me instantly."

Both Katie and I say at the same time, "Thank you."

"Cinda, tomorrow I'd like to meet with you again to talk in more detail. When's a good time?"

"I work the early shift tomorrow. Do you want to meet me around noon? I can ask for a longer lunch if you think you need more time."

I can feel Katie's eyes on me. She can't believe that I'm even thinking about going to work tomorrow. But, I need to get things back to normal, back to normal...*back to normal.*

"I'll take whatever time you can give me. You just tell me how much time you have and I'll get you back to work when needed. You two try to get some rest. I can tell you're tired. There are police officers everywhere in this neighborhood. With this panic button, you're safe. This guy won't be stupid. He won't try anything tonight."

I believe him, or at least I choose to believe him.

What choice do I have?

"Thank you. I hope to God you're right," I say as Katie and I walk the men to the door.

I don't want them to leave. I do NOT want to be alone in the house.

"Oh, and get some curtains or blinds for your windows. Immediately. First thing tomorrow. Especially for your room, Katie. As a matter of fact, nail up some sheets, like in Cinda's room. It's not about what looks tacky. It's about your safety."

I take in a breath. He's right! I get it now. I get why everyone's been telling us to put up blinds.

What idiots we are. What were we thinking?

Katie locks the door behind them. I walk through the house and turn off all the lights so no one can see inside. With our porch light shining through our front windows, we can see well enough to get around. I walk through the house making sure that each window and door is locked. Katie walks past me with her arms full of my "violated" bedding and tosses the pile in front of the basement door. I shake my head and smile because she's obviously planning on doing the wash tomorrow.

"Thanks, Katie. But don't bother, there's no way in hell that I'll ever, EVER, sleep in those sheets again."

I grab the top sheet off the pile and drag it into the kitchen. Taking a knife from a drawer, I pierce the center of the sheet, pull at the hole and tear the sheet in half.

"Here, Katie. This is for one of your windows. I'll hang up the other."

I get the box of tacks out of my nightstand and then head into her room. We tack up the half-sheets over her windows. I'm willing to use every sheet I own to cover up the living room windows too. But I'm exhausted. I need to go to bed. I need to try to get some sleep.

I go into the bathroom to wash my face and brush my teeth. Katie and I do our usual dance around the bathroom space. To give her more room, I brush my teeth while I walk around my newly arranged room. Flashes of last night, *well...this morning*, go through my head. I try to shake them away as I go into the bathroom to spit into the sink.

Before I go to bed, I call my mom. She will want to hear about the detective working on my case. I tell her about the panic button to reassure her that the police are protecting us.

It doesn't reassure her.

"Oh, honey, why don't you just move back home. You and Katie can stay here." Her emotions reach deep into my gut.

"Mom. Mom. I have a job. Katie does too. We can't just get up and leave. They promise us we're safe."

"Well...I'm sure Grammy and Grandpa would take you in. Or call Aunt Margaret and Uncle Lou; they have room. Maybe even Uncle John...."

My mom means well, but I am not going to move into any of my relatives' houses. It is hard to explain. She won't understand. I barely understand it myself...but if I show any weakness right now...if I cave in, I may never come out of it.

I may not feel brave, but I need to be brave. I must show my family that I'm strong—strong and brave, independent and confident...*an adult.*

I must show Bob that I am not afraid of him.

"I gotta go. I love you, Mom. I'll call you tomorrow."

"Cindy, sleep with a knife. The biggest one you have."

Next, I call Scott. He answers immediately, as if he's sitting next to the phone waiting for my call. It warms my heart to think of it.

"I wish I could be with you right now. It doesn't feel right having you alone up there."

"They installed a panic button. They promise it will keep us safe, at least safer than without it. There are lots of policemen in our neighborhood too."

"This sucks. I'll be there tomorrow, as early as I can." We say our usual long and drawn-out goodbyes which gives me a warm glow inside my freezing, frightened body.

Tonight, I'll try to think of Scott…instead of Bob.

After I hang up, I give the phone to Katie.

"Here, I have a panic button. You have the phone."

Back in my room, I remake the bed with clean sheets and a different bedspread. But when I lay down, I'm positive I won't sleep. My heart is racing. Every time I close my eyes, I relive Bob lunging at me and I hear my scream. That awful animalistic sound of terror, *my terror*; it's everywhere, echoing off my walls, vibrating inside my skull. I toss and turn, trying to silence it.

I take a pillow to cover my head. What used to be a habit, an easy way to block out noise, is now a life-threatening memory. My breath is hard to come by. With each gasp, I tell myself I'm safe.

You're safe. You are S A F E.

I reach up to the panic button, I feel it. *Yep, it's still there.* I need to practice reaching for the button. I practice while on my back, then my stomach, then on my side with my back toward the button.

What if I don't wake up in time to push the button? I need to find a way to wake me up.

If Bob sneaks into my room, I need to wake up with enough time to push the button. I need to rig up a type of booby trap…a booby trap that will make a loud noise, wake me up and warn me.

One that might scare Bob away.

I turn on my reading light and look around the room for objects that will work. I've never built a booby trap before, so I'm not sure what I should use. After some searching, I find what I think will do the trick. Sliding my dresser closer to the door, I put my curling iron on top and wrap its cord around the door handle. My theory is, if Bob opens my door, the curling iron will fall off my dresser, swing down and crash into the door. My hope is, it will make a loud enough noise to wake me up. I test it. The crashing sound cuts through the silence.

Yep, it works.

"Katie," I quickly yell. "It's just me! I'm rigging up a booby trap to wake me up if Bob comes back."

"A booby trap? OK, well, it'll wake me up too. I promise I'll come running this time. Plus, I have Buffett to protect me."

As I crawl back into bed, a frightening thought occurs to me. Has Bob been watching us tonight? Did he see the detectives in the house? Has he noticed the police cars everywhere? Is he pissed that we called the cops? Does he know we are alone?

Shit…it's going to be a long, long night.

Chapter 17

THE NEW NORMAL

My alarm clock blares me awake. It's already morning. Somehow, I must have fallen asleep. Yet, I don't feel refreshed. I can't possibly function at work today. I glance over at my booby trap to see that it's still set. *It is.* I try to fall back to sleep, but I'm hit by a wave of panic.

What if something happened to Katie last night?

I sit up in bed and listen. I had a booby trap to wake me up. Katie had nothing.

Nothing. I hear nothing. Is that a good sign or a bad sign?

I can't trust or just assume that Katie is safe.

I thought I was safe yesterday, and look what happened to me.

As quiet as I can be, I undo the booby trap and open the door. I shriek in surprise when Buffett jumps at me, hisses and runs away.

"You spazz of a cat!" I hiss back at him.

Then remembering that Buffett was inside Katie's room last night, I can't help but be freaked that he's out.

Oh God, please let Katie be all right.

I tiptoe by the bathroom door and look at the window. It's still closed and the towel is still tacked to the molding. Maybe I should just barge into Katie's room, but I don't have any way to protect myself or Katie. I creep into the living room. The front door's deadbolt is still set. I tiptoe into the kitchen. Nothing has changed since last night. I check the back door and see that it's still locked. But the basement door is unlocked. I panic. It was locked last night.

Is Bob in the basement? He's been down there before….

I think of Bob's sneering reference to the pile of strange clothes down there. *He wanted me to know that he knew of those clothes…. Oh God, could they be his?* This thought makes my already nervous stomach churn even more. I wrap my arms around my belly, willing myself to continue my search through the house.

Thinking of those clothes makes me think of my own pile of laundry. I look around the kitchen and see that it's missing. A wave of relief fills me...*Katie*. With caution, I open the basement door and listen. I can hear the washing machine going. Katie got up early and started the laundry. I head back to Katie's bedroom and with confidence in her safety, knock on her door.

"You don't need to knock," she calls to me.

I open her door. She's sitting on her bed reading. She smiles at me.

"Could you sleep?" she asks gently.

"Not really. I was worried about you when I saw Buffett running loose and your door closed."

"Well, I couldn't sleep either. I'm so wigged out over this whole thing."

I sit on her bed just as Buffett comes running in and pounces on it. He's telling us he's hungry. We both laugh at him.

"I got up early and started the laundry."

"I noticed. Thank you. Umm...I don't think I can go into work today. I mean...I thought I could handle it...but I'm thinking no way, now."

"Do you need me to stay with you?"

I say nothing because I want her here with me. I can't stand the thought of being alone, but I can't possibly ask that of her.

"I think I'll stay home too," she says, reading my mind yet again.

I head into the kitchen to call work. As I reach for the phone, it rings. "Hello?"

"Hey Cinda, this is Detective Redmond. We talked about meeting today during your lunchtime, but could we do it sooner? I don't want you to forget some of the details."

"I'm not sure I'll ever forget. I'm going to call in sick today, so we can meet whenever."

"Great, that works then. I was planning on coming over to look around the outside of your house anyway, but if you're going to be home, we can talk there. I should be there around ten o'clock."

As soon as I hang up, the phone rings again.

"Cindy, it's your dad. My purpose in calling is..." he pauses...like he always does and it makes me smile. "I've been thinking about what you told me yesterday. So, I'd like to come up to see you and look around your house. I'd feel better if I did."

"Sure, Dad. Oh, and, Detective Redmond, the one assigned to my case, will be here around ten o'clock. You can meet him."

"That will be nice. I'm leaving now. I'll see you in an hour."

"Katie," I yell as I start to punch in my work number. "My dad will be here in an hour and Detective Redmond at ten. So…you can either go to work or hang out with us."

"I'm staying!" she calls out.

Before I can get the number for work into the phone, it rings in my hand.

"Hello."

"Hey, Babe," it's Scott. He doesn't need to announce himself. "I'm going to take off from work early today and head up to Portland."

"OK. Dad is coming too and Detective Redmond. Maybe they'll still be here. You can meet the detective. Babe, it'll be so good to have you here. Thank you."

When I hang up, I think about the three men who just called, each wanting to come to my house, wanting to ensure my safety, wanting to protect me.

Thank God for these men.

My phone rings again. I can't help but laugh.

"Cindy, it's Mom. I just couldn't sleep last night. Worried, worried. How did you sleep?" Her voice fluctuates in tones as if she is singing to me through the line.

"Not well. But I did sleep somehow. The detective is coming today. So is Dad and so is Scott."

"I'd be up there too," she says with a heavy sigh. "If only Jerry felt better."

"Don't worry, Mom. Jerry needs you. Love you. I gotta go get ready before everyone arrives. Say hi to the sibs for me."

I hang up, call work to tell them I'm not coming in, and then head into the bathroom to shower. I scrub my skin pink attempting to remove anything and everything that may have accumulated on me over the past 48 hours. The water is extra hot and fills the bathroom with steam. I refuse to open the window.

When my father arrives, I show him around the small house. Giving him a tour feels very different than when we gave the mothers theirs.

Seems like a lifetime ago.

"How did he come in?" he asks.

"Through the bathroom window," I say, as I lead him into the room.

"A towel?" he notices the towel covering the window. He peeks into my room and then Katie's and into the living room, "Sheets on bedroom windows and nothing on your living room windows?"

"Yeah, we need to get some blinds or curtains or something."

"Not a problem. We'll take care of that today. In the meantime, can I take you girls out for breakfast?"

There are many things I love about my father, but the one thing that I love the most is how he uses food to show his love for someone. This isn't just a casual invitation to breakfast.

He wants to take care of us.

We hop inside his blue Jeep Cherokee and drive to a local breakfast place. Inside, the restaurant is warm and smells of bacon and maple syrup. Outside, leaves are blowing around in the crisp fall air. I try my best to enjoy the scenery and the company and make small talk. But really my mind is dominated by thoughts of what Detective Redmond wants from me today.

Dad interrupts my thoughts. He raises his orange juice glass and waits for us to do the same. He makes a toast.

"Here's to being brave! Being brave and smart! Cindy, here's to you!" There is emotion behind his words and I'm touched.

We clink our juice glasses together.

Here's to being brave and smart...

Chapter 18

THE INVESTIGATION

The rest of the meal we eat in partial silence, each of us deep within our own thoughts. When we arrive back at the house, it isn't long before we hear a knock. My father answers it. I make a quick introduction between Detective Redmond and my father.

"Ken, nice to meet you. I'm sorry about what happened to your daughter. I want to assure you that we're doing everything in our power to catch this creep and protect her in the process."

"Cinda," he says as he turns his focus onto me. "I've been walking around your neighborhood to get a feeling for it. I also walked around the outside of your house. It wouldn't have been easy for the guy to have climbed into your bathroom window. It's been raining, and there are no muddy markings on the side of the house below the window. There is nothing that was left behind that could have been used to give him a step up. I don't believe he came in through the window."

He pauses to look at his notes. "The report says that the back door was unlocked, but it also states that he left through the back door. Are you sure that all your doors were locked before you went to bed? I don't see any signs of any forced entry from the outside."

"We only have two ways into our house," I tell him. "The front door has to be locked for it to remain shut. The back door is never used, so we always keep it locked. When I came out of my room after he left, the bathroom window was open. I checked the doors and noticed the back door was unlocked."

I walk him through the house and as I do, he asks more questions. When we come to the basement door, I tell him about the pile of clothes down there. I tell him that during the night of the attack Bob told me he knew they were there. We walk down into the basement and Detective Redmond rummages through the pile. My dad and Katie follow us.

"These seem to be men's clothing. So…, this guy, he knew about these? Do you have any idea who they belong to?"

"I don't. But he knew they were here. He seemed familiar with this house. He acted like he'd been in here before."

"The landlord says that if the old tenants don't claim the clothes, he'll throw them out. But that hasn't happened yet," Katie says.

"I'll be calling the landlord and I'll find out what I can about the previous tenants. And I'll get him to change the locks." Detective Redmond makes a note in his pad.

"I've called our landlord many times already," Katie interjects. "I've asked him to fix the hole in the wall, take away the clothes, and I just talked to him to tell him what happened to Cinda. I even asked if we could have a dog. I thought a dog would be great protection, but he said no. Which is ridiculous. He told me he'd get around to the rest when he can."

"Yeah, he hasn't been much help since we moved in," I agree.

"There's a hole in the wall?" Dad asks.

Katie leads us back upstairs, out of the basement, through the kitchen, to the corner of the living room. She lifts the circular tray she had hung over the hole.

"This is the hole I mentioned yesterday when you and Detective Cooper were here," I tell Detective Redmond. Then to my dad, "When the guy woke me up, I thought he was here to fix this hole."

"Can you tell me more of that night?" Detective Redmond asks.

The four of us sit down together in the living room. Detective Redmond sits on the couch with me, and Dad and Katie sit on the dining room chairs Katie brought in. I begin my story from the beginning. It's extremely awkward and uncomfortable answering these questions in front of my father. He'll hear more of the details I purposefully left out the first time I told him. I worry it might scare him more, but I need to be honest with my detective. I decide to pretend my father isn't in the room and only look at the man asking me the questions.

Yet...even with wanting to be honest with the detective, I still censor the story. I'm not sure Detective Redmond needs to know...*what I did*. I most certainly don't want my dad to know that I invited a violent man into my bed...*while I was naked*.

I fear they won't ever really understand. How could they?

My heart aches for their understanding. I wish I could tell them what and why I did what I did. But I don't get it myself.... I don't get how I could have taken such a risk. *If Buffett hadn't scared him away....* I push the thought away.

Stop dwelling on the what ifs....

The detective continues to ask questions, write notes, then replays the scene I just spoke about, back to me. It's a ping pong game of memories. I hate it.

"Based on this information, I'll be touring the nearby homeless camps and see what I can find out. I'll walk the neighborhood more today, with eyes peeled for anything or anyone that fits this description."

When he gets up to leave, he reaches out to shake my father's hand.

"Ken, while you're here, would you please make sure these young ladies get blinds up over their windows?"

"Already on top of it. We're planning on doing that today."

"Cinda, I'm going to schedule a meeting with you and our forensic sketch artist. We need to get a drawing of this guy. I'll call you about the time. Most likely it will be tomorrow."

I walk Detective Redmond to the door and we agree to talk tomorrow. I haven't known this man for very long, but I feel an intense attachment to him. I'm desperate for an adult to take control and make things better. This man is offering me safety, protection, and kindness. I'm so grateful that he's the one assigned to my case.

He is MY detective. MY savior. MY protector.

My detective. My Detective Redmond.

It isn't long before Scott arrives. We all pile in my dad's car and go shopping for blinds.

We find the perfect solution at an import store: white rice paper shades with thin wavy strips of bamboo running horizontally through them. They hang from hooks, are close enough to the correct width and seem to be long enough. They'll add texture and charm to our living room. Katie and I love them.

As we get back into the car, Dad says, "Next, we need to go to a hardware store to get a drill and screwdriver."

"Dr. Stevens, I have a toolbox at home," Katie informs him.

My father gives Katie a look of surprise and nods. When we get back to the house, Scott and my dad go to work hanging the blinds. They start in Katie's room, then mine and then in the living room. They don't fit exactly. There is still a gap along the edges where they hang side by side and they don't reach completely to the bottom, but they're better than nothing. On the kitchen windows, Katie and I nail up new dishtowels to the lower part of each window frame. The bright colors on the towels add life to the dull, dark kitchen.

When my dad gets ready to leave, he wraps his arms around me and holds me longer than normal. I can feel his heart beating next to mine. I can feel him sending me his love.

"OK then. Lock up behind me," he says, quickly turning on his heel to leave. It appears he's working on not showing any emotion, which makes me an emotional wreck. But like my father, I won't expose it.

We lock the door behind him, raise and lower the blinds to test them out, make sure the other doors and all the windows are locked—*again.* It's become a routine of ridiculous repetition, but we have no choice.

Later, Scott runs to the store for dinner supplies. After cooking a simple meal, we take our plates to the couch and turn on the TV. We watch "The Love Boat" and then "Fantasy Island." The shows are a great escape from the stress. With the blinds covering the windows, we can watch TV with ease because…*Bob can't watch with us.*

When Scott and I head into my bedroom, I feel an unfamiliar anxiety creep up inside me. I try to push it aside, but it's difficult. I'm safer with Scott here and that should help me feel more relaxed and secure. But I can't help but dwell on the last time a man was in this bed, or the last time a man touched me.

It's Scott, Cinda. This is Scott…not Bob.

I feign that I'm tired. He seems to understand the unspoken words and just holds me. I'm still awake as his body relaxes and his breathing turns into a steady rhythm of sleep. In the darkness, my mind races. I must figure out a way to keep Bob away…to banish him from my mind— *from my bed.* I can't allow the memory of him and what happened to get inside me and pollute my sanity and my relationship with Scott.

Not tonight…not any night.

Chapter 19

THE DOG

Scott leaves the next morning while it's still dark out. I peek between the blinds and watch him walk up the hill to his car. I wonder if Bob is watching him leave. I fear that Scott might not be safe and I'm prepared to push the panic button if I need to. He leaves without incident and I relax.

I crawl back into bed hoping to sleep a few more hours. I can't. This room, even with my furniture switched around, even with Scott having been here, is still a keeper of memories that won't leave. Sitting around my house gives me too much time to dwell and the dwelling isn't helping me feel safe.

It's time to get back to normal!

I need to get back into my routine. I need to get back to normal as quickly as I can. The best way I can do this is to go back to work. I get out of bed, choose my outfit for the day and head into the bathroom. When I get out of the shower, Katie is up making coffee. She's eager to get back into her usual routine too. She heads out to work before I do, giving me free rein of the house. This is the first time I've been alone since Bob entered my bedroom.

It seems so much bigger when I'm alone in it.

Fortunately, Buffett runs up and purrs at my feet. His attention reminds me that I'm not completely alone. He's telling me that his breakfast is gone. He's telling me, with his purrs and meows, that if I give him more food…he will be my best friend. I want him to be my best friend…*for life*. I'm happy to feed him more. His enthusiasm makes me laugh.

It feels good to laugh.

The phone rings, and I jump. The tension I'm feeling is obvious despite a momentary reprieve. Detective Redmond is calling to tell me that my appointment with the forensic artist, Janet Frances, is scheduled for this afternoon at three o'clock. I thank him and hang up.

What will it be like to see Bob's face in a drawing? Oh God, I don't want to see him again, even in a drawing.

When it's time to go, I gather up the sales reports from my department at Meier & Frank. I'd been working on them last week...*before*.... I push the memory aside. After I slip the papers into their appropriate manila folders, I stretch a couple of thick rubber bands around the stack to keep the pages from slipping out. Buffett is not happy when he sees me heading toward the door. He blocks my path. I need to shove him aside with my foot then quickly close and lock the door. As sad as it is to leave him, I'm relieved to be out of this house.

I take a moment to stand on my front porch and look around. I haven't walked in this neighborhood alone since Bob bragged about watching us. My legs feel unsteady—but there is no choice—I must get to work and I need to walk to the bus to get there. The air is crisp and clear as I take in a deep breath and force myself to move forward—*ready, set, go.* I avoid the broken step by jumping over it and onto the sidewalk. Straightening my back, I raise my chin and head up the steep hill. I'm pretending that nothing has happened. It's an act, but in case he's watching me, I will appear to be confident.

Ready. Set. Go. Just get to the bus.

As I walk, I pull at one of the rubber bands and release it against the top file. It makes a loud but soothing snapping sound.

Snap, snap, snap.

I'm far more nervous than I want to admit. The feeling of being vulnerable is new to me...*I don't like it.* The more I snap at the rubber band, the easier it is for me to take the next step. It creates a rhythm, a steady pattern of stepping and snapping.

Step, snap, step, snap, step, snap.

When I reach the corner at the top of my street, I pause to decide which way I want to go—straight, or turn right. I decide to turn right. I keep snapping at the rubber band, as I walk in front of the large blue house on the corner.

Out of the side driveway, a black and white dog runs toward me. Startled, I freeze. Worried that he might not be friendly, I reach out a hand to let him smell me.

"Hey there, boy. Where did you come from?"

Strange...I've never seen this dog before.

A dog running loose in this busy neighborhood is unusual. It isn't safe for him. I'm concerned he might run out into the road and be hit by a passing car. I look around, wondering where his owner is, but there seems to be no one looking after him. He walks over to a nearby bush and lifts his leg. When he's finished, he stares at me.

"Good boy. Now, go home. Go home." I point back toward the direction he came from.

He doesn't move. Instead, he continues to stare at me. I need to get going to my bus, but I'm worried for his safety. I'm not sure what to do. I'm pissed at his owner for being so careless.

"Stay," I command. "Stay."

As I start to walk past, I keep an eye on him to make sure he doesn't leave the sidewalk or follow me. He doesn't move. So, I go back to snapping at the rubber band and keep walking—*snap, step, snap.*

Over the sound of the snapping rubber band, I hear a man's voice calling out. I'm relieved. The dog's owner is taking responsibility. I continue walking and snapping, when I hear the man call the dog's name again, louder this time.

"Cindy! Cindy!"

I freeze. My entire body tenses.

Did I just hear my name?

I look over my shoulder at the dog to see if the dog recognizes the man's voice—to see if in fact, the man is calling this dog. But the dog isn't moving or looking in the direction of the man's voice. Instead, he is still staring at me. The dog then looks up toward the second floor of the blue house, possibly where the voice came from. He then looks back at me.

I'm totally freaked. I'm frozen in place. I don't know what to do…or who is calling…or who is being called—*me or the dog.* Although, I'm sure I heard the name, Cindy…I don't want it to be true. I don't want this to be Bob calling my name.

Crap, crap, crap. Just get to the bus. Just get to the bus.

I decide that I'm imagining things. I decide that the dog's name is close to Cindy. I decide to get the hell out of there.

I turn away from the dog and the blue house and pick up my pace. With nervous energy, I snap at the rubber band with purpose. It makes a loud cracking sound. My hope is that whoever is calling can hear the loudness of the snaps and assume I can't hear his voice over the noise.

I try to control every muscle in my body, willing it to walk, when what I really want to do is run. I try to make it appear that I'm calm and cool and collected. I want whoever is calling out to me, or the dog, to think I didn't hear him. If this is Bob calling me, I do NOT want him to see me totally wigging out.

Shit, shit, shit. Snap, step, snap, step, snap, step. Shit!

I walk quickly along the sidewalk, turn left to cross the street and walk the block up to the bus stop on the corner. The bus comes just as I approach. I take a seat. Once the doors shut, I can safely look back from where I just came from.

No one has followed.

No dog, no man, no Bob.

Chapter 20

THE SKETCH

When I get to work, I avoid my coworkers and sneak unnoticed to my register. I pull out Detective Redmond's card, pick up the phone on the counter and punch in his number. I leave a message with the woman who answers, telling her about the dog. I leave my work number for him to call me back.

The department manager, Kara, approaches me as I hang up. There's a look of concern on her face. When I called her yesterday to tell her I wouldn't be in, I also told her a bit of what happened. She promised to keep it to herself and to support me in any way I need.

"Kara, hey, I need to go to the police department and do a sketch drawing of this guy at three o'clock. I don't have a clue how long it will take, but I'll come back to work as soon as I'm done. I hope that won't be a problem?"

"Are you kidding me? No problem at all. I'll come and cover for you when it's time."

A few hours later, Kara shows up to take over my shift. With worry still on her face, she asks me how I'm doing. I tell her that I'm looking forward to getting outside and walking without any fear of being followed. I see her cringe. As I head out, she wishes me luck.

Luck...yes...I'll take some of that right now.

When I arrive at the police station, I give the receptionist my name. I tell her that Detective Thom Redmond made an appointment for me to meet with Janet Frances. She calls Janet's desk to tell her I'm here.

"An officer will be out soon to escort you back," she says as she gestures for me to sit in one of the chairs, but I stay standing.

Within minutes an officer shows up and leads me through a maze of desks covered in piles of paperwork and individual computers. Plainclothes detectives sit at their desks either interviewing someone or staring into their computer screen. Police officers roam around the room. The noise level is loud: phones ring, machines hum, walkie-talkies spew static, and voices—lots and lots of voices collide in the air around me. It's overwhelming and intimidating. As I follow him, I notice people turning to watch me. I feel embarrassed—worried that they may think I'm a criminal.

We walk up to a desk where a woman is sitting. She stands when she sees us approaching. Despite my nervousness, I'm taken in by her appearance. A small gasp escapes me because she is breathtakingly beautiful. She's almost as tall as I am. Her piercing blue eyes are painted with sparkling azure eyeshadow and massive amounts of mascara. Her long blond hair is teased and curly, pinned up at the temples with hair combs. Her smile is huge. Her lips are painted a dark glossy pink, making her teeth seem even whiter. I can't help but smile back at her in awe.

She glows.

Janet reaches across her desk to shake my hand. I look at her flawless, manicured fingernails and am embarrassed by my own chewed up, torn up nails. I'm caught speechless. I don't know why…but I just am. I can't help myself. I snap out of my trance when I realize she's speaking to me.

"I'm sorry. What did you say?" I ask embarrassed.

"Cinda Stevens, correct? Detective Thom Redmond sent you?" Her voice is warm and inviting.

I nod.

She gestures for me to sit in the chair next to her desk. When she sits back down, I watch as she positions a sketchbook in front of her and slides over a jar of charcoal pencils. With a fluid motion, she picks out one of her pencils and flips open the book. She dates the page in the upper right corner. She turns the paper over and writes Detective Redmond's name and mine on the backside.

"Here's how it works. I'm going to ask you a whole lot of questions to help you remember what this guy looks like. Thom Redmond hasn't shared any information with me, so I don't have any preconceived ideas of this guy. OK?"

I nod, still speechless.

All the other noise and distractions in the room seem to have vanished. She has my attention. She is so pretty, so kind, so calm. I decide that I'll do anything she asks of me.

"Let's begin. Try to remember that first moment you saw him. You can close your eyes if it helps."

I close my eyes and try to re-see the moment Bob first woke me up. It feels strange to have my eyes closed, sitting in a chair in front of a stranger in a strange place. I immediately open them and give her a look of apology. She smiles like it's nothing and nods for me to continue. I close my eyes again and instantly a flash of Bob lunging at me comes into focus. I re-hear my scream. I gasp. I open my eyes. I so want to please her…but now…I'm not so sure.

I'm not so sure I can do this. I'm not so sure I want to do this.

"It's all right, Cinda. Take your time," Her voice soothes my anxiety and I'm grateful. "It takes a while to get the hang of it. Let me ask you some questions. Was there anything that stood out immediately to you? Was there anything about his body or on his body like a tattoo, or about his hair, his clothes, anything about his appearance that you noticed first thing?"

"Well…," I hesitate, not eager to remember, afraid to hear the scream again. "It was really dark. He broke into my house at around three in the morning."

She encourages me to put myself back into that moment and to see him in my room. I decide to not close my eyes this time, and work to see the images with them open.

"He's standing at the end of my bed…." I want to go on describing the scene but realize that it's not easy to do with my eyes open. I close them again and I see my room more clearly. "My bed and box spring are on the floor so I'm looking up at him, yet he doesn't seem to be a large man. He has a slight build."

"Good, Cinda. What's he wearing?"

"He's wearing a light colored, long sleeve, button-up shirt and jeans."

"What else do you remember about his clothing?"

"His jeans are torn up."

I open my eyes. She hasn't drawn anything yet. I suppose it's because we haven't talked about his face.

"Cinda, you're doing great. Close your eyes and take your time traveling back to that moment. I imagine that this is very difficult for you, but if we can get a good picture of him, the chances of catching him are greater."

I close my eyes and the memory of Bob standing in my room comes flooding back. I open my eyes to avoid reliving the confrontation and find her calmly looking at me. Janet nods. I close my eyes again.

"I want you to trust that you are completely safe. He can't hurt you here. I promise you…," she pauses. "Can you tell me what color his skin is? What color is his hair?"

"His skin is light colored. He's white. He's wearing a knit cap."

I open my eyes to give myself a break.

This isn't fun. It sucks.

"This isn't so easy. I mean, it was really, really dark. I talked to him for quite a while. Actually, I kept him from doing whatever he came to do for over three hours."

I ramble on attempting to avoid reliving any of the violence— avoiding any of the moments Bob lunged at me, avoiding any of the moments I couldn't breathe.

I watch her eyes grow big.

"Really, three hours? You had to have had a good look at him then."

She's not going to let me get away with the rambling and avoiding.

She's going to make me remember, like it or not.

I continue, "Well…, when my eyes adjusted, I tried to get a good look at him. The problem was…that every time he thought I was looking at him, he attacked me again."

I stop talking because I see a flash of him pulling my robe over my head. All I can see is red. I sit with the image for a bit because it doesn't seem to want to leave. I can feel my chest tighten. I take in a deep breath and shake my body to loosen the memory's grip on me.

"At one point, I sat with him on my bed and moved my hands around, hoping he would watch my hands. This gave me a chance to look at him."

"Can you give me more details about his face? Go back to that time, when you were sitting with him on your bed. Tell me, what's the shape of his face?"

I close my eyes and put myself back on the bed. I had just removed my bathrobe and am gasping for air. The air is cold on my naked body. Bob is stunned, sitting across from me. I see myself using my hands to talk. I look closely at him and try to zoom in and focus on his face.

This time, I'm not afraid to remember. Something is different this time. It's as if…it's as if Janet is sitting on the bed with me.

She's looking at Bob with me.

"His face is oval, narrow, but his nose is wide, like maybe it's been broken before. His eyes seem light. They must be light colored because they don't look dark."

"He's wearing a knit cap? Can you see anything unusual about the hat?" I swear her voice is coming from the bed next to me.

"His hair must be long. I think he has a ponytail shoved under his hat because I can tell that there is a bump under it in the back. I can see light colored curly hair sticking out from under his hat."

I want to ask her if she can see his hair too. But then Bob begins to crawl toward me. I smell his breath. I lean back to avoid the confrontation—both in the memory and in my chair. My body starts to shake with the memory of what comes next.

"Oh, my God, I remember his smell…his hands!" I whisper, emotional pain shoots through my body.

"Cinda," Janet's soft voice brings me back to the present moment. "Open your eyes. Come back to me."

When I open my eyes, my mind slowly replaces Bob's repulsive face with Janet's beautiful one. I feel tears building up behind my eyes; one tear escapes and rolls down my cheek.

I can't believe this. How did this become my life? This just can't be real. This has to be a dream, a fucking bad dream!

She hands me a tissue box.

"This must be tough, but you're doing a great job. How about we take a quick break for a minute? Would you like something to drink? Some water, a Coke, tea, coffee?"

I can't help but giggle through my tears at the offer. She seems confused by my reaction, so I share with her why it's sort of funny. I share with her the offers that I made to Bob—of steak and coffee and Katie's awful iced tea.

"We know how to make it here," she says with a gentle laugh.

"Maybe some coffee, thank you." Maybe the wait for the coffee will prolong her need to keep asking me to remember.

She signals for someone to bring us two cups of coffee. While we wait, she turns her tablet toward me and shows me what she has drawn so far.

"When you look at this, does it resemble the way you remember him?"

I look closely at the picture. It's very strange to see Bob in a drawing. She's captured everything I remember. Fortunately, seeing him in one dimension doesn't seem to trigger a reaction. I suppose I thought seeing Bob in a drawing would bring him back to life. It doesn't and I'm relieved.

Bob doesn't jump off the page at me.

"Yes, that's Bob. You've drawn everything I remember."

"Bob? How do you know his name?"

A man interrupts us with two Styrofoam cups of steaming dark liquid. The coffee smells delicious. I pick up one of the cups and hold it close—it brings comfort as I had hoped. The smell reminds me of Katie and my stress begins to ease. I won't drink it. My opinion of coffee hasn't changed, but I sample a sip anyway. It's awful. I just needed something in my hands to distract me...from my emotions, from my memories...*from the picture of Bob.*

I tell her how I came about naming him—*that man, that criminal, that intruder, that rapist*—Bob.

"Clever. Tell me, what was his reaction to your offers of food and to calling him a name?"

She leans back in her chair and sips her coffee. It seems like we're taking a break from the composite drawing. I hold the cup of coffee close to my chest. I can feel its steam on my face and take in a deep breath of its aroma.

I tell her the rest of the story...making sure to keep from sharing the scary parts, the naked parts. She seems to be awed by my story. Her reaction intrigues me.

"Cinda," she says, with her emotions on the surface. "I've seen many women who have been brutally beaten and bruised. I've had to sit with them and help them remember what their attacker looked like. It isn't easy for them and it isn't easy for me. But the fact that they survived means we get a chance to capture their perpetrator in a drawing and hopefully use it to get him behind bars. If I can help you do the same, I will have done my job well. Your story is an amazing one. You're a very brave young woman. Thank you for sharing your story with me."

She signs the bottom of the drawing and puts her pencil back into the jar. She then opens the top drawer of her desk and pulls out a can of something and sprays the drawing. It smells like hairspray. I suppose it's to keep the charcoal from smearing.

"I'll pass this on to Detective Redmond when I see him later today."

Janet stands. I do the same. She puts her hand on my arm and she looks at me with her beautiful eyes. I surprise myself by giving her a hug. When she hugs me back, I don't want to let go. I can't explain it, but being with her has altered me in some profound way. As I walk back to work, I can still feel her hug and smell her floral perfume. It's as if that glow of hers has penetrated my shell. I feel like maybe…I might just be all right.

I feel hopeful.

Chapter 21

THE STRANGERS

It's been over two hours since I left work. I decide to grab a quick bite to eat and walk around downtown to recover and regroup from my session with Janet. Then, I make my way back to Meier & Frank.

When I do show up, Kara comes running over.

"I'm surprised to see you come back," she says. "I assumed since you were gone so long, you'd be gone for the rest of the day."

"I wouldn't do that without calling you. It took a lot longer than I expected. I'm sorry. Plus, that guy…he knows where I live; not where I work. I'd rather be here."

I see her cringe. It seems to bother her whenever I mention or hint at what happened. She gives me a piece of paper with a note on it.

"Detective Redmond called a few times," she tells me what's in the note as I read it. "He says that he got your message about the dog and is concerned. He'd like to talk to you before you head home. It's a good thing you came back here first. You can use one of the buyers' offices in the back. They've all gone home."

I head to the back hallway—dark and narrow—where the department walk inside the first door. In the middle of the office is a rolling rack filled with samples of spring clothing. I run my hands along the bright fabric as I walk to the desk. The colors and the texture of the fabric against my fingertips feel nice, it makes me smile. I'm reminded of innocence and youth, spring breaks and sunshine.

Until I remember that it's not me anymore—innocence, youth, gone. A wave of sadness rushes over me.

Damn you, Bob!

I pick up the phone and dial Thom Redmond's number. As I wait for him to answer, I take a colorful blouse off the rack. I hold it up to myself and look in the mirror.

"Oh God, I look awful."

My eyes are red and puffy and dull. *Dull?* I look closer. The dullness is real. The life and sparkle that once shined from my eyes seem to have vanished. The sight depresses me even more, especially as I remember the beauty and sparkle of Janet's eyes earlier.

This victim thing...it IS noticeable. Will the sparkle ever return...to my eyes... to my face...to my life?

I put the hanger back on the bar, wishing I'd never picked up that shirt.

"Thom Redmond here," his voice is now so familiar it slows my heart down to a steady beat.

"It's Cinda Stevens, returning your call returning my call."

I laugh awkwardly and I hear him respond with a soft chuckle as well. It's a dance between the personal and the professional.

"So, Cinda," he clears his throat, changing the conversation to professional. "I understand that you had an incident this morning with a dog. Can you tell me about it?"

I tell him about the dog that came running toward me from the side driveway of the blue house on the corner. I tell him that a man called out from that house for the dog. I tell him that the dog's name sounded like, "Cindy."

I can hear the scratching noise of him taking notes. When he's finished, he gives a heavy sigh. An awkward silence follows.

I fill in the void by saying, "I just got back from the police station. I spent two hours with Janet Frances."

"Two hours? Wow."

"Yeah, I know, right? But for whatever reason, it took that long. She was unbelievably patient while I tried not to freak out."

I think about her trick of sitting on the bed with me, looking at Bob.

"Yep, that's what makes her good at her job. I have your composite sketch. I'm looking at it now. This picture will help. Is he black? I thought you said he was white."

"No, he is white."

"He looks like he has black features."

"He is white."

"I'll make sure the officers patrolling your neighborhood have this in their cars. They can take it when they ask around. I'll also have them pass it out to the local businesses near your house. Hopefully, someone will recognize him. I'm going to go down to your neighborhood right now and ask about a black and white dog. When are you off work?"

"I'm here until closing. I'll be catching the 9:30 bus, if I can get out of here in time."

"Cinda, you have a car, correct? I wish you'd drive to work and home."

I get what he's saying. I'd feel a lot safer in my car too.

"Parking downtown costs a fortune and finding parking in front of my house is nearly impossible. I'd most likely still need to walk three blocks to my house from my parked car, like I do from the bus."

"Can you meet tomorrow? I've found that the more times someone retells the story, the more they remember. How about over lunch?"

"My lunch will be around three."

"OK, I'll pick you up out back. See you then."

I finish out the day helping customers and hanging new merchandise. When my shift is over, I close out the register and say goodbye to my co-workers. I'm exhausted and an hour will pass before I get home. Outside, the dark and cold add to my misery. With the hood of my jacket over my head, I hold the collar tight for extra warmth. My pace is quick as I walk the two blocks to the bus stop, weaving in and out among people headed to their own destinations. I barely notice them.

A homeless man approaches me. I pay him no mind and walk around him. I hear him spit and then feel a wet splat on top of my foot. I look down and see a blob of disgusting mucus run down my nylon stocking and into my shoe. I turn and glare at his back as he walks away.

Really? Really! Seriously, are you freaking serious?

I have nothing to clean it up with, so I bend down and take off my shoe. I attempt to shake it out but his phlegm has spread so thin I can't do anything about it. With a defeated grunt, I put the shoe back on and continue walking. I'm pissed off and completely grossed out.

Homeless prick! Really? Really, what the hell? Why is all this shit happening to me right now? I'm so tired of this shit. So. Freaking. Tired.

There are many locations in town where I can catch a bus to take me home, but at night I prefer this one. It's lit up with streetlights and always crowded. Tonight, the corner is packed. I stand with other professional and not-so-professional people waiting. Many people are sitting on the edge of a large round cement fountain, which isn't flowing. Stairs to the entrance of a nearby building have people sitting, waiting, on them. I have nowhere to sit.

I stand.

I'm standing in spit. I'm angry. I'm tired. Being a victim has infiltrated all parts of my existence. No one offers me a seat, validating the unfairness of my life. I scowl and pull my arms even tighter around my chest. All I want to do is go home and crawl into bed. I want to sleep…I need to sleep. But home is a fucking scary place.

My life sucks.

Out of the corner of my eye I see a man walk in my direction. When he approaches me, he stops and says something that I don't understand.

"Sorry?" I snap back at him.

How dare he invade my space!

"Someone as beautiful as you shouldn't be frowning."

What? Really? Seriously? You're picking up on me?

I glare at him. But then I see that his face is kind. His smile is gentle. I feel that he's waiting for a response. I attempt to smile back at him, but he seems to want more.

"You are too beautiful to be frowning. Smile."

Something stirs inside of me. I feel my mood begin to shift. I look into his kind eyes and get the sense that he's being sincere. I'm thinking that he genuinely wants me to feel better. I'm able to manage a weak smile and in doing so, I thank him. He smiles back, and with a respectful nod he walks away.

Today, Janet used her calm and soothing ways to ease my fear and tension. This stranger just did the same. Both events feel mysterious. Both people seemed to positively influence me and lift my mood. When the bus pulls up and I climb the steps, I barely feel the slime in my shoe.

I am ready to face my frightening house.

Chapter 22

THE ATTEMPTED BURGLARY

I rush home after I get off the bus. When I enter, I set down my purse on the coffee table, toss my jacket on the couch and kick off my disgusting shoes. I reach up my skirt, pull my nylons off and throw them in the trash under the kitchen sink.

"Katie? Are you home?"

"In the bathroom. Be out in a minute."

Katie comes to join me in the living room. Her body is wrapped in a robe, her hair wet.

"Nice robe," I tell her, surprised. I wonder if she bought it new or has always had it.

"So how did it go today?" she asks while toweling dry her hair. "Did you meet with the sketch artist?"

"As a matter of fact, I did."

"And…?"

"She had me close my eyes and visualize that night. She asked me questions and drew what I said. Bit by bit, Bob appeared on her paper."

"Wow! Like in the movies."

"Yeah, maybe, but I have to admit…it was freaky weird to have to think about him again and then to see him in a drawing. Oh, my God! I almost forgot. This morning, on my way to the bus, a dog ran out from the side of the blue house up on the corner. I've never seen a loose dog in this neighborhood before. Have you? But the weird part is that the owner called its name and its name sounded just like Cindy!"

"What? There's a loose dog in the neighborhood? One named Cindy? Weird coincidence." Then after a short pause she says, "Or…was the person calling you? Oh, my God, do you think it was Bob calling you? Did you tell Detective Redmond?"

"Yes. He said he was going to ask around the neighborhood today. I haven't heard yet what he found out. God, what if it was Bob calling out to me?"

I walk into my room and find my pajamas. I shudder when I see the red pull-over robe. I push it aside.

I should throw it away.

"Are you done in the bathroom? I need to take a shower. Some asshole bum spit on my foot. I feel filthy all over!"

"What? Gross! What is it with homeless men and you? I'm done with the bathroom. Go for it."

What IS it with homeless men and me?

After I shower, I go sit on the couch next to Katie. On her lap is a bowl of popcorn. The smell is intoxicating. I grab a handful and hum in delight as the buttery taste fills my mouth. She's watching a new show called "Hill Street Blues." I get sucked into the storyline—Chicago police catching criminals.

Let's be careful out there...agreed!

When the show ends, I take the empty bowl into the kitchen. Since we don't have a dishwasher, I place it in the sink and turn the faucet on. As I wait for the water to get hot, I glance out the small windows. Despite the streetlight, it's unusually dark outside. I see a man standing across the street, his back to me. He's looking up at the side of the house in front of him. Something's strange, not quite right about him. I call Katie over, turn off the kitchen light and point him out to her. We watch as he searches for something along the sidewalk and under the trees. He picks up a long branch.

"What's he doing?" she whispers.

"He's up to no good. Look at how he's checking out the window."

All the houses on this street are built on a steep hill, putting their first-story windows above either a garage or an enclosed basement, like ours. The house across the street has a broken, unusable garage under theirs. We watch as the man reaches the stick up to the window and pushes it open. He takes a few steps back, runs forward, jumps and scales up the garage door. He then grabs the base of the window frame and pulls himself into the house.

"Oh my God! Do you think that's Bob breaking into their house?" Katie screams.

"I have no idea! What do we do? We have to do something! We have to help those people!" I reply in a panic.

"I'm pushing the panic button!" Katie yells and runs away into my room. From my room, I hear her yell, "I'm pushing it! I'm pushing it! Oh my God! Oh my God!"

She runs back to my side and looks out the window with me.

"What happens now?" she asks.

Within a minute our phone rings. It's the police dispatch making sure we have an emergency. I quickly tell her what we just saw. She informs me that police are already on their way.

We watch two police cars come screeching around the corner and come to a halt across the street. Their lights are flashing and sirens blaring. When the officers get out of their cars, they turn their sirens off but leave their lights on. One of the officers walks up the steps to the front door. He has his hand on his holster. The other officer stands under the open window.

Someone must have answered the door because it appears that the officer on the porch is talking. We wait to see if he makes an arrest. He doesn't. I'm relieved and disappointed at the same time. My neighbors don't seem to be in danger, but I wish I had caught Bob in the act. A few minutes later, the officer walks back to his car and talks to the other policeman. Together, they walk across the street to our house.

"Shit! Why are they coming here?" Katie screams, as we both duck down below the window, hiding.

"Beats me! I wonder if we overreacted by pushing the panic button. Do you think we're in trouble?"

The sound of knocking, even though we're expecting it, startles us. We crawl out of the kitchen then stand to open the door.

"Miss. Miss," the officer says nodding at me and then at Katie. "We understand you called 911 regarding a potential break-in across the street?"

"We pushed the panic button, actually," says Katie. "We saw the guy breaking into the neighbor's house!"

"It happened to be the owner. He locked himself out," the officer informs us.

"Oh." Katie and I say at the same time.

For some strange reason, I'm embarrassed by them being here. The whole neighborhood is probably watching us right now.

Bob is probably watching us.

"We're on alert. We're aware there was an attempted burglary in this neighborhood, so we're glad you called. We're taking every call seriously. Ladies, have a safe night and lock the door behind us." He tips his hat and they walk back to their police car. We watch as they drive off.

"On that note, I'm going to bed," says Katie,

"I'm leaving the dishes and doing the same."

I go into my bedroom, reset my booby trap of the curling iron on the dresser and crawl into bed. I go over the day's events—the dog, my name being called out, the sketch of Bob, the homeless man spitting on my foot, a stranger complimenting me and now witnessing a man breaking into his own house.

This was the longest day of my life. Who lives like this?

Instead of resting, my mind starts to think about the police. Having them here again disturbed me. Instead of bringing me security like before, this time I'm bothered.

Why?

I'm bothered by what the officer said. I'm bothered that he called what happened to me "an attempted burglary." He had to have been referring to me, to our house, to what happened here.

Why did he call it an attempted burglary?

Maybe he didn't know it was our house that got broken into and didn't want to scare us. Maybe he did know, and was just being polite or cautious.

The more I think on this, the more upset I become. What happened to me was NOT a burglary. That man tried to rape me! He tried to kill me!

I didn't say anything—*as is my pattern.* I didn't ask what the policeman really meant—*as usual.* I wasn't brave enough to speak up—*as usual.* So now, I'm stuck not knowing.

I continue to dwell. If they're calling it an attempted burglary... then maybe they don't take what happened to me seriously...maybe they don't believe me. The difference between an attempted burglary and an attempted rape is extreme.

What the hell?

I'm dismayed...even disheartened. I decide I'll casually bring it up with Detective Redmond when I see him next. Maybe he can help assure me that the police believe what I said happened.

My detective will help me understand.

Chapter 23

THE
UNDERSTANDING

The next day at work, Detective Redmond picks me up during my lunch break. I meet his car out back of the department store where the delivery trucks park. When I get in, he hands me an envelope.

"What's this?" I ask, as I open the envelope's flap.

"It's something from my wife and me. She felt you might need a pick-me-up. But before you get into that card, I want to tell you that I asked around your neighborhood about the dog. No one I talked to owns a black and white dog. And what's even stranger, is that no one has ever seen a dog in the neighborhood that fits that description. No one has heard of a dog named Cindy."

"What does that mean?"

"Well, it means to me...the dog must have been a stray. And...it wasn't the dog the man was calling."

He pauses, giving me a chance to register what he has said.

"Do you think that it was Bob calling me, then?"

I will not be scared. I will not be frightened. I will not be...terrified.

Regardless of how hard I try to control my emotions, I can feel my body tighten and shake.

"We're going to assume that the person who called your name is this 'Bob.' I've told the officers and the 911 agents to be on alert. Cinda, if he is still monitoring you, he'll make himself known and we'll get him," his tone is serious, adamant.

"Last night we pushed our panic button," I have a sudden need for him to know this.

"I wasn't aware of that! Why?"

I tell him what Katie and I saw happen across the street. I tell him that later the officer came over and told us it was only the owner, climbing into his own house.

"You did the right thing. I'm relieved that it wasn't your Bob breaking into someone else's house."

"Yeah, me too…I guess. It was strange and creepy to see him climb into the house. He opened the window with a stick. Exactly like you thought Bob would have opened ours. It's just so weird…I mean what are the chances of seeing that happen? Especially so soon after Bob climbed through our window?"

"Yes, it is strange. I'll make a point to talk to the officers and find out what they learned from the man who answered the door. Perhaps there is something there."

I want to bring up the policeman's comment about the 'attempted burglary,' but I don't want to sound petty or childish. I don't want to appear ungrateful or complaining. But I need clarification. I swallow hard and ask.

"I have a question," my voice is timid despite my attempt to sound confident. "When the officer came to our door, he mentioned that an attempted burglary had happened in the neighborhood. He said that all the officers are on alert. I'm sure he meant our house. But…why did he call it a burglary?"

"That's standard. We refer to any form of breaking and entering as a burglary."

I'm partially satisfied with his answer, but not really. It doesn't seem right to call what happened to me 'breaking and entering.' It makes me wonder…*if he believes me, if the police believe me, if they believe my story, believe that I was almost raped and murdered?*

I sit quietly, debating what I should say next, if anything. I decide that I need to tell him everything that's bothering me. I take in a breath and try to bring up the subject.

"There's something else….. I have something else on my mind…," My voice cracks, but I refuse to cry, "You believe me, right? I mean…it wasn't a burglary. He didn't just break into our house. He really did try to hurt me. I mean…like…umm…don't get me wrong…I'm grateful for all the police help and yours…there are policemen everywhere…but it's just so hard…it's just a lot to understand…and then for him to call it an attempted burglary. It just doesn't seem right. It's just a weird thing to call it. That's all I'm trying to say."

My heart is racing while it is also breaking—*it's just so hard…it is just a lot to understand.* I hold my breath, fearful I said too much. Fearful I showed too much weakness. I look down at my lap, at the envelope. In the corner of my eye I can see him glancing over at me. He makes a quick decision to turn the car. I grab onto the door handle to keep from falling toward him. I look up and see that we are in a Burger King parking lot off Burnside Street. He pulls up behind a car in the drive-thru line.

"Is this OK?"

"It's fine. I don't care where we eat."

I don't care about eating anything right now. He hasn't responded to my comments. His silence is making me anxious.... Did I insult him? Is he mad at me? Does he understand my confusion?

I wish I hadn't said anything. I should have kept my mouth shut.

When we get to the window, I ask for a cheeseburger, fries and a Sprite. He orders for both of us and pays. I try to pay him back but he won't let me. He still hasn't responded to my comments, making me even more self-conscious and embarrassed.

I speak up, "I'm grateful for everything you've done for me. I am...I am...I am. I just wonder...if the police are frustrated that they need to protect two girls whose house was only 'burglarized.' I worry...that because I wasn't hurt...they don't take what happened to me seriously. And I'm really embarrassed by all the attention...even though I want it and need it...it's overwhelming. I kind of don't feel like I'm worth all the attention." The last part comes out as a whisper.

Again, silence from the man sitting next to me....

I want to crawl into a hole and hide. I've poured my heart out to my detective. I've confided in him things I've yet to say out loud to anyone.

And he says nothing.

The food attendant hands him our sack of food through the car window. He hands it to me. Still not talking, he drives back around the building, into the parking lot and backs into a parking space. He turns the car off, removes his seatbelt and turns to face me.

Oh God, what is he thinking? What is he going to say?

"Let me see if I understand. You're concerned that we don't believe you? That I don't believe you? You say that since you weren't raped or beaten or killed, that you don't deserve any of the attention you have received from the police? Am I understanding you correctly?"

I can only nod. I refuse to look at him and instead stare at the sack of food on my lap. I can't swallow. The lump of embarrassment in my throat is too big. He must be able to see the shame all over my face. I want to turn myself invisible. I wish I could transport myself someplace else. I wish I could take back what I just said.

"Cinda," his voice is stern, serious. I can feel his eyes still on me. I look at him, then quickly back down at the food. "Let me help you understand something. Yes, we believe you. This is *why* there are so many police officers around you and your neighborhood. Every one of them wants to keep you and Katie safe. Let me make something else perfectly clear— what could have happened to you that night didn't happen because of how you handled yourself. Not everyone in the same situation has the wherewithal, or the common sense, or the calmness to behave the way you did. Of all my years in the police force, I have never met anyone who handled such a frightening situation like you did. It is a very unusual story, because you are a very unusual girl."

I sit quietly for a moment, the warm sack of food on my lap offering me comfort. I think of Janet Frances's comments about my story and now the things Detective Redmond is saying. I also remember my parents' reactions when I told them...*none of their expressions have to do with blame, shame or embarrassment or not believing me.* The consistent emotion they express is...*maybe...perhaps...*awe.

Perhaps...my story IS unusual.

I realize that the unusualness is NOT in the *not* being raped, beaten or killed, but is instead in the *act* of preventing it from happening. The unusualness is in the story of spending three hours outsmarting a monster.

Here in the Burger King parking lot, inside a car, with my detective next to me, a wave of acceptance and realization begins to settle my insides. I finally look at Detective Redmond. His eyes are still on me. I can tell he is monitoring my thought process.

I get it. I get it now.

"Thank you," I whisper.

The emotions I have been experiencing are not correct. I should not feel shamed by what happened to me. There is nothing shameful about nearly being killed or raped. I *have* been harmed. What I experienced was frightening and serious and dangerous—*it still is.*

I did nothing wrong. I am not guilty. I am not responsible for Bob's actions. I should not feel embarrassed by the attention and the protection I'm receiving from everyone right now.

I deserve it. I need it. I am still in danger.

I'm so glad I had the courage to say something. I'm so glad I had the nerve to speak up.

"Read the card," he says.

I pull the envelope out from under the sack of food and slide out the card. It's a Halloween card. On it is a cartoon of a cat in a witch's hat. On the inside, it wishes me a *"Purrfectly Happy Halloween."* A handwritten note says, *"You are amazing, stay safe,"* and is signed by him and his wife. I'm truly touched.

"Your wife knows about me?"

"Yes…a little bit. There's not much I can tell her for privacy reasons. But, yes, she knows what you did to save yourself. I wanted her to know. It's valuable information for her to know."

"Wow…. Well, tell her thank you," It isn't the hot food on my lap that is making my face flush.

My detective told his wife about me.

"I will. Hand me my food. Are you willing to answer some more questions?"

I reach into the sack and hand him his burger. As I hand him the small sack of French fries, our eyes connect. I smile, a bashful but genuine smile of thanks. I'm not embarrassed anymore.

Of all the detectives that could have been assigned to my case—how lucky that I got this one.

My Detective Redmond.

Chapter 24

THE GROCERY STORE

My conversation with Detective Redmond in the Burger King parking lot changes everything for me. Where I had been feeling torn into multiple emotional pieces, I now feel a sense of solidness. Where I had been feeling weak and unworthy, I now experience a new sense of confidence.

We finish eating our lunches as I answer more of his questions. After, he takes me back to work. As I finish out the workday, I can feel this difference. I seem to stand straighter, walk taller and I make a point to look people directly in their eyes. I hadn't realized it, but I'd been avoiding eye contact with others. I think I was afraid they would see that "victim sign" lit up behind my eyes; that they would know I had been attacked.

Interesting…. Curious…. Strange…. It makes no sense.

I don't understand…. Why should I feel less than or abnormal because of what happened to me? Why should I feel like I need to hide from it? Or, hide it from others? Why is there so much shame wrapped up in what happened?

Do other victims feel this way?

Detective Redmond has helped me see that my thoughts are wrong. He seems to want me to feel proud of myself. Proud? Proud. I need to change my attitude about this. I need to believe in myself again. If what I did was unusual, then maybe…there are other things I can do too.

If I could handle Bob, then damn it…I can handle anything.

When my work shift is over, I head home on the bus. When it reaches my stop, despite the fact that I'm back in the scary neighborhood, there is a lightness in my stride. The overhanging sense of dread seems to have been lifted. For whatever reason, I'm not as fearful of my walk home. I decide to take advantage of my good mood and explore the small grocery store on the corner, just a block from my bus stop. I have yet to visit it and since we are out of milk and bread, it's a perfect reason to finally check it out.

The street lights illuminate my way along the sidewalk. The quaint little store is painted white with a large vintage sign protruding out from its corner. Striped canvas awnings hang over the front windows shading an outdoor fruit and vegetable stand. The produce has already been brought in for the evening, but the store is still open.

As I walk in, the door jingles my arrival. The clerk stocking a shelf in the front row greets me with a warm hello. It appears that we are the only people in the store. I find a jug of milk and loaf of bread, grab some coffee for Katie and choose a couple of candy bars. The clerk makes small talk with me as he rings up my purchases.

"I haven't seen you in here before," he says. "Do you live in the neighborhood?"

"Yeah, I do. We moved in a few weeks ago. I live a few houses down."

That seems to satisfy him. While he puts my items into a bag, I look around the charming little store. It doesn't have a lot, but it does seem to carry the basics and a few gourmet items. When I look back to give him my cash, I notice a black and white drawing of a man's face hanging on the bulletin board behind the register.

My picture of Bob.

Fear shoots through my body. Shame overwhelms me all over again. All my newfound composure is tossed out the front window. I'm instantly afraid about what this clerk might know. For some reason, I don't want him to connect me with that drawing. Is he aware that a girl in his neighborhood had been assaulted?

Will he know it's me? Will he see the victim sign over my head, behind my eyes?

Then another thought occurs to me, one that reaches inside my bones, grabs hold of my gut. What if Bob has seen this picture? What will Bob do when he sees this picture?

Oh God. I'm in even more danger.

I look at the clerk and see that he's still waiting for me to hand him money. I ask about the drawing.

"What's that?" I say, pointing to the picture, trying to sound casual.

"What's what?" His eyes follow the direction of my finger. "Oh that. The police dropped that off today. I guess some creep broke into one of the houses in the neighborhood. They've been asking a lot of questions and showing this picture around door to door. Didn't they come to your house? He must have done something pretty bad, because they seem really intent on catching this guy."

His words repeat in my head.

"He must have done something pretty bad, because they seem really intent on catching this guy."

I smile at the clerk as he hands me change and then the bag of groceries. I thank him and say goodnight. I can hear him lock up the store behind me. As I walk around the corner and down the two blocks to the house, I think of his words.

"He must have done something pretty bad, because they seem really intent on catching this guy."

His words bring me back to the conversation I had with my detective in the car. They rekindle the sense of confidence I was feeling before. I want to hold on to this feeling.

I need to hold on to this feeling.

As I walk, I stew over my ridiculous behavior. I don't understand my reaction. I'm bothered by it. Regardless of what Detective Redmond said, I can't seem to shake this shame thing, this feeling guilty thing, this feeling like I did something wrong. Why couldn't I tell the guy that I was that girl who got attacked? Why do I feel the need to keep it a secret?

I can't figure myself out.

I mean…it makes sense that I'm scared. I can wrap my brain around being afraid…afraid of what Bob might do…*to me*, if he sees that picture. If he finds out that I can identify him, that could really piss him off.

It could give him another reason to come after me.

Bob made it clear…he'd been watching us. So, he's had to have seen the police, the detectives, now the drawing…. He's got to know that I've reported him.

I race home, looking over my shoulders, down side streets, behind bushes. I don't relax until I get inside the house. Katie is watching TV. I tell her about the picture in the store. I tell her about what the clerk said to me. As I put the groceries away, I confide in her about all the insecurities I've been feeling. I tell her about confiding to my detective. I mention his serious tone and response. I mention that it helped me feel better.

"Cinda, you are such a freak! Can't you see that what you did was remarkable? And of course, they're taking you seriously. Why wouldn't they? How silly that it took a grocery clerk in a store and your detective in a Burger King parking lot for you to see that!"

"Yeah. Yeah. It's just weird. There are so many different emotions going back and forth in my mind. I need to start believing in what you're saying, in what my detective told me. If I'm to get through this,

I need to stop being so freakin' afraid." I take in a breath and with determination state, "OK! My new motto is this: *If I could do THAT...I can do ANYTHING!*"

"Shit, yes! If you can beat Bob at his own game, then hell yes, you can do anything!" Katie agrees.

If I could do THAT...I can do ANYTHING! If I could do THAT...I can do ANYTHING!

I walk into my bedroom but keep talking, "Oh yeah, on a negative note, Detective Redmond says that there isn't a dog in the neighborhood that fits that description, or a dog named Cindy."

"What does that mean?" she calls back to me.

"That it was more than likely Bob calling me." I shudder; my positive resolve is diminishing quickly.

If I could do THAT...I can do ANYTHING! If I could do THAT...I can do ANYTHING!

"What the hell!" she yells and comes into my room.

"He said they're putting more patrols out," I say in an attempt to reassure her as well as me.

"Cinda...," Katie looks frightened.

If I could do THAT...I can do ANYTHING! If I could do THAT...I can do ANYTHING!

I shrug...*my mantra isn't working very well.* Remembering what my detective said about the dog, about it being Bob that called me, is sinking in. As if I'm hearing it for the first time. I'm petrified. My body hurts from it.

Bob was trying to contact me. Oh, my God; will he try again?

I'm freaked! My mantra is NOT working.

Katie asks, "What did Detective Redmond say? What are we supposed to do?"

"He promises we're safe. Detective Redmond said that since Bob is watching us, he'll slip up and the police will catch him."

This is all so bizarre. It's all so exhausting. It's all so crazy-making. A few moments ago, I was in control, now I'm not. Katie and I keep going back and forth between feeling normal and panicking...normal...panicking.

In a desperate attempt to get my equilibrium back and help Katie get hers, I say, "I'm going to call Scott and fill him in. Then I'm going to try to sleep. I've got my booby trap and a panic button, you have the phone and the best watch-cat on the planet."

We both force a giggle and say goodnight. Detective Redmond told the truth; police cars are all over our neighborhood tonight. They were there when I got off the bus, and when I left the store.

They know who I am. Who we are.

It should make us feel safe. But it's also a constant reminder of the danger we are in.

I call Scott and fill him in on the events so far. He tells me that he is nervous, afraid, worried. I can feel his fear through the phone. I know he's not the only one upset. My mom has called daily. My dad reminds me he's just a phone call away. I love each of them for their concern, but their distress panics me more.

I can NOT bear the thought of anyone I love living in fear because of me. I'm frightened enough as it is. I don't have it within me to take care of their emotions too. So, I make it a point to tell them—convince them—that I'm fine, I'm all right, I'm OK, I'm safe, all is well, don't worry. This seems to appease their apprehension—*I hope….*

I think it works because they need to believe me.

They choose to believe me.

They prefer to believe me.

I need them to believe me.

I need to believe it myself.

I. Am. Fine.

Chapter 25

THE ENCOUNTER

The next morning, I wake up to the sound of the shower. When Katie is done, I take over the bathroom. There is plenty of time to get ready since I don't need to be at the bus stop until 11:30. I'm working the late shift again.

I wave Katie off to work, then head into the kitchen to fix myself some breakfast. We keep the rice paper blinds closed all the time. They help me feel safe and I don't mind being alone in the house like I did before. I take a few moments to play with Buffett. When it's time to leave, I give Buffett some additional food and warn him not to tell Katie.

I lock the door and stand on my front porch, looking up and down the street. Rush hour traffic has cleared. I head up our street just as a police car drives by. When I get to the corner next to the blue house, where I saw the dog, I decide to not go that way. Instead, I walk straight up the street toward the grocery store.

As I walk along the side of the store, I admire the large, colorful murals of produce painted on the wall of the building. The murals add charm, giving the market an old-fashioned feeling. I think about the night before and the drawing of Bob behind the counter. They want him caught as much as I do. I feel a partnership with them. Having a homeless man breaking into people's homes can't be good for business.

When I come to the corner, a man is inserting a letter into the freestanding blue mailbox which is in front of the store. It's a tight squeeze between the mailbox, him and the fruit stands. I wait for him to finish so I can easily pass. It takes a while for him to notice me, but when he does, he doesn't apologize for blocking my way, instead he gets all weird. First, he has an expression of surprise…which then turns to…maybe…familiarity…*like he knows me*. I don't know this man and his strange reaction makes me uneasy.

Am I going to be afraid of every man I meet on the street now?

I give the man an awkward smile and walk around him. I push aside any feelings of uneasiness—*I will not be afraid of strangers!* As I pass the store, I get curious to see Bob's sketch again. I pause to peer through the front window of the store. I lean over the vegetable stand while cupping my hand around my eyes to avoid the window's glare. Instead of seeing inside the store, I see in the window's reflection. The man from the mailbox is looking at me. I monitor him in the reflection as he comes toward me. *What is it with this guy?* The uneasiness inside me grows. I give up on the sketch and head away from the store and the man, down the block to my bus stop.

When I get to the corner, I look back beyond the grocery store, to see if the bus is coming. Thankfully, the man is crossing the street. I watch him, for no other reason than to fill my time. He stops on the opposite corner of the intersection, then crosses the other street, heading away from me—*good, he's leaving.* But then he does something strange. He stops on that third corner and turns to look down the street in my direction. He starts to pace back and forth and seems to be talking to himself. The uneasiness I felt earlier comes back.

This man is not normal.

I look beyond him down the street, wondering why my bus isn't here yet. I glance back at the strange man. He has just crossed the street, still on the other side of the intersection, but is now crossing back over to the corner where I first saw him, at the mailbox. He has taken an unusual, counter-clockwise route for getting back to the store. I assume, I hope, that he's forgotten to buy something. But…instead of going into the store, he heads down the sidewalk toward me.

He is smiling, when he reaches me. I smile politely back at him. Since I don't want to carry on a conversation, I look down at my feet. Rarely do I share this stop with someone else. I don't like it. I pull my coat closer around me because things suddenly get freezing. The man rocks from one foot to another and I assume he's cold too.

I glance at him out of the corner of my eye. He isn't dressed for the weather. His jeans are baggy, hanging on his thin body. He's wearing a worn-out denim jacket that can't possibly be warm. He's not wearing a hat and his frizzy grayish hair is blowing in the damp breeze. If he's going downtown…why didn't he dress warmer?

I'm growing more uncomfortable by the minute, and this man standing next to me isn't helping my comfort level. He moves closer and mumbles something I don't understand. I take a casual step backwards to keep a non-personal distance between us. I am not interested in having a conversation, nothing about my body language is inviting him to do so...but he's talking to me regardless.

He continues to mutter and mumble nonsense. Still ignoring him, I raise my head to look for the bus's location. It's almost here...*thank God*, but it's still a few blocks away. In a swift move, he steps into my line of vision, as if he's demanding I pay attention to him. His movement feels threatening. A shot of panic surges through me.

Something is not right about this guy.

A soft breeze blows right at us. I shudder because of its coldness, but also because the gust carries with it a whiff of this man's breath, followed by a strong scent of his body odor.

I smell unbathed skin, stale alcohol and musty cigarettes.

I've smelled this before.

This smell, this man, is BOB!

Chapter 26

THE CANDY MAN

Every ounce of me wants to scream, to run, but I don't. I can't let him know that I know who he is. His earlier strange behavior makes sense now. He's fully aware of who I am. He's known since I came around the corner and first saw him.

How could I have not recognized him?

I recognize him now. I'm familiar with him now. I know him, now

Shit, shit, shit. What do I do? What do I do?

The bus arrives and I quickly leave his side to board it. I'm desperate to get away from him. I'm desperate to get to work and call Detective Redmond. I mentally beg him to stay at the stop...*stay, please stay.* Behind me, I hear him get on. I hear the bus driver greet him. He's going to follow me to work.

Oh God, oh God, oh God.

Even though there are plenty of empty seats, I walk toward the end of the bus and sit down next to a woman. I do this to prevent him from sitting next to me. I see him sit near the front of the bus in a side seat, with his back along the window. He has a clear view of me, and me of him. I don't know where to look because I can feel his eyes glued to me. I try to avoid looking in his direction. I debate as to whether I should say something to the woman I'm sitting next to, or to the bus driver. But decide against it. I don't want to endanger them or myself.

I can't trust what Bob would do.

I try my best to pretend that it's just a normal commute. I make small talk about the cold weather with the woman next to me. Fortunately, she's friendly and responds. But I'm not listening. My mind is racing with thoughts of how to escape.

I can't risk him finding out where I work.

I can't get off the bus at Meier & Frank.

I need to take the bus to The Galleria, where I told him I worked.

Shit, shit, shit.

I stay on the bus as it drives past my usual stop. When it arrives in front of The Galleria, I stand to get off. I glance toward him, just long enough to see that he's watching me. He appears to be preparing to stand too. As soon as the back doors of the bus open, I exit.

Once my feet hit pavement, I sprint through the automated main doors of the mall. I hear them close behind me. This means he's not inside the building yet. In case he follows me, I pretend I'm late for work and look at my watch. I rush through the small mall, looking for a place to hide. On my right is a candy store. Just as I'm about to pass its entrance, I duck inside.

In the center of the store is a large display. I hide behind it. I try to catch my breath, praying he didn't follow me. Carefully, I peek out from behind a stack of plastic bags filled with pastel pink and blue cotton candy puffs. They are balanced high on top of a large cotton candy machine. I must look ridiculous, but I don't care.

From my hiding place, I peer through the display, looking at the crowd outside the store's front window. There are too many people in the mall to see if Bob is among them.

Oh God, what do I do?

"What are you doing?" asks a male voice from behind me. It has a slight laugh to it.

I freeze—so does my heart—so does my breath. He's found me.

I remind myself that I'm in a public place. *I'm safe.* I'll scream if I need to. I swallow hard, gathering courage to confront him. I stand and turn around.

"Miss?" says the voice again. "Can I help you? Can I help you find a particular flavor of cotton candy?"

I almost weep in relief—it isn't Bob. It's a boy, about my age, wearing a pink apron and a smile.

"Can I help you?" he asks again.

He must see something in my expression because his expression changes when he sees my face. I don't have it within me to pretend nothing is wrong.

I DO need his help.

"I need your help," I tell him almost crying.

My fear is choking me. I can feel my body quiver along with my voice. I don't want to scare this guy. I don't want to appear overly dramatic. I don't want to appear weak either.

I have no choice. I have to tell him.

"I need your help," I tell him again, my voice shaking, my emotions raw. "A man attacked me a few days ago. He followed me here on the bus. I'm hiding from him. I'm too afraid to leave in case he's out there."

"Are you serious?" He says loudly in surprise, and then in a whisper, "Oh my God, seriously?"

He comes closer and looks through the cotton candy display with me. Our shoulders are touching.

"What does he look like? Do you think he's out there?"

This clerk is odd, a good kind of odd. He's friendly…a bit too excited. His closeness feels nice, but he's also a distraction…a distraction I can't afford to have right now.

"I don't see him. It's too crowded out there. I'm not sure if he got off the bus. Can I stay here until I am sure he's gone?"

"Do you want me to go scout the mall and see if I can find him? I can walk around and look for him!"

"Really, you would do that? That would be great. Can you leave the store, though?" I ask as relief floods over me.

"Heck, yeah! I'll just tell Miss Fussy Pants over there that I'm going on a break. I'll tell her to leave you alone. You stay put."

I give him Bob's description in detail. He then walks over to the girl at the counter. He points to me and I see her eyes grow big. When he walks by me, he gives me a double thumbs-up. He's on a mission now. I watch him walk out into the mall. His pink apron is easy to track as he mingles with the shoppers and peeks into store windows. He's taking it so seriously and yet trying to appear nonchalant. I worry that his actions are a bit obvious and might attract attention. But then I realize that Bob would only be looking for me.

I glance over at the counter. The sales girl is staring at me. When we make eye contact, she turns a shade of bright red and turns her attention to the opposite wall. Sitting in front of her is the store's phone. I need to call my detective, but the counter is in full view of the mall. I would be vulnerable. I can't risk Bob seeing me.

I turn my attention back to the mall. I watch as my partner in pink rides up the escalator backwards. He looks toward the store and winks at me in an overly dramatic way. He then surveys the crowd from his higher perspective. When he gets to the top, I lose sight of him.

A few minutes later, he returns.

"The coast is clear. I scouted the entire mall and didn't see anyone who I thought was your bad guy. You are officially safe to go." He puffs his chest up in a superman pride pose.

He then leans in toward me and says, "That was kind of exciting. I wish I could've found him. I was ready to call mall security if I did!"

"Mall security," I swallow the laugh that wants to escape. "Yep that would have been helpful."

Oh...you have no idea...this is so much bigger than mall security...police, detectives...a panic button.

I reach out and place my hand on his shoulder to thank him. With animation, he pantomimes a message: ah-shucks-it-was-nothing-ma'am.

"Good luck," he says. His tone is sincere, backed with a touch of emotion.

At the candy store's entrance, I scan the crowd. Not seeing Bob, I leave the store and race to the back entrance to the mall. I glance back toward the store and see that the pink-aproned man is watching me get away. He waves goodbye just as the automated door shuts behind me.

I look at my watch—I'm late.

I need to get to work so I can call my detective.

I need to tell him what happened.

I need to tell him to fucking catch Bob!

Chapter 27

THE BUM DETECTIVE

I sprint the four blocks toward Meier & Frank. I duck behind a delivery truck and peek around it to see if Bob is following. I don't see him.

Once inside the store, I try to compose myself as I ride the escalators up to my floor. I go directly into the back offices, find a vacant one, and pick up the phone. Detective Redmond answers. I do my best to remain calm, but my voice is shaking, cracking, giving my fear away as I tell him everything, in every little detail.

He's quiet as I ramble on in my panic. When I finish, he speaks in a slow, calm tone. "Cinda, I'm glad you're safe. That was smart to go to The Galleria, to lead him away from where you work. But I wish you would have called me from the candy store. We could have searched the premises, both inside and outside. There could have been a better chance at finding him. Remember, I said that if he is monitoring you, he'll make his presence known. He just did that. He's going to do it again, and I want to be there when that happens. Are you sure you weren't followed to work?"

"I don't know if he got off the bus. I don't know if he followed me into the mall. I don't believe he followed me here. Detective Redmond...I didn't know that guy on that corner was Bob! Why didn't I recognize him? What do I do?" I can't hide my desperation.

"Stay at work. You are safer there than anywhere else. Do not leave the building, not for lunch, a break, for anything. Promise me you will stay where you are," his voice is stern and commanding, kind and protective. "I'll call you back in a few hours. I need to figure out what to do next. Do not leave until you hear from me. Got it?"

"Got it. I will not leave," my voice cracks and my hand shakes as I hang up the phone.

I gather my wits about me and head back out onto the sales floor. I try to pretend that nothing is different, that nothing is wrong. I do my best to get through my day by helping customers, ringing sales and not collapsing into the fear. I'm a nervous wreck. I'm on constant alert for a denim jacket and frizzy hair.

Three hours later, Detective Redmond calls.

"I've got officers driving around your neighborhood looking for a man that fits your description. I've met with the bus driver and showed him your composite drawing. Unfortunately, he doesn't remember seeing the guy."

"OK…," I'm not sure how to respond.

"What time are you off? Will you be taking the bus home? If so, can someone walk you to your bus stop downtown? I don't want you to be alone."

"I'll close out at 9:00 and be out of here by 9:30. I will be taking the bus home. It's only a two-block walk to the bus. I won't be alone; the streets are somewhat crowded at night. I usually get home around 10:00."

"If you can get yourself an escort to the bus stop downtown, I'd feel much better. Here's the plan for when you get off the bus in your neighborhood. I'll be waiting for you across the street. I'll be undercover, dressed as a bum. I'll have a shopping cart filled with stuff. If you see me, don't acknowledge me. I'll keep my distance, but I'll follow you home. Once you go inside, I'll monitor your street to see if I can spot anyone watching you. If the coast is clear, I'll come and knock on your door. Do NOT open it unless you're sure it's me. Do you understand?"

"Yes, I think so."

"Good. I'll see you later tonight."

When I hang up the phone, my entire body is shaking. My detective is going undercover and wearing a disguise. I feel like I've just jumped into a horror movie.

I set my emotions aside so I can keep working. The rest of the day goes by in a fog and I grow more and more apprehensive as the time gets closer to leaving. When the time arrives, I do my best to count the money and close my register without any complications. As scattered as I've been today, I'm surprised and grateful that my money and sales match.

I put on my coat and wave goodbye to my co-workers. I decide to not take the elevator because the thought of being confined inside a small space sounds like torture. I've had enough of that already. I take the escalators down. Their slow pace and steady hum is soothing—*if that's possible.*

The security guard unlocks the door and holds it open for me. I want to ask him to walk me the two blocks to my bus stop, to ride the bus home with me, to stand outside my house and be my personal security guard. Instead, I smile and say thank you as he locks the doors behind me. When I hear the click, separating security and me, I let out a cry of desperation— part whine, part whimper, almost a full-on howl. The tension is too much to hold in. I yearn for human support. I lied to Detective Redmond. I told him I'm not alone downtown, that downtown is crowded with people. But right now, I am…I am very much alone.

I scan up and down the street in front of Meier & Frank. I see no man with frizzy hair waiting for me. I must somehow find the courage to get to my bus—to my detective…to my detective who is dressed as a bum, waiting for me.

One, two, three, go!

I walk the two blocks weaving in and out of people. The bus arrives as I approach. I look for Bob on the bus. He isn't there. During the 30-minute ride to my neighborhood, I replay the events of the day. I wish I would have called Detective Redmond from the candy store—maybe they would have caught Bob.

As the bus pulls up, sure enough, across the street is a homeless man with a shopping cart. I assume that this is my *bum-disguised-undercover-detective.* Just as instructed, I don't acknowledge him when I step off the bus. I pretend he's not there. As I head down the street toward my house, I can hear the wheels of the shopping cart clanging along the sidewalk. He is following me home.

I walk the three blocks to my house when an awful thought occurs to me. Could this be Bob following me? I didn't get a good look, because I was following instructions and trying not to pay attention.

What should I do?

I pick up my pace until I reach home. I hop up the steps, unlock the front door and burst inside. I slam the door shut, push against it and relock it. I startle Katie and her boyfriend Perry who are sitting on the couch watching TV. They laugh, but then stop when they see I'm on the verge of hysterics.

"Cinda, what's wrong?" Katie asks, concerned.

I sit on the coffee table in front of them. I am blocking "Dallas," but they don't seem to mind. As JR and Sue Ellen are having a yelling match on the TV screen, I tell Katie and Perry about running into Bob at the bus stop, then him following me onto the bus, the candy man's pink apron and about Detective Redmond being dressed up as an undercover bum outside.

"That is if it wasn't Bob who followed me home!" Fear chokes my throat.

Perry's voice is a yell. "You've got to be kidding!"

Katie says nothing. She's obviously too scared and worried to speak.

Perry turns to the window behind him and raises the blind to look out.

"Perry, don't! Detective Redmond doesn't want us to draw any attention to him! Once he checks out the neighborhood, he'll come here. And... what if it was Bob? We don't want him to be clued into anything."

Perry lets the blinds fall closed and turns back around. He says, "Well, your detective is looking for Bob. So, if Bob was the one following you... then he'll be caught. Right?"

"You have a point," I say.

A whine comes from Katie, "This just gets stranger and stranger. Every day. This is non-ending."

Perry asks, "You really think the guy at the bus stop this morning was Bob?"

"Yes! I'm positive. I got a whiff of his body odor. It's Bob, I know it for sure."

Twenty minutes later a knock comes. Perry jumps up and opens it before I have a chance to tell him he's supposed to ask who it is. Standing under our porch light is my bum-disguised-undercover-detective.

Yes, it was my detective at the bus stop...not Bob.

I see a police car drive by behind him, *one of many tonight I'm sure.* I invite him into the house and close the door. He tells us that there is nothing, no one suspicious out there tonight. He seems disappointed. I'm disappointed. I introduce him to Perry.

"Glad to see you here. Having a man in the house right now can make a difference." He shakes Perry's hand.

Detective Redmond turns back to me. "Cinda, what's your schedule tomorrow?"

"I work the morning shift for a change. I'll be catching the bus at 8:30."

"I'm off tomorrow, but I'll have another detective contact you in the morning. If this guy tries to approach you at the bus stop tomorrow, we'll nab him."

"OK...so...he'll call me at home in the morning? Before I leave for work?"

"Yes. I'll make sure he connects with you before you leave. I'm going to snoop around some more in your area tonight. If he's out there, we'll catch him."

Perry says he should get going too, but something tells me he's also going to be snooping around the neighborhood. When he leaves, Katie and I don't know what to do with ourselves but go to bed. The last thoughts on my mind are a prayer.

"Please God, have them catch Bob tonight."

Chapter 28

THE UNDERCOVER COPS

Early the next morning, from the recesses of my sleep, I hear a distant ringing. Confused, I listen…wondering why that sound is in my dream of pink angels sitting on top of clouds made of cotton candy. Then I remember the phone call that's meant to come today. It's my phone ringing. I'm awake. I leap out of bed, struggle to undo my booby trap, and sprint to the phone.

"Hello?"

"Miss Stevens, this is Detective Richardson. I've been updated on your case by Detective Redmond. I understand that you were approached on the street yesterday by your assailant, or someone you believe might be him. Is this correct?"

"Yes."

"I understand you'll be riding bus route 43, three blocks northwest of your house, at 8:30 this morning. Correct?"

"Yes."

Maybe I'm just tired, but I don't like this man's manner. He's not friendly or warm or comforting.

He's nothing like my detective.

"We'll be monitoring the actions in your neighborhood this morning," he continues. "We'll be watching your bus stop location very carefully for anyone who fits your description of the man who approached you. We also have the composite drawing of your alleged perpetrator."

"OK…," I say.

I want to get him off the phone. This detective seems so condescending. It's as if he doesn't think this is important…as if taking care of me is a nuisance to him.

"There will be two of us. We'll be in an unmarked car and position ourselves nearby, within sight of your bus stop. We need to come up with a strategy, a code, some way for you to signal us if you are approached by this man again. Do you have any suggestions?"

"What?" I ask. "Do *I* have any suggestions? I don't have a clue."

"We need to agree on a signal, a signal that will inform us that the man who approaches you is your perpetrator. Our goal is to apprehend him on the spot."

"Well, don't ask me."

My detective takes care of me…this guy is causing me even more anxiety and stress and I don't want any more of it. I can't handle any more of it. This guy is asking me to do shit that's supposed to be his job.

"Do you have something that you can drop, perhaps your purse?" he suggests. "We're looking for something that would be obvious to us, but not too obvious to the suspect."

"I have multiple purses—small, large, medium. What do you recommend?" I tell him. My irritation and discomfort are rising.

"Whatever you think you can drop without being obvious."

"I have a clutch that I can use. Perhaps I can carry that?" I say, grasping for ideas. "Since it doesn't have handles, it would be easy to drop and not look suspicious."

I feel my body stiffen and as my muscles tighten, the shivering comes. I'm stressed. I'm worried. This detective does not make me feel safe. He's ordering me to be the bait that entices Bob to show himself again. He's using me to lure Bob into a trap. He's requiring me to be vulnerable and exposed.

If this fails…what happens to me?

"That purse sounds like it will work. So, to repeat the plan: We'll be driving around your neighborhood this morning looking for anyone who fits the description of this suspect. At 8:10, we will park our car within view of your bus stop and wait for you to arrive. We ask that you do not draw attention to us, if you see us. If anyone approaches you at the bus stop, we will not make a move unless you drop your purse. If you do drop your purse, we'll immediately apprehend the suspect. Do you have any questions?"

I just want him to shut up!

"What if I make a mistake? What if I accidently drop my clutch and you arrest the wrong person?"

"Do you feel that you will do that?"

YES!

"No, I don't," I lie as I think of that poor man who was a suspect in the back of the police car.

"Very well, then. In a couple hours," he says and hangs up.

I sit at the kitchen table and try to catch my breath. Buffett comes under the table and rubs up against my legs. If Buffett is out, Katie must be up. Sure enough, I hear the shower running. The cat's purring is soothing. I prepare his breakfast and some toast for me.

When Katie finishes in the bathroom, I head into the shower. As water rushes over me, I go over Detective Richardson's plan in my head.

Shit. This is crazy weird!

My days have been nothing but crazy since…since this shit happened to me. They haven't been the same, or normal, for what seems like forever. Right now, I hate my life! I hate that THIS has become my life. I get out of the shower and head into my room and get dressed. In the back of my closet, I find my clutch on a shelf. I swap out the items from my larger purse and put them into the smaller one.

Katie has already left for work so I have the house to myself. I can rehearse *the plan* without embarrassing myself. Holding the clutch under my arm, I walk around the house practicing a variety of ways to drop it by *accident*. I pretend to fumble inside of it for a lip gloss and let the clutch accidentally slip out of my hands. I pretend I'm cold and tighten my coat around my middle, causing the purse to fall. I imagine people approaching me at the bus stop—people who aren't Bob.

Don't drop the clutch. Don't drop the clutch.

I then imagine Bob coming up to me.

Drop the clutch! Drop the clutch!

I drop the clutch. It's easy enough to do, although it feels awkward. My head is filled with questions, all stemming from my insecurity and worry about messing up. What will I say when I drop my clutch? I can't just stand there and pretend I didn't notice I dropped it. But if I pick it up too quickly, the detectives might think I made a mistake. Shit, what if Bob picks it up for me? I have never acted before, but this is the most important acting job I'll ever have.

This is freaking I N S A N E!

A quick glance at my clock and I see that I need to get moving. I've put it off as long as I can. I put on my coat, lock the front door behind me and head up the street. I'm running a bit late and hope that the detectives aren't angry that I'm not on schedule with the plan. As I get to the corner with the blue house, I see a car with two men drive in my direction. They both see me at the same time. Their reaction gives them away. It's easy to assume they are my new undercover detectives. Following Detective Richardson's instructions, I pretend not to notice. I do notice when they turn up the next block.

When I get to my bus stop, it's not long before I see the same car park about a half block up the side road. The two men are looking right at me. They're so obvious that I want to laugh.

My bum-disguised-undercover-detective drew less attention than these guys.

The bus comes almost immediately after I arrive. I board and find a seat. I look through the bus window and watch the detectives follow my bus for a few blocks, then turn off in another direction.

As I ride to work, I scold myself for not being at the bus stop earlier. Perhaps, if I hadn't procrastinated…if I had gotten to the bus stop earlier… if I hadn't been so nervous about being part of Detective Richardson's plan…if I wasn't so afraid of seeing Bob again…Bob would have had time to find me. Maybe my change in working the morning shift versus the evening shift today screwed up the chances of Bob finding me. Either way, I'm disappointed…I didn't handle it well…I should have been braver…this wasn't a successful sting operation.

I'm disappointed.

Bob wasn't caught.

Chapter 29

THE EYES

Throughout the morning at work, I have trouble shaking off the disappointment. The phone rings and I am grateful for the distraction. I'm even more grateful and surprised to hear Katie's voice on the other end.

"Hey Cinda, I'm downtown and thought I'd come by. Can you do lunch?"

We meet upstairs on the tenth floor of Meier & Frank in the Georgian Room. It's an elegant restaurant, and feels like a perfect way to treat ourselves. Katie's eager to hear how the sting operation went. Unfortunately, there isn't much to say. So instead of celebrating the arrest of Bob, we decide to pretend our life is normal. We're just two normal teenagers, spending way too much money on a meal. We gossip and giggle away the hour.

Katie walks me back to my department and decides to stay and shop. I get busy helping multiple customers at the same time. I rush back and forth from the fitting rooms to the floor to satisfy each customer with either a different size, style or color. I love this part of my job. It fills a need to solve problems for other people, a need that seems to be amplified right now.

As I'm flipping through the rounder of dresses, looking for a holiday dress, size five, in red instead of black, I notice two women turning into the department from the escalator. I find the dress, but before I run it back to my waiting customer, I make eye contact with them. I indicate that I'll be right back to help them. One of the women smiles at me in understanding. She has a light about her that's familiar, but it takes a few seconds for me to place her. Then I do! It's Janet Frances, the forensic sketch artist. I wave to her, excited. I run into the fitting room to give the customer her dress and then rush back onto the floor.

I can't believe I get to see Janet again. After our time spent trying to recreate Bob's face on a piece of paper, I haven't been able to stop thinking about her. When I get back out onto the floor, I search the department.

I don't see her. I rush over to Kara and ask her if she helped the two women who were just here. She says she didn't. I race to the escalators to see if they're heading up or down to the next floors.

I don't see her.

More disappointment.

I understand why she left…I guess I do. It would make sense…that once she recognized me…she would respect and honor my circumstances. I suppose she would assume…that I wouldn't want her to expose my stressful personal experience inside of my professional place of work.

But she's wrong.

I had hoped to see her again and thank her. She did more for me than just a drawing of that man. Her tenderness, her gift of traveling through time with me and her support changed me for the better.

More disappointment.

I find Katie shopping for a blouse and tell her what just happened. She's disappointed too. She would have liked to have met this woman I've talked about so much. I help her pick out a blouse and then ring her purchase through the register.

"Too bad that Janet Frances left without speaking to you," Katie says, as I give her a hug goodbye.

"I'll see you tonight. We can do dinner since I'm off early."

When any woman with blond hair comes into the department, I get my hopes up that she will be Janet. But she doesn't come back. The rest of the day goes by with the heavy cloud of disappointment hovering over me. I'm not sure what to do to get it to leave.

When my shift is over, I'm eager to leave. Maybe some fresh air will clear things up. I wave goodbye to Kara and log out of the register as my replacement steps behind the counter. Because of the time I'm leaving, I can catch the bus at a different stop. I like this bus stop; it's just up the street.

There are three different bus routes along this block and mine is in the middle. Next to the first stop, a group of guys, maybe in their twenties, are hanging out. They have a boom box blaring. They're rowdy, probably drunk or high on something, and are rudely harassing every person that passes by. Wanting to avoid them, I don't cross the street at the corner. Instead, I walk up half the block on the other side of the street, then cross over in the middle.

It doesn't matter.

They spot me anyway. When I get onto the sidewalk, next to my bus stop, the pack directs their attention toward me. They strut around me, throwing out sexual innuendos. I do my best to ignore them, avoiding eye contact. I try to move away from the male mob. Then one of the men steps directly in front of me. In a macho and threatening manner, he glares at me. His stance is daring me to notice him.

I'm scared...more scared than I want to admit.

I'm also pissed.

I'm pissed and I'm tired of men picking on me.

I decide to glare back at him. Our eyes lock. I expect to be intimidated, but instead I'm mesmerized. His eyes are the clearest, coolest, greenest, most beautiful eyes I've ever seen. I'm so taken in by their beauty that a gasp escapes me. I can't turn away. He doesn't try to break away either.

There is a connection here that I can't explain.

Then a strange thing happens. In his eyes, his beautiful eyes, I experience a complete sense of peace and awe...perhaps even reverence. There's a deep recognition of some kind...yet I'm certain we've never met. I've never experienced anything like this, like him, like these eyes.

I'm frozen in place, in time.

He is too.

He takes a few steps back and one step sideways. This breaks our eye contact and the intense connection. He's allowing me to pass.

"I'm sorry," he whispers. He's looking down at his feet.

"Don't do that to people. It's not nice," I whisper back.

I walk past him and onto the waiting bus. After I find my seat, I look over my shoulder at him and his group of rowdy thugs. His buddies are razzing and teasing him. They're laughing and pushing him around. I notice that he isn't acting so tough anymore. I straighten up in my seat still feeling the beauty and awe and reverence and peace his eyes seemed to pass on to me.

What was that?

Who was that?

Chapter 30

THE LETTER

When I get home, it's still early evening. I see that Katie has put today's mail on the coffee table. I call out to her, but there's no answer. Buffett comes to greet me, purring and circling around my feet. This poor cat is starving...*again*. He follows me into the kitchen. There's a note from Katie next to the phone telling me to call her when I get home. I feed Buffett, not worried how many feedings he's had today. His gratitude is adorable.

I head back into the living room and sit down on the couch to look through the stack of mail. The new issue of *Seventeen* magazine catches my eye. I flip through the glossy pages filled with holiday flair. I fantasize what it would be like to be at one of those holiday parties, looking as cute as the models do. I toss it aside and go through the rest of the mail. I flip through bills and junk mail, then come upon a letter addressed to me. It appears to be a personal letter since the address is handwritten. I turn it over and see the name "Ron," but no last name or return address. Curious, I rip it open and unfold the paper.

The letter starts out *Dear Cindy*.

Since Cindy is what I was called while growing up, this letter had to have been written by either a family member or a friend from high school or earlier. Curious, I skim down to the end of the letter to see who it's from. It's from Ron, a childhood friend. He was a nice guy.

I go back to the beginning of the letter and read it. Ron proceeds to thank me for being such a good friend, especially when he felt like he didn't have any. The letter ends with a request to see each other again.

This letter is strange.

Ron was popular and had a lot of friends. Even though the letter is nice, I'm confused. Ron and I haven't spoken for years so why would he reach out now?

This is totally weird.

I put the letter down and pick up the new issue of *Glamour* magazine. I start to flip through its pages. I again fantasize about looking like the models, when the phone rings. Thinking that it's probably Katie, I go to answer it. As I pick it up, I hope it might be my mom so I can ask if Ron contacted her to get my address.

"Hello?"

"Cindy? Hi. It's Ron."

"Ron?" I ask, surprised. "Hi Ron, how are you?"

How totally weird to have him call right now.

"Good. I'm good!" He says with a cheerful tone.

His voice is not familiar. The Ron from my childhood has a deep and low voice. Something tells me that this isn't the same Ron, but I don't know another Ron. Who else could it be?

"What's up?" I ask, trying to find a tactful way to figure out who this is.

"I was wondering if you got my letter?"

"Yes, as a matter of fact, I just read it and then you called."

"Good. I was hoping you found it on your coffee table."

I freeze.

Every hair on my neck is standing at attention. Warning bells are going off in my head. My intestines twist and cramp. My chest tightens. I can't breathe.

How the hell did he know the letter was on my coffee table?

This isn't Ron from my past. I am positive.

This is Bob!

My mind is racing. I glance at the windows to ensure that the blinds are closed. They are. They always are now.

Oh, my God, how...? He had to have seen the letter in the pile.

How did he know about the letter? How did he know it was from my friend Ron? The truth sets in.

Bob's been in my house.

He's been in my house, rifled through my mail—*and God's knows what else.* I glance around the house, looking for things that look like they've been moved. Nothing seems obvious. Then it hits me...he called right after I got home. He had to have seen me walk home from the bus. He's watching me now. He's watching the house now.

He knows I'm alone.

Then, just as during the attack, everything starts to move in slow motion. My mind slows down, my entire body calms. This strange phenomenon gives me time to think, time to figure out how to handle this.

I look at the facts: I'm not safe. I need to call the police. I could push the panic button. I need to get him off the phone. I need to do this without making him suspicious that I know who he is. I can't afford to make him angry. I can't let him know I'm scared.

Careful, Cinda, tread carefully.

If Bob is watching me while he's on his phone, then he's using a pair of binoculars or is on a portable phone nearby. He might be able to see through the gaps in my blinds. He might be able to see my silhouette through the thinness of them. It's possible. They are, after all, rice paper. I must playact this out, not just fake it on the phone with him.

An idea comes to me…a way to get Bob off the phone without clueing him in to the fact that I know who he is.

Call-waiting!

"Ron," I say, faking enthusiasm. "I'm so glad to be talking to you, but my call-waiting is beeping in. Let me get the other line and then we can talk. I'll be right back."

I don't give him time to respond. I push the button on the phone. It's the same button to either connect to a second call, *if there is one*, or hang up. Since there isn't a second call, I hang up on him. Hanging up on someone, when trying to answer the call-waiting line, happens all the time. So, it won't be unusual or suspicious to have it happen now.

In case he's watching, in case his binoculars are focused on me, I pretend to connect to the *fake* second call. I pantomime a conversation with a nonexistent person on the nonexistent other line. I pretend to laugh and talk. Then, I pretend to click the button to go back to him, to Ron, to Bob. I bring the phone back to my ear and then pull it away to look at it. I act out disappointment that we've been disconnected.

Oh God, if he's watching, I hope he believes me.

I decide against calling the police or pushing the panic button. What could the police do if they came? I don't know where he is. I don't know where to tell them to go. If the police showed up right now, it would piss him off. He would know that I know who it was on the phone, that he'd been in my house…I'd be in greater danger.

I'd be in greater danger.

I'm not safe to leave the house either. My car is parked a block away. I'm sure he'd confront me. On the phone, he seemed eager to talk to me.

I'm trapped. Trapped inside of my own house.

I shouldn't be alone, though. I should call Katie home. I go into the kitchen and call the number she left me on the note. It's Perry's phone number. Perry's mother answers. I ask her if Katie is there.

"Is this Cinda? Is everything all right?" She asks with the concern of a mother.

Her concern makes me want to cry out.

No, I'm not all right, I'm scared to death!

"Yes, I'm fine. Please, is Perry or Katie there? Can I talk to Katie please?" I speak in the calmest voice I can muster, but I hear my panic.

"Hold on, Cinda."

I can hear a muffled sound. She is covering the receiver as she tells her son that I sound upset.

"Cinda, you OK?" Perry asks.

"Perry, can you and Katie come home please?" Despite my attempt to remain calm, I begin to cry. "I just got a phone call from the guy that broke into my house. I'm sure it's the same guy, and I'm scared to death."

"We'll be right there," he says, and hangs up.

I grab Buffett and go into my room. I booby-trap my door and sit on my bed with my back up against the wall. I'm ready to push that panic button if I need to. For 20 minutes, I wait…listening for any kind of noise. I wait…playing scenarios in my head. What will I do if Bob barges through my front door? Is he just outside ready to strike? How can I defend myself if he does? My breath comes in gasps, and my heart is racing. I hold one hand over the button just in case, Buffett held firmly in my other.

I hear a key in the door. I freeze. I hear the door open. I hold my breath. Katie calls out my name. I'm so relieved that I jump off my bed, undo the booby trap and both Buffett and I come scurrying out of my room. Perry is carrying a baseball bat and it warms my heart in appreciation.

I'm hysterical. More hysterical than I've been yet. My body is shaking, my emotions are on the surface, my voice cracks as I tell them the story. I show them the letter.

"Bob had to have been in the house!" I exclaim, trying to control the hysteria. "He had to have gone through the mail, because he found this letter from Ron. Then he called, pretending to be Ron. What a freak! Who does that? I wouldn't have figured it out, if he hadn't slipped up and mentioned the coffee table! I'd have kept assuming he was Ron from my childhood! Oh, my God, he's been in our house!"

I take in a deep breath and hold it to stop my ranting and look at them. They are both staring at me. I can see their minds racing. Katie's fear is written all over her face, her eyes wild. Perry's back straightens, his jaw clenches. He tightens his grasp on the bat, ready to use it, ready to fight, ready to protect Katie and me.

He speaks first, "Cinda, I don't think it was a slip up. He's playing a mind-fuck game with you. I think that this Bob is trying to scare you. I think he said that on purpose, so you'd discover that he'd been in this house. So, the question is…how did the son of a bitch get in?"

He takes off through the house with Buffett hissing and chasing him from room to room. Katie comes and stands right next to me.

"Should we call the police?" she asks, with her voice cracking, "Should we push the panic button?"

"Not yet," I share my reasoning with her. "I'll call Detective Redmond in a minute."

We watch as Perry checks every window, every door, the basement—all are locked, all are secure.

"That son of a bitch must have a key," he yells.

Katie speaks up, "The detective told the landlord to change the locks on the door. But that hasn't happened yet."

I ask the next obvious question, "But…how did he get our phone number?"

Katie goes to the phone and holds it up. She points to the inserted slip of paper that has our seven-digit number written on it. We stare at each other in disbelief.

"A house is supposed to be a safe haven, but right now it feels like a torture chamber," I breathe out these words. "I don't feel comfortable calling the police. I think it will make things worse for us if Bob sees them here. But I'm going to call Detective Redmond."

I punch in his number, which I now know by memory. He's already left for the day, but he gave the receptionist instructions to contact him at home if I called.

Thank God! Thank God!

It isn't long before the phone rings.

We all jump, afraid of who might be on the other line. I answer it, as Katie and Perry lean in to listen.

"Hello?"

"Thom Redmond here. Cinda, what's up?"

There is a unified sigh of relief. Katie and Perry go sit down at the kitchen table.

I tell my detective everything, including why I didn't call the police or push the panic button. He doesn't seem to approve or agree. *It may not make sense to him, but it does to me.* He says that he'll send an undercover officer, in an unmarked car, to watch over our house tonight. I thank him—*maybe he's just appeasing me, or maybe he sees my point of not wanting to piss off Bob.* Either way, I'm so, so, so relieved—relieved that he's listening to me, relieved that he's not sending cops, but relieved that he *is* sending secret cops.

Right before he hangs up, his voice turns tender, "Cinda, I'll call you in the morning. Make sure all your doors and windows are locked. Do not, I repeat, DO NOT answer the door for anyone. Do you understand? Don't hesitate to push that panic button if anything and I mean ANYTHING scares you."

My hand is shaking as I push the button on that phone to cut me off from my safety line. Tears run down my cheeks as I try to breathe through the stress. Katie comes to my side and puts her arm around me. I can feel her shaking too.

Perry stands up from the table, "So…then…how about a drink?"

"We don't have anything," Katie says.

"Humph," Perry's disappointment is shared by all of us. A drink would be helpful.

Perry walks into the living room and turns on the TV. "Come on, you guys. Let's make some popcorn and watch a show."

What a sweet guy; he's trying to distract us. Katie stays in the kitchen to make popcorn and I go sit next to Perry on the couch. There is nothing on TV that grabs our attention. Perry leaves it on some news station, but suddenly stands and starts scanning the room. I pop off the couch with a shot of panic.

"Perry, what's wrong?" I ask him.

"If Bob has a key, we need to find a way to secure the doors!" he yells. *He's right!*

He and I slide the couch over to block the front door. We run into the kitchen, past Katie making popcorn on the stove, to move the dining table in front of the back door. The smell of popcorn is filling the air. My stomach growls in either stress or hunger, and it occurs to me that I haven't eaten dinner. I don't care. I can't eat anyway. I don't think my stomach will allow anything inside of it.

"Perry, are you staying the night?" I ask, hoping he will.

"Yes. I'll stay. I don't think you girls should be alone in this house," he answers.

I'm more than grateful to have him in the house. It will be easier to sleep with him here.

But who am I kidding? No one is going to get any sleep tonight.

Bob has a key!

Chapter 31

THE LAST STRAW

In the middle of the night, I undo the booby trap and sneak out of my room to go in the kitchen for a drink of water. I'm startled to find Perry sleeping on our couch. He jumps up, baseball bat in his hands, sees it's me, waves and lies back down. I get my drink of water and go back to bed. I leave my bedroom door open because I don't want Perry to feel alone. Katie's door is closed to keep Buffett inside her room and off Perry.

A few hours later, I wake up to the sound of voices, and am warmed by their soft chatter. I walk into the kitchen to the smell of fried eggs, toast and coffee. Katie and Perry are sitting at the table eating. They stop talking and look up at me when I enter.

"Do we dare ask you how you slept?" Katie asks.

Perry smiles in a polite way.

I must look like crap. I feel like crap.

Concern for me is plastered on their faces and I attempt a smile to put them at ease. The smile doesn't hold, though. I can't fake it. I hardly slept last night and I am exhausted.

I am exhausted. EXHAUSTED and tired of this shit!

I pop in a piece of toast and scoop out the leftover eggs from the frying pan. I sit down with them at the table.

"Thanks for staying over last night, Perry. I really appreciate it."

"No problem," he says. "This is so unreal. Isn't it? I can't believe that this can happen here in Portland. Well, I guess it can, but I can't believe that this can happen to someone like you."

"Yeah, I never thought this could happen to me."

Katie says, "I'm still freaked out by the thought of Bob being in our house. When I think of him snooping through our mail...it makes me wonder what else he's been snooping through? I mean...he knew about the clothes in the basement...what else does he know about us? What the hell! Right?"

"I'm pissed that your landlord hasn't done anything to help you guys," Perry states.

"Not even change the locks on our doors!" Katie fumes, "He acts like he doesn't give a shit about us. Not once has he made any effort to help. He's totally aware of what's happening. I've called, the detective has called and still he doesn't seem to care. What an asshole!"

"Yeah, I don't get it either," I agree. "I'd better go get ready for work. I'm not sure how I'm going to make it through the day, but I feel safer there than here."

I take my dishes to the sink then head to my room.

After I'm dressed, Perry offers to drive me to work. "I've got to take Katie back to my parents' house to get her car anyway," he says.

I accept with gratitude. If Bob was watching us last night, there's a real chance he would approach me at the bus stop today.

Katie finishes washing the last dish and places it on the drying rack. She looks out the window and says, "There goes another police car. They've been driving past our house every few minutes. It's a merry-go-round of cop cars."

The three of us put on our coats and get ready to leave when the phone rings. We freeze. We stare at each other and then at the receiver— *what if it's Bob?* No one moves to answer it. Perry decides to pick it up.

He pushes the button and yells into the phone, "What! What do you want!"

"Thom Redmond here."

"Hold on, please, sir, thank you, sorry, here's Cinda," he says, handing the phone to me. "It's your detective."

I take the receiver from Perry.

Without any small talk, Detective Redmond gets straight to the point. "Cinda, there are police that will follow you to your bus. Once you get to your work, stay there. I recommend that Katie do the same. Consider your house a danger zone. It is apparent that this guy is not going to leave you alone. You and Katie NEED to find a safe place to stay, a different place to stay for the time being, until we can catch this guy. Is there any place you can stay?"

"Yes. I have family that lives in town."

"Good, call them. Now."

After he hangs up, I look at Perry and Katie and tell them we need to pack our bags and find a temporary place to stay.

"He called our house a danger zone. He doesn't want us back here."

Katie stares at me. I turn and run into my room and throw items into a bag. Katie does the same. We meet back in the living room and place our bags by the front door.

Perry takes control. "I'll go get my car and double park it out front. Katie, get Buffett's stuff together. You guys can stay with me, at my parents' house. It'll be fine with my mom." He slides the couch out of the way, then leaves. We lock the door behind him.

Katie and I watch out the kitchen window. Another cop car drives by. When Perry pulls his car up, Katie grabs Buffett and heads outside. I take his kitty litter box. Perry rushes inside to get our suitcases. We lock the door and race down the steps. Perry places the litter box in the trunk and tosses the bags next to it. Katie slides into the front with Buffett, while I climb into the back. Perry throws his car into gear and we are gone.

As he drives through rush hour traffic, I dwell on Detective Redmond's words.

Danger zone.

"What the hell!" I scream out. "I've had enough of this bullshit! That letter! That phone call! It's the last straw!"

Katie looks back at me and I see Perry's eyes on me in his rearview mirror.

"Why the hell are we still in this house? Katie! I hate it! I hate everything about that house! I want to move out of that fucking house permanently! NOW!"

Enough! I have had E N O U G H!

"I agree!" Katie says, her voice calm to balance out my frenzied tone.

"Let's get the fuck out of this nightmare! NOW! I don't want to go back!" I yell. Her balancing therapy isn't working.

"OK. OK…let's figure this out. We need to give a month's notice…." Katie, as usual is being practical.

But I'm not practical right now!

"I'm not staying in that house one more day! Not one more minute! I want to move out of that place now!"

Perry interrupts, "You can move in with my parents. Seriously, they've already offered."

I see Katie reach over and rub his leg in affection. She likes Perry a lot, but to move in with his parents could be awkward for her.

"Thanks, Perry," I tell him, making eye contact in the mirror. "But I bet we can move in with my grandparents."

I look over at Katie and say, "I'll call my grandmother when I get to work."

Katie nods and says, "I'll call the landlord and give our last month notice."

Perry pulls his car up to the curb in front of Meier & Frank. I leave my bag with him since he'll be picking me up after work. I lean over the back of the front seat and take Buffett from Katie's lap. He's wonderfully warm and his purr touches my heart. I hold him close to my chest and kiss his head.

"You are such a great cat. I love you." I put him back on his blanket next to Katie, slide out of the car, slam the door and wave goodbye.

I ride the escalator up to my department. When I get to my register, I don't bother taking off my coat, or logging in. I call my grandmother.

"Grammy, hi, it's Cinda. You know about what happened to me, right? Mom told you about the guy that broke into my house and attacked me… right?"

She hesitates. I assume it's because she's not sure how to respond. I imagine it's too uncomfortable for her to talk about. But I don't have the patience to make her feel better. I get straight to the point.

"Would you mind if Katie and I moved in with you for a while? I mean, until we find another place to live? It'll only be for a couple of weeks, no more than that. I promise."

The pause is long and I'm not sure if she heard me, or doesn't like the idea. I can't politely wait for her to respond.

"Grammy!" I snap impatiently. "Did you hear me? Things are a little scary right now and we need a safe place to stay."

"Of course, of course, sweetie. Move in as soon as you can."

I'm so relieved I could weep. I can leave the nightmare behind me.

Before my shift is about to end, the phone rings in my department. It's Detective Redmond.

"I have scoured the neighborhood. I have revisited the homeless camps under the bridges near your house. I have asked door to door. I can't find anyone who fits the description of this guy. He's hiding from us and that makes him dangerous. I'm tempted to have a policeman positioned outside your home full time."

"You don't have to worry about it. We're moving in with my grandparents. They said we could move in tonight. So, that's what we're going to do."

"That sounds like a good plan," he sounds relieved. "When do you get off work? I'll send an officer to monitor your home while you pack up."

"I get off at five. Katie's boyfriend is picking me up. We've already packed a bag. Katie is giving the landlord our last month notice."

"Good girls," he says, and hangs up.

I barely make it through the day, but somehow, I do. After my shift ends, Perry and Katie are there, waiting for me behind the store. I tell them that my grandmother agreed to letting us move in with her.

"We can move in tonight. But she doesn't want any pets in her home."

I look at Katie. I mouth the words, *I'm sorry*.

"That's fine. He stayed at Perry's today while I went to work. Perry's mom loves him." Katie assures me.

I'll miss that precious, spastic cat.

Then she says, "Oh, yeah. I called the landlord and yelled at him. I tried to talk him into letting us move out now. He said no. What an ASS! So, I gave him a month notice and hung up on him."

Perry suggests we go out to dinner and strategize a plan. He takes us to the Red Robin off Burnside Street. We decide that since we have a month to find another place to live, we can leave our furniture where it is until the time comes to move. If we are going to live with my grandparents for at least a month—*which I want to do starting now*—we are going to need more than the clothes we packed in our overnight bags.

Perry pays for our dinner, then we pile pack into his car and he drives back to our neighborhood. He pulls up in front of the house and watches us walk inside. He stays in the street until Katie and I run through the house making sure it's safe—*as in…Bob-free*. Katie gives Perry the thumbs up and he leaves to park the car.

I pull out my other suitcase and fill it with as many clothes as it will hold. I fill multiple paper grocery bags with toiletry items and shoes. Katie does the same. When Perry returns, he escorts me to my car and helps me load my suitcase and bags into the trunk of my silver Honda Accord. I get in my car and wait—with the car doors locked—while he loads Katie's stuff into his car. Her car is still at his house.

We caravan up into the elegant southwest hills of Portland. I knock on the large wooden door of my grandparents' Tudor-style home. My grandmother answers and we're greeted with warm hellos from both of my mother's parents. Inside, we are greeted with the warmth of their house. It's more than just the temperature. I breathe in the lemony smell of Pledge that waxes the wood floors, moldings and furniture. It is the smell of home.

It is the smell of safety.

My grandfather helps us unpack our cars and carries our suitcases upstairs. Katie and I follow with the extra bags. He guides us into a room with twin beds, two antique dressers and a desk. He sets one suitcase on each bed, then turns and hugs me, clears his throat, pats my back with firmness—*pat, pat, pat*. As I unpack, I look around the room. It's warm and inviting. After Katie unpacks, she turns to leave with Perry to go get her car. She whispers that she'll probably stay with him tonight.

"Is that all right with you? You're safe now," she asks.

"Of course, do what you want and need to do. Give Buffett a hug for me."

I walk them to the front door and wave goodbye. I still need to call my parents and Scott to fill them in. I turn back into the house and let out a long-held breath. It's a breath I feel like I've been holding for weeks now. As the breath is released, I feel a wave of security come over me.

I'm truly, really, totally safe...finally.

Chapter 32

THE TRACKS

Two weeks go by without any drama or trauma. My life is easy again. Our room is perfect; the beds are comfortable. Katie doesn't stay there every night, so I have the room to myself more often than not. Because my grandparents go to bed early, on the nights I work late, I come home to a quiet house. I use this time to sit on their back porch and take in the spectacular view.

This house is built on the backside of a hill. It is four floors high; the main floor is above a daylight basement, and below that, the cellar, and a hidden bomb shelter. Above the main floor are three bedrooms, a nursery and two bathrooms.

During the day, I can see Mount St. Helens, which last year blew her top off, and the majesty of Mount Hood. The cityscape is down below and at night the sparkling lights make it appear mystical and magical.

Somewhere down there is also the nightmare of my house.

On workdays, I catch a bus for downtown by first walking along a meandering street that weaves through large old homes. The bus ride takes me down scenic Vista Boulevard, onto busy Burnside Street and into the city. The people I ride with are all middle-aged, briefcase-carrying professionals in their business suits. The bus is clean and smells fresh. Amazing what a change in economics can do to a bus's environment and a young woman's attitude.

Katie's schedule is busy, and since she's mostly at Perry's, I don't see her much. The occasional times when I do see them both, Perry promises me that Buffett is happy. Every now and then, I go for a visit and sneak treats to Buffett. On my days off, I drive down to visit Scott and my parents. We don't talk about Bob...we pretend that nothing has happened.

One afternoon during work, Katie calls to remind me that we need to be out of our house by the end of the month. Being the constant planner, she suggests we pack up on the Monday after the Thanksgiving holidays. I have that day off. She thinks she can get that day off. Scott and Perry have both offered to help, and Monday works for them too. The plan is to move her stuff into Perry's parents' garage and mine into my grandparents' basement.

Thanksgiving arrives and my extended family decides to spend it at my grandparents' home. I appreciate this since my work schedule doesn't allow any time for travel. The tradition of having holidays spent in this home is priceless. My aunts, uncles, cousins along with my mom, stepfather and three siblings arrive for a beautiful reunion. No one mentions anything about my incident and I'm grateful. I can pretend that nothing ever happened. Only one of my aunts mentions that she's glad I am living with her parents.

I am too...I am too.

On Monday, I wake up dreading the day. Today, I must face that evil house again. I procrastinate leaving. I'm going to be late, but I don't care. I don't want to be the first one there, and risk being alone.

I do NOT want to go back to that place, to that neighborhood, to that...Bob.

As I get into my car, it begins to snow. The soft, lightweight flakes most likely won't stick, so I'm not worried about driving in it. With the whiteness floating in the air, the dreaded drive becomes somewhat beautiful. When I enter the neighborhood, the dusting of snow on everything makes the place look different...even peaceful.

By the time I drive around the block and find a parking place, I am only about 10 minutes late. No one seems to mind or notice. Katie, Perry and Scott, who drove up to help, are already loading the heavy stuff. I sit in my car and observe as the men load our couch into the van. I look around, wondering if Bob is watching them like I am. I'm fearful of getting out of the car in case Bob is nearby. I don't want him to come near me——ever again.

He wouldn't do that with the guys here. Would he?

I see Katie waving. She's holding something up for me to see. To my surprise and delight, she's brought Buffett. I jump out of the car, grab Buffett from Katie and spend another five minutes cuddling with the cat inside the house. After I'm done, I pass Buffett off to Katie, take a deep breath and force myself to go into my room. When I walk in, I look around. There is a pile of empty boxes on my mattress. I shudder when I see my bed.

This sucks. This sucks.

A couple months ago, Katie and I were excited to move into this house and prove to the world——*to our parents*——that we were independent and grown-up. Now, we can't get out of here fast enough. And instead of being independent, we're living like fugitives with my grandparents.

This sucks. Damn you, Bob.

I'm a mixture of emotions. They swing from a pendulum of concern about being back here in this scary room, all the way to disappointment that it didn't work out the way we hoped. I'm pissed. I'm scared. I'm sad. I'm eager to leave. I'm ready to be done with this hell hole and wish it would have ended differently—back and forth, back and forth.

Where do I go from here?

Sighing, I assemble the boxes and pack my remaining clothes and knickknacks. I don't have much stuff, so it doesn't take long. I tape the top of the boxes shut, write on the outside what's on the inside and carry them out one by one to the front porch.

Perry and Scott stumble past me with the dryer. I watch them struggle to get down the steps, avoid the broken one and load the machine into the back of the U-Haul. When they're done, Perry comes up to me and between heaving breaths, he asks me a question. "What do you want to do with that pile of clothes down there in the basement?"

"Leave them. Leave them for the next tenant to worry about."

He laughs and says, "Can do."

Scott comes up the steps. He's breathing hard. I rub his arm in thanks for his hard work and he kisses my forehead. I can smell his sweat, his body odor, and again I can't help but compare his delicious smell to that of another.

He and Perry head into my room next. They carry out my mattress and then my box spring. When they're done, I walk into my empty room and see the panic button hanging on the wall all by itself. The button is a glaring reminder of why it was installed, how the police anticipated Bob's return and why we're moving. It seems like ages ago that Detective Cooper installed it and I met Thom Redmond for the first time.

Scott and Perry return to grab my dresser and then my nightstand. I pull up the rice paper blind to look outside my window. I remember the day my dad bought these for us and replaced the sheets that once hung here. Outside, beyond the sidewalk and the busy road is Interstate 5. Traffic is buzzing by our little house on the corner. I lower the blinds. The landlord informed Katie that we needed to leave them even though we bought them and they aren't permanent.

He's a prick. But he can have them.

I go into Katie's room. Her dismantled bed frame is leaning up against the wall. Her mattress and box spring are already in the U-Haul. I pull up her window blind to peek outside. There really is nothing out there but the large vacant lot between us and the blue house. I appreciate how different, almost beautiful, the scene looks covered in white.

In the snow, I notice a line of tiny paw prints leading from the backside of our house across the lot. Curious about what kind of animal might have made them; I decide to check it out. I carefully walk down our slippery front steps and around to the side of the house and find the beginning of the tracks. They look like a cat's. Then I remember Buffett. The doors have been wide open for over an hour now. Buffett must have escaped.

Oh no! Shit! Buffett!

Afraid that Buffett is loose, I follow the tracks across the vacant lot. Green grass peeks through where Buffett's warm pads have melted the snow. I call out his name over and over, hoping that he'll come to me.

He doesn't.

Worried, I continue following his tracks. They lead me to the backside of the blue house. The tracks come to an end at a makeshift plywood door, covering an opening into the house's basement. It hangs loose on a set of hinges and is painted the same blue as the house. An unlocked padlock is looped through a latch holding the door in place. A missing corner in the lower left creates an opening big enough for a cat to sneak into. Buffett's tracks lead right into this hole.

"Buffett. Here kitty, kitty. Come on boy," I call out, bending down to the small opening.

He doesn't come.

I can't tell what is on the other side. Is this a storage unit…a shed…a garage? I step back to examine the house. I have never really looked at it closely before. From this side, it is three stories high. Because of the angle of the hill, I am on the same level as this basement. A set of outside stairs run up the backside of the house from the sidewalk. There is a door at the top. I notice that a room number or address hangs next to it. It must be one of multiple entrances, indicating the house has been converted into apartments.

"Damnit Buffett, please come to me," I call out again.

I'm so troubled about Buffett being lost that thoughts of Bob have completely slipped my mind. I forget that I'm alone, that I may be in danger and that Bob may be watching me right now. All I care about is finding that beloved cat.

I debate if I should climb the stairs and knock on the upstairs door. I decide against it because Buffett isn't up there. *He's down here.* I crouch down and try to peer through the hole. I can barely see anything. I look at the lock just hanging there and lift it from its latch. The plywood door swings open on its own. Inside is what looks like a storage room, a garden shed of sorts because the dirt floor is covered in a black tarp.

"Buffet. Here kitty, kitty," I call out in a whisper.

I continue whispering Buffett's name, not wanting to draw attention to my trespassing. I walk in a little bit farther. There is enough light to see a set of stairs running up the middle of the building. Banisters run along the perimeter leading to what appears to be entrances to the multiple rooms.

I call for Buffett again, this time a little louder.

Nothing. No Buffett.

Suddenly, I hear a sound coming from upstairs. I freeze. I'm about to get busted.

Oh crap! Shit, shit, damn.

It's too late, I can't hide. I look up. I'm ready to apologize, ready to explain what I'm doing here. A man is looking over the banister, down into the basement. The darkness hides his face from me.

"Hello!" he calls out.

He seems friendly enough.

"Oh God, I'm so, so, so sorry. My cat got loose and I followed his tracks to this door. It wasn't locked, so I thought I'd peek in to see if I could find him," I stammer, embarrassed and scared at being caught.

"I haven't seen any cat around."

"I'm so, so sorry. I'm so embarrassed. I don't usually do this kind of thing but I'm just so worried about finding him," I stammer.

"It's OK. I'll help you look. Give me a minute. I have to go get my shoes on."

Before I can say anything, he turns to go back into his apartment. When he does, the little bit of light reflects off the back of his head. His hair is wild and frizzy, maybe gray or a light blond.

That hair…I know that hair.

It's *his* hair.

Bob!

"It's fine! No need to help, we can find him on our own," I call out, trying hard to not reveal the panic I feel.

Oh God! Get me out of here.

In a frenzied rush, I take the few steps backwards, back outside. I close the door and hook the lock through its latch. Instead of leaving it unlocked like I found it, I lock it. I run down the lot, sliding in the snow, until I get to Perry's side. Katie walks up.

"Everything OK?" she asks, concerned.

"Katie," I say on the verge of tears. Words spew out of my mouth. "Buffett got loose! Oh my God. I followed his tracks into the blue house next door, but I couldn't find him. I don't think he's there, he didn't come to me when I called. I'm afraid he's lost. Katie, I'm so sorry, I couldn't find him."

"What? Cinda, Buffett isn't loose. He's been locked in the cab of the U-Haul the entire time. We wouldn't let him run loose while we're packing up. He's fine. Calm down."

"Really? Are you sure? Because there were tracks…in the snow! They led to the blue house! I followed them!"

I look over my shoulder, afraid that Bob might be there.

"I'm positive. I just checked to make sure he's staying warm. He's curled up on a blanket. He's fine."

Just then Scott walks up to us. "Van's all loaded. Cinda, how about you lead the way to your grandparents' house? We'll unload your stuff first. Then Katie and Perry can head to his parents'."

Do I tell them or not? Do I tell them or not?

NOT!

I'm not going to tell them. I'm not going to scare them, or alert them to what I just saw—*who I think I just saw.* Scott and Perry would go after Bob. I can't risk that or putting them in danger. I will not endanger anyone for my sake. Not now. Not ever. The sooner we get out of here the better.

I just want to get out of here….NOW!

"Good idea! Let's go!" I yell, a bit too eager.

I grab my keys out of my coat pocket and race to my car. I jump in, lock the doors and start the engine. I watch Scott get into his small pickup and Katie and Perry jump into the U-Haul. Katie holds up Buffett for me to see.

I'm relieved to see Buffett, but that's not enough to stop my heart from racing. I don't care whose tracks I followed, or what made them. Since they're not Buffett's, I just don't care. Buffett might be safe, but we're not. We must get out of here.

Come on…come on…let's go!

Perry flashes his headlights from the U-Haul indicating he's ready. I pull out onto the road and stop at the sign on the corner next to the blue house. Bob's not running out of the house to find me. *Thank God!* With Scott and the U-Haul behind me, I lead the caravan and watch as the blue house—Bob's house—disappears from my rearview mirror.

Good riddance Lair Hill. Good riddance house. Goodbye hole in the wall. Goodbye pile of clothes in the basement. Good-fucking-bye Bob! May it all burn to hell!

The wave of relief I feel, mixed with the adrenaline of what and who I just saw, is overcoming me. I'm by myself. I no longer need to be brave. I no longer need to pretend. I no longer need to hold it in.

I begin to cry hysterically—giant heaving sobs, gasping for air. I scream obscenities—one after the other after the other. I let it all out—two months of pent-up stress, fear, anxiety.

When I arrive at my grandparents' house, I wipe away my final tears and take a deep breath.

I am free!

I have escaped my nightmare!

I am done…done…done!

Forever done!

Locked Up

When I snapped that lock shut on the blue house's basement door, I locked it to guard me against Bob. I also locked it to separate myself from those two months.

I bury those memories deep inside of me and they're locked up tight. I hide the key. I hide the key so even *I* can't find it…way under the fluff of my future.

A future I am craving.

My future will not include Bob, a frightening small house, a panic button, a pile of stranger's clothes, a red robe, a mysterious note, an unusual phone call…or..:the memory of a silhouette…and a scream.

I say goodbye to a gray ninja cat, an amazing detective and an incredible best friend. I'm not so sure I could have gotten through that nightmare without them.

I purposefully seal away all the memories—the bad and the good together. With determination and a commitment to myself, I will never, ever, break that seal or open that lock.

Ever.

I'm done.

I don't know when I'll see Katie again. She's headed back to Oregon State University to finish up school. Scott is leaving soon too. He's joined the Army and is headed to boot camp in just a week, then overseas.

I've put on blinders. I am moving forward toward my future. I plan to live with my grandparents while I keep working for Meier & Frank. There is a private school in town, Bassist College, which specializes in merchandising management, fashion design and interior design. I've requested information to apply. I can't wait to see what comes of it.

What will my life look like now?

Now, that I don't have to worry about Bob.

It is over!

Done!

Until....

Part Two

THE HEALING

The Perfect Storm

A perfect storm analogy can be described as this: Combinations of minor events accumulate and lead up to one huge, unforgettable, life-changing moment. My perfect storm begins to build in November of 1993 and it gathers momentum when I am between the ages of 31 and 35.

Up until this time, I live life as if nothing traumatic had happened when I was 19. I behave as any normal young woman in her twenties would, or so I believe. I ignore all impulses to remember my frightening past. I am a master of disguise— the most successful kind—because the person I am fooling the most, is ME.

But...some memories are impossible to ignore.

These five years in my early thirties are filled with minor storms building and building, one on top of the other. Some events are painful and come at me with a fierceness I'm not prepared for. Others give me hope, even support...a safe place to ride out the storm...but then don't hold true to their potential. I'm caught inside of a whirlwind of emotional highs and lows, days of light and dark, nights of dreams and demons. The major storm arrives with a gale force that threatens to crumble my denial, flatten my resolve, destroy my sanity.

Until...

...until I have no choice...no choice but to collapse and surrender to the power of this perfect storm. I get sucked into its cyclone and deposited back to that awful night in October 1981.

What happens when I land is undeniably holy. An unforeseen and unseen divine and mystical force catches me. It holds me safe as it guides and leads me through a profound and sacred ritual of healing.

With this ritual comes an awareness that perhaps there is a unique way to respond to life's tragedies...a sacred way to heal from life's traumas.

This is not a story of forgiveness, for that might have been expected. What I am guided to do goes far beyond forgiveness. What I experience is unexpected, it is unique and sacred; it is life-changing and saving.

This is the second part of my story.

This is the story of my healing.

Chapter 1

THE CALM BEFORE
THE STORM

When Katie and I move out of our rental house in late November of 1981, we have no intention of ever going back. I have no intention of ever unlocking that door to my past. I have no intention of ever unearthing that key I buried deep inside me.

After we leave that awful neighborhood, I lose contact with my Detective Thom Redmond. Even though he knows where I work and how to get in touch with me, I have no intention of connecting with him again.

I never tell a soul what I encountered in that blue house during our move. Bob is never caught. The ramifications of my actions matter not to me. It doesn't occur to me that I am leaving a dangerous felon unpunished. It doesn't occur to me that I could be putting other women at risk. It doesn't occur to me that he might track me down, find me, continue to stalk me. I have tunnel vision and all I care about, all I can think about, all I want is to leave it behind…shut it down…deny it happened.

With determination, I do not let my past dominate or dictate my life one more day.

The investigation ends, my case is filed away.

I am done.

I'm moving on.

I am adamant about focusing on my future.

I will not be a victim to what Bob did to me. I'm not faking it; it's not pretend. This determination is real—as real as I can make it. This is my way. I don't care if it's right or wrong and I don't know enough to question it. The years go by and the memories I have of the attack are minimal, or at best controlled. I am successful at keeping my past locked away. I believe and behave like everything is normal.

I'm a strong-willed woman and claim my independence with a vengeance. My willpower is mighty. My stoicism is even mightier. I show no vulnerability to anyone, not even to myself. The pep talk I give myself is constant.

If I can do THAT, I can do anything.

When I share my story, which I do, I tell it from a very unemotional place. I skim the surface, making it just scary enough. Then I quickly move to the end where I outsmart the villain.

I make plans. I make important plans for my future—Bassist College, retail management, travel, friends, Scott, maybe even marriage and a family—none of which have anything to do with letting those two lousy months in 1981 back into my life.

Then one day, my guard begins to waver. My life begins to change. The quote: *"Life is what happens to us while we are making other plans,"* becomes a reality and messes with my resolve.

Life is not going to leave me alone until I take notice.

Life is not going to allow me to hide any longer.

Life…reaches for my attention.

Life…has different plans for me.

Chapter 2

THE FIRST MINOR STORM

In 1991, Scott and I decide to get married. We spend months planning the celebration to be held on New Year's Eve of that same year.

We hold our wedding and its reception in Cheatham Hall at the World Forestry Center in Portland, Oregon. Fir trees, white lights and white poinsettias create the ambience of a winter wonderland. The wedding party is dressed in elegant black and I'm wearing my mother's wedding dress. The party, which is our life, is about to begin. Together.

"I do," I say to the man I've loved most of my life.

Scott smiles and holds my hand.

"I will," he says back.

"I now pronounce you husband and wife," says our minister and family friend as he finalizes our marriage vows.

"Finally," whispers someone in our wedding party.

I'm not sure who said it, but it could have been a collective comment from the crowd who came to witness our commitment to each other. After all, it's been 13 years since our first date as juniors back in high school.

We walk down the aisle to a standing ovation of cheers and clapping and congratulations from 150 friends and family members. Our life together has been and promises to be a whirlwind of adventures. I suppose that's to be expected when you marry your best friend.

Before getting married, Scott serves in the Army for four years, two of which are in Germany. When he comes home, he attends Portland State University. I continue working full time in retail at Meier and Frank while getting a degree from Bassist College. I leave Portland for a retail management job in Seattle, while Scott remains in Oregon to continue his education. In 1988, Scott graduates and I quit my job. Together, we drive cross-country from Portland to New Orleans, then fly to Belize to retrieve my father's chartered sailboat. We ship the boat back to Scott's parents' farm in Oregon and spend two years renovating it. During this time, I get a second degree from Oregon State University. After the sailboat is sold, Scott and I move to Seattle and then north to Anacortes, Washington where we both find work in the sailing and boating industry.

After we marry, our careers take us to Sunnyvale, California where we settle in for three years. My merchandising career has me traveling around the country, setting up new stores for a boating equipment supply chain. Scott is the manager for one of the stores within this same chain.

Our careers are fulfilling and fun and consume our time...until I become pregnant.

In November of 1993, Eric is born. When I hold this baby in my arms, I experience a love that I've never experienced before. I vow to keep this prince of a boy happy and healthy...*and safe, safe, safe*. I know now what it means to be fiercely protective, to be so in love that I would risk everything for it, for him. Everything seems right in the world.

And then it doesn't.

During the time, a young 12-year-old girl goes missing during a slumber party at her home. A man sneaks into her house and kidnaps her. The story hits the media. Parents are worrying about the safety of their own children. As a new mother, I feel sympathy for the girl's grieving parents.

One afternoon, while I'm sitting on the couch nursing Eric and watching Oprah's show on TV, a news report interrupts, telling us that the kidnapper of the missing girl has been captured. They give us the horrific news that the kidnapper admits to having killed this beautiful, innocent child.

"How did this man finally get caught?" a reporter asks the detective.

The detective goes on to say that a forensic sketch helped to identify the kidnapper and lead to his arrest. The TV shows a cut screen of both the killer's mug shot and the composite drawing. They are almost identical.

"We brought in a forensic artist from Oregon," says the detective.

Being from Oregon, I turn up the volume. A reporter is interviewing the artist. When he introduces her. I freeze in my chair.

Oh, my God, that's who drew Bob!

She looks the same. She has the same voice, the same calmness, the same beauty, the same light surrounding her.

In this moment of recognizing her, twelve years come colliding back on me. I'm buried in emotion. My body shakes as I'm taken back to Janet's desk in the Portland Police Bureau. I can smell her perfume and feel her presence all over again.

I relive the scenes of her talking me through that night. I begin to remember everything—everything about those awful two months. The memories come flying back. They blow toward me with such force that the gust takes my breath away.

Damn, damn, damn it!

I thought I had locked it up for good, sealed the memories away and buried the key forever. But it's all back.

Although she made me feel safe many years ago, seeing her again puts me in a whirlwind of panic. The timelines between now and then become blurred. It's as if I'm 19 all over again...feeling the same fear I haven't felt since I left that neighborhood.

Damn, damn, damn it!

I do my best to get through the day. When Scott gets home from work, I tell him about seeing my forensic artist on the news. I don't tell him about my reaction.

"That's a weird coincidence. I'm glad that creep got caught," he says.

When we go to bed, I have trouble sleeping. I toss and turn, trying desperately to block out what is coming...*who is coming.* Just as I begin to drift off, I see him...*I see Bob.* He's standing at the foot of my bed, lunging at me and warning me to shut up. I hear my dreadful scream...*that guttural, animalistic scream.*

I sit up in bed, feeling the terror and the panic all over again. I check the inside of my cheeks to see if they're bleeding, but only feel the slight scarring.

Bob's not here, Cinda. Bob's not here.

The rest of my night is filled with nightmares. Memories of his horrific body odor fill the room. His rough, dry hands are on my body. I gasp for air, as pillows and a bathrobe are suffocating me, strangling me.

In the morning, I pretend to still be sleeping when Scott kisses me goodbye as he heads to work. I don't want to tell him about my night terrors—*they're only temporary*. I don't want him to worry—*his worry will amplify my own*. This is something I can and will get through. I will NOT allow Bob back into my life.

Not now. Not again. Bob is not allowed to enter! Not this time!

I get up and check on the still-sleeping Eric. I take an extra-hot shower and scrub every inch of my body, hoping the pain of the heat will overpower the pain that my emotions are bringing to the surface. Standing in the thickness of the steam, I scream. I scream out in desperation to release all the fear that's returned. I scream because I refuse to have it dominate my life again. When I get out of the shower, I wipe the mirror clear. I look at my reflection. My entire body is pink, my face blotchy with emotion.

"Cinda," I say looking directly into my eyes. "You will not…do you hear me…you will not…let this…let Bob…control your life again!"

With determination and a mission to move forward, I take in a deep breath, throw my shoulders back and do what I do best when I'm stressed. I start my day in a methodical, thought-out, step-by-step manner. I put lotion on my body. I pull on my underwear. I put one leg into my jeans and then the other. I feel the panic rise inside of me again. I swallow it down. I snap my bra around my back. I pull a shirt over my head. I have a flash of Bob strangling me with my red bathrobe. I ignore it. I quickly pull my shirt down. I tuck it into the top of my pants, resolved to tuck away the memory.

Keep it tucked away, Cinda. Keep it away.

Eric calls for me. He's hungry. I walk into his room and coo at him as I pick him up. I take him to his changing table and change his diaper. I then head into the family room and turn on the TV. I sit down to nurse him.

This is my life now…Scott and Eric…dinner, diaper changing and breastfeeding. This is where I will focus my energy…my thoughts…my attention.

The TV is filled with disaster after disaster, violent show after violent show and it feeds my stress level. I turn the TV off.

"I will protect you from all the awfulness in the world. I promise you. I will," I say, as a vow to Eric and perhaps more to myself. "You are safe."

As I nurse Eric, I look in his eyes. His face, his life, his everything is so innocent. He has yet to be touched by the evil that lurks in every corner...the evil that's lurking in the back of my mind.

I can sense you, Bob. Damn you to hell!

Chapter 3

THE SECOND
MINOR STORM

A year goes by and I do my best to keep the memories at a distance. It's easy to do since I live in California. Sunny Sunnyvale doesn't look anything like Portland. But in 1994, Scott gets a promotion that requires us to move back Portland. I'm anxious about this move. I'm afraid that moving back will amplify the memories that are sneaking back. I make a vow to myself that I will not let that happen.

The good news is we will be able to raise our son close to family. We buy a small, charming two-bedroom house in the West Slope neighborhood. Since I no longer work outside the home, I begin to nanny my two nieces. I'm now surrounded by young, rowdy, happy children. To add to the chaos, we adopt a Golden Retriever puppy, Hannah.

I love everything about my life. I love these kids, this dog, my house, my husband. The memories take a back seat to the hectic pace of my life.

I continue taking care of my nieces for over a year. When my older niece starts half-day kindergarten, her mother drops her off at school in the morning. In the early afternoon, I pick her up and bring her back to my house. During pick-up, parents gather into friendly groups outside, waiting for the class to be dismissed. Since I'm not one of the mothers, I usually keep to myself and watch the younger kids play in the school's playground.

One afternoon, I decide to bring Hannah with me. While Eric and his cousin toddle around on the school's play structure, one of the moms leaves her group to play with the puppy.

"Oh hello, aren't you beautiful?" she says, giggling in delight as Hannah shows appreciation for the attention.

Thinking she's talking to Hannah, I don't pay much attention to her. My eyes are on the kids. But then I realize she's asking me a question.

"Sorry?" I ask, giving the woman my attention.

"What's her name?" she asks again.

"Hannah."

Then I recognize her. I recognize the mother that's petting Hannah. It's Katie.

I can't believe it. Katie!

"Katie! Oh my, God. Katie!"

"Are you serious? No way! Cinda! What are you doing here?"

She stands up and gives me a hug. My body swims in emotions. I'm almost dizzy with them.

It's Katie! She looks just the same!

"I'm picking up my niece from her kindergarten class!" I force the words out.

"No way, I'm picking up my son! How crazy is this? They're in the same class!"

I'm so surprised and happy to see her I can't stop smiling. It's such a shock that I'm trying to keep from tipping over. This reminds me of the time Scott surprised me after returning home from his Army assignment overseas. It was such a surprise that my knees buckled and I became light headed. He hadn't been home in almost two years.

I haven't seen Katie for 12 years. After leaving that neighborhood, I left behind everything and everyone. Unfortunately, that included Katie. By now, I have no idea what she's been doing. What's happened in her life?

Just then the school doors open and a stream of kids come running out.

"We have to get together for coffee!" she says, looking over the sea of children's heads for her son's.

She reaches into her purse, pulls out a paper and pen and writes down her phone number. When she hands me the note I giggle to myself...*she hasn't changed.*

"Here, call me! I should run, we have an appointment to get to," she gives me a giant hug and bends down to pet Hannah goodbye.

"Absolutely! I will call. I promise!" I yell over the chaos.

I see my niece. She's found Eric and her sister on the playground and is leading them up the stairs of the slide. I take off running toward them to avoid a potential catastrophe. I pull the younger ones off the stairs and scold the older one. Tears spew out of all three children, but I don't mind. My heart is racing. Not because of the dangerous act of three cousins, but because of seeing Katie again.

I load up the kids into our blue Jeep Cherokee, the one that my dad used to own, and head home. I try my best to keep my mind on the road, but it wants to focus on Katie. Memories of my time with her come flying at me like debris. I try to dodge them because if one makes contact, it will be embedded—and then I'll need to look at it.

I don't want to look at any of them. I don't want to remember.

But they're coming anyway.

I see us meeting for the first time at Oregon State University. I remember us laughing and giggling over the silliness of boys. We were so innocent. We were so happy.

I see her brave and free spirit walking naked around our house and me wishing I could be more like her. I remember her bolting upright in bed, hysterical, crying when I tell her I was almost raped. I hear the crackle from the policeman's walkie-talkie in my ears all over again. It fills the entire car with static electricity.

The storm of my emotions is coming. I can feel it. I'm afraid I won't be able to spare myself from its onslaught. I need to find shelter. I need to find a way to keep this storm from landing. Maybe seeing Katie again isn't just a chance; maybe…maybe we were meant to find each other. Maybe I can find moorage, put down the anchor, and ride out the storm with her.

We rode out the storm together before….

I arrive home with the kids sound asleep in their car seats. I use this quiet time to sit and think. I remember riding in Katie's car…she's driving me home so I can tell my parents. I remember when Katie took control and helped me through the shock when it finally came. I remember Katie being my grounding agent throughout those two long and scary months.

Maybe she can help me get through this storm too.

Maybe Katie can help.

Chapter 4

THE THIRD
MINOR STORM

A couple of weeks go by. I still carry the piece of paper with Katie's phone number, but have yet to call. I'm embarrassed. I'm concerned she'll be hurt and angry that I lost touch with her and stayed away for so long. And I'm frightened. I'm frightened beyond what I can easily explain. What if...being with her uncovers that long-buried key? What if...being with her unlocks that door to my past? What if...being with her triggers again the emotional onslaught that seeing Janet Frances did? What if...after all these years of avoiding the memories, being with Katie brings them all back?

Could I handle that?

When I finally get the courage to call, she's delighted.

"Cinda, I'm so glad you called! I'm sorry I had to race off so quickly, especially after not seeing you for years. I hope you weren't mad. It's just that I had an appointment and I couldn't be late."

"No, I wasn't mad! I was worried you'd be mad at me. So, do you still want to get together for coffee? I'll have my two nieces and Eric, so maybe we can get all the kids together and they can play while we chat?"

We set up a time that following week. We meet at the kids' school. Then I follow Katie to her house a few miles away. The big five-bedroom house fits her growing family. I learn that she broke up with Perry after she went back to school. Later, she graduated from Oregon State University, held multiple jobs, married, had two boys, divorced and is now remarried and pregnant. Life has been good to her. She beams with happiness.

So much has happened to her, so much I've missed out on.

I get her caught up on my life. She is thrilled that Scott and I finally got married. When I tell her where we live, she laughs. She'd been inside our house during the realtor's showing. She and her first husband used to live a few blocks away, so she knows the area well. We're in awe of how close our paths were to crossing before they finally did.

The reunion is beautiful and heartfelt. When our visit comes to an end, we agree to meet on a regular basis.

During our next visit and for the many that follow, we sip coffee, talk about our husbands, chat about life as a mother and let the kids play. Every time we get together, I thank my lucky stars for bringing her back into my life.

"I remember you used to hate coffee. Do you remember?" Katie laughs as she pours me a cup, "But now, you have seen the light. Welcome to the dark roast side!"

"You're right! I did hate coffee...," I try not to remember too deeply because if I do, I may need to remember all the stories that go with me and coffee...*and Bob.* "That seems like a lifetime ago. Well, I love it now. At least it isn't your iced tea we're drinking!"

We both laugh.

This happens when I'm with her. We share bits and pieces of our times together back then, but we avoid the main topic. We avoid talking about the attack and those scary days that followed. I don't know if it's even on her mind like it is on mine. Is she avoiding bringing the subject up as much as I am? Does she think bringing it up will be too painful for me? Does she think that I would rather just ignore it...forget it? Does she wonder if I've resolved it... am at peace with it? Or has she forgotten all about it?

Is that even possible...to forget?

I crave to talk to her. I crave to ask her. I crave to bring up *that* time... but have no idea how to approach the subject. It's as if the younger me, the 19-year-old me, is screaming for attention, is wanting her old friend back, is needing to be understood by perhaps the only person who can. And yet...I'm afraid if I start talking...I don't know how either of us will respond. My desire to keep the memories hidden seems to make them even more dominant. The more I keep them pent up inside of me...the more insane I feel. If I bring up the subject...will I open the gate and cause all the memories to come flooding out of me? If this happens...can I control it, can I control them...can I control me? It's an unsettling battle and I don't know what to do.

So, I do nothing. I stay quiet.

For months, for almost a year...*I stay quiet.*

During this time, I get pregnant and Katie gives birth to her daughter. Like me, she loves being a mom. When she's not aware, I watch her. I watch her with her kids. Her kids are her everything, just as Eric is mine. Yet, every time I see her pick up one of her children, swing him around, tickle her belly, nibble on their checks, I feel a pin pricking the bubble of time we are in. I sense another bubble hovering above with a different scenario playing in it. The overhanging question of...what if things had played out differently for us that night of the attack?

In our present space, the memories swirl and spin around us when we are together. As hard as I try, I can't keep Bob's words from landing in the room. They haunt me. They weigh heavily on my mind and heart... those awful frightening words he said right before he attacked: "You're not who I thought you were."

What did he mean?

I'm afraid of what he really meant. I'm afraid he meant to go into Katie's room that night. I am afraid of what might have happened if he had.

I sense Bob's tentacles creeping out from the past and into my time with Katie and her kids. I need to find a way to prevent him from completely slithering in. I must keep her safe from my memories, from my nightmare...from *this* memory...*from Bob*.

Visit after visit, it as if the emotional teeter totter tips up and down, up and down—from my desire to keep it all to myself—to the part of me that wants to talk to her, share with her, remember with her. She is the only one, the *only* one, who knows my story, who lived it with me. At night, after a day with Katie, my nightmares are far more active and alive... and they're growing worse.

It's time I talk to her.

It's time.

During one of the coffee playdates, I finally get the courage to bring up the subject.

"Katie....do you ever think about the night that Bob broke into our house?"

"Sometimes...," she's busy picking up toys but stops to think about my question. "I suppose you do, though."

"Yeah, I do."

Katie tosses the toys into a basket, then looks at me. I'm sitting at the island in her kitchen. She comes over and sits on the stool next to me.

"Lately, it's been dominating my thoughts. And my nightmares are back. Nightmares of that night. It's awful."

"Cinda. I'm so sorry. That has to be terrible."

Her expression is that same gentle and worried face from before—familiar and comforting. I had become dependent upon it, so many years ago. My heart is warmed to see it again.

So far, so good.

"A couple years ago, I saw Janet Frances on TV. Do you remember me talking about her back then? She drew the sketch of Bob."

"Yes! I remember you talking about her and the sketch. The sketch looked just like him."

I visualize the sketch in my head. I vaguely remember what it looked like.

"Since they never caught him, there's no knowing for sure," I stop talking...*what did she say?* "Wait. What do you mean, 'you think it looked just like him?'"

"Oh...well...I guess I never told you. Months, maybe a year, after we moved out, I was back in Portland with a friend from school. I took her by the house and drove around the neighborhood. We saw a man standing on the corner near that small grocery store. Do you remember that small country grocery store on the corner?"

"I think I do," I work on visualizing our old neighborhood and that store.

Then, I remember it! I remember it all very well—the store, the mailbox, Bob at the bus stop. The memories from the days after the attack come storming toward me. I can feel my body responding to the force.

Cinda, get out! Get out of those memories!

"Well, I swear to you, Cinda. I swear that that man looked just like your composite picture. I yelled to my friend, 'I think that's the guy! I think that's the guy!'"

"What? You think you saw Bob?"

"Yes, isn't that crazy? He had on a knit hat with fuzzy hair sticking out, just like you remembered. I swear it was Bob. He looked just like the picture. When we came back around the block, he was gone. We drove around looking for him for quite a while. I didn't call the police because I didn't know where he went. Huh...funny that I'm all of a sudden remembering this."

I'm at a loss for words. I'm not sure what to do with this information. Is there anything I should do with it? I can't be upset that Katie never told me; we had lost contact. What would I have done if she had? *Nothing*. And it's too late to do anything now.

Katie breaks the silence. "So…you were telling me about seeing the sketch artist on TV."

"Oh right. Seeing Janet again after all these years triggered the memories…the memories I thought I had gotten beyond. Having them back is awful. After not thinking about that night for so long, it's scary how it's coming back with a vengeance. It's like I'm being followed, haunted almost. It won't leave me alone."

"Like you're being haunted?"

"Yeah, it feels like that. I don't know how else to explain it…," putting my feeling into words is hard, trying to be tactful when I want to blurt them out is harder. "The memories won't leave me alone, no matter how hard I try. Then I find you, as if by chance. I wonder…if I…, if we…, were to talk about it, it might make things easier. But I don't want to scare you or make you uncomfortable."

"Well, sure, Cinda, of course. We can talk about it, if that will help. I'm not sure how much I remember, though. But I can listen."

A wave of relief flows over me. I can finally talk about the night and maybe in doing so, I can release the pent-up stress and anxiety. I first bring up the simple things like the house, the lack of blinds, the hole in the wall. I skip to the trip down to see my parents. I laugh at the undercover detective and the failed sting operation. She laughs too. The more I talk, the more I remember, the more I'm able share.

It's obvious it hasn't impacted her as much as it has me.

But…there is still that one thing I need to get off my chest…the one thing that's been haunting me most of all—Bob's comment. I take in a deep breath. It's a difficult topic to talk about and I can feel the emotions begin to well up in my throat.

"Katie, since seeing the artist on TV, I've spent a lot of time thinking about this…. Back in 1981, I didn't know much about anything. But now, I'm beginning to understand…that I think I was the one meant to deal with Bob.…"

"What do you mean? Why?"

I take in another deep breath.

"Somehow, someway, I had the wherewithal to fend him off, to beat him at his own game. I don't know how I was able to do that, but…if it had to happen, it was best it happened the way it did. It was best that he came into my room that night."

"What are you saying?"

"Katie...there's something I don't think I shared with you about that night. One of the first things I remember Bob saying to me...when he broke into my room was: 'You're not who I thought you were.'" I pause, I wait, I continue, "Katie, I think he thought I was someone else. I think he thought he came into the wrong room."

I watch her face closely. I watch her eyes grow huge as her brain registers what I've told her. I watch as my nightmare of *what ifs*, become her own—what if Bob had gone into her room, what if he had attacked her, what if she screamed and tried to fight him off, what if he tried to quiet her?

In my imagination...it doesn't end well.

I reach over and place my hand on hers. I lock my eyes to hers. Her entire body stiffens. Panic surfaces on her face...it's the same panic I've seen on mine.

"Aren't we lucky that that didn't happen?" I say with sincerity.

It is essential for her to comprehend how fortunate it was for both of us that Bob came into my room. I believe this with all my heart. I don't believe Katie could have fended him off. I don't believe she would have lasted three hours with him.

Our kids come running into the kitchen, then chase each other back out. Her gaze follows them. I can guess what she's seeing—a potential world without them in it. The possible loss is too much, too unbearable, too unfathomable for her to take in. The thought is far too frightening for her to consider or process.

She can't and won't do it.

I should have foreseen this. I watch as it comes...the realization of what might have happened. I watch as the concept overcomes her...I can't stop it. I watch as she shuts down...her wall of defense goes up.

My intention wasn't to scare her, but it did. She doesn't have it within her to talk about it one second more. The discussion is over.

I must respect and honor her reaction, her emotions, her defenses. After all, I've had many years to work through this part of the story. She's hearing it for the first time. I wish I hadn't said anything. I was wrong to bring it up.

What gave me that right?

As much as I understand, I'm devastated. I try to change the subject. Fortunately, the kids come into the kitchen and Katie jumps up to fix them a snack. As soon as they are done, I know it's time to go.

I hug her goodbye and leave her warm, friendly and safe home feeling more lost and more alone than ever. I am on a spiral toward darkness and I needed someone to talk me out of it. I hoped it would be Katie. I hoped she could do for me now what she had done for me back then—be my sanity during an insane time.

But she can't be that for me this time. I've ruined the chances of her help.

As I drive away, I feel as if I am on an island all alone, surrounded by a sea of giant, frightening waves of emotion. They are rising around me and I am about to be consumed.

When I get home, I share some of the stories with Scott. Just as I couldn't tell him everything when I was 19, I'm careful of what I say. I don't want to trigger in him what just happened with Katie. Things between us have been wonderful. Our intimacy has been wonderful. I don't want to suck him into the mounting tsunami of my psychosis and risk all that is good right now.

If I go down, I go down alone.

Chapter 5

THE FOURTH
MINOR STORM

We continue to live in our adorable West Slope home. I'm still watching my nieces. Eric has started preschool. My pregnancy is going smoothly. Hannah is a well-trained and surprisingly calm member of our family. I wish I could say the same for me.

My coffee dates with Katie become farther and farther apart. I don't bring up the past with her again. Yet, I've continued to stress, worry, and remember things I don't want to remember. My memories hover above me like a dark cloud waiting to drop its contents. I carry an invisible umbrella…hoping and praying that I'll be protected from the fallout.

Throughout this time, my aunt Nancy stops by often to visit, check in, and let her daughter play with the kids. I look forward to when she comes because our conversations are deep and meaningful. We have become good friends since she married my uncle in 1988. She is a chaplain at The Living Enrichment Center (LEC), a new thought, nondenominational church. She knows how to talk about uncomfortable subjects with ease. My hope is that maybe, during her next visit, I can talk to her about all I'm going through. If there is anyone who understands, it will be her.

She'll understand, because when she was 22 she was also violently attacked. Many years ago, when I first met her, she asked about my assault and then told me about hers. She was the first person I talked to who had experienced something similar. I didn't realize how much I needed someone to understand my story.

There are three things I remember about that long-ago conversation. The first was how she told her story without any shame or embarrassment.

The second was how she set out to help herself recover by becoming an advocate for other victims of rape. The third was how she used this advocacy to train the Portland Police in rape victim sensitivity.

It's a story that I will never forget.

"How did the police treat you?" she asked me.

"They were my knights in shining armor. They were totally cool. The detective that was assigned to my case was awesome. Why?"

"When I was raped, the police treated me as if I were the criminal. They made me feel like it was my fault that I was attacked. It was handled poorly. They were so insensitive, that it felt as if I had been assaulted a second time. I'm glad to hear that your experience was different."

"That's awful. I'm so sorry. But no, that's not how they treated me! They were all very respectful."

"After my incident, I wasn't going to have another woman experience what I went through. Multnomah County hired me to head their Rape Victim Advocate Program. I did that for two years. Then, I taught classes on rape victim sensitivity for eight years at the Oregon Police Academy. I trained over 1,800 police officers. The police officers and even your detective may have gone through my training."

When I heard this, I couldn't believe it. The coincidence was just too weird, that this woman, now my aunt and friend, may have trained the policemen and detectives who helped me during that time. I didn't even know her then, but her impact on my life is considerable now.

When she comes to my house on one of her routine visits, I make a snack for the kids and we go outside to the backyard for a picnic. I decide to bring up this past conversation. I hope that maybe she can help me get through this awfulness. Maybe she can offer some of her wise advice on how I can get rid of these nightmares…and get rid of Bob.

She seems to have done well in her recovery. Maybe she can help me with mine.

"Nancy, do you remember when we talked about the time that guy tried to rape me?"

"Of course, I do. Why?"

"Well…" I stumble over the words because I don't want to appear silly or over dramatic. "It seems like you've been able to recover from yours, and I was wondering how you got through your nightmares. That is, if you had them, of course. I just thought I was over it…but it's back with a vengeance. My nightmares are back."

"Nightmares, huh…? Of course, I had them, but it's been so long that I don't dwell on it like I did."

"Well, he haunts me in my dreams. When I wake up, I feel like I'm fighting an invisible demon during the day."

"I can relate, believe me. It's to be expected. It never really leaves us. It does get better with time, though. Days, even months, go by where I don't think about it and then…BAM! It shows up for no reason. But then it goes away again, and my life recovers. You'll be OK. I promise. Have you talked to Scott about it?"

"No, not really. I don't want to worry him. As far as he's concerned, I'm over it and have moved on with my life."

"I get it. Sometimes when other people worry about us, it can actually make us more afraid. But I'd strongly recommend that you tell him what's going on. He's such a good man, Cinda. He could help."

"If things get worse, I will."

I won't.

I won't bring it up to Scott. I have no intention of worrying him. What could he do for me anyway?

He can't climb into my dreams and slay the dragon. Only I can do that.

"You know, the LEC has beautiful beliefs and strategies that help people recover from trauma. They believe that there is a spiritual solution to every problem. There truly is. Maybe the relief you're looking for can be found there."

"Spiritual solutions?" I ask laughing. "What do you mean? I'm not religious and don't really want to go to church."

"LEC is a different kind of church. We believe more in the spiritual aspect of religion than the dogma of it. We practice and incorporate and welcome all beliefs, practices and religions under our roof. It's very accepting and open-minded. You're more than welcome to join me some Sunday. Their services can be very enlightening and might offer you some guidance. Or, if you would be interested, I have tapes of their services you can listen to at home."

"Sure, listening to cassettes could be interesting. Why not? I am open to try anything that might help."

I'm doubtful, though. I can't possibly see how spirituality can help me with my mental and emotional state.

"Great! I'll bring a cassette over each week after I get a copy."

A week later, as promised, Nancy brings me a cassette of that Sunday's service. She tells me about the topic and shares interesting stories about her work at the center. The cassettes and our conversations around them are about topics that are new to me. They include meditation, mysticism, laws of attracting and manifesting, transformation and healing through energy work, positive affirmations and more. I have no idea what Nancy is talking about, but I am fascinated and intrigued because I can see the positive impact it is having on her.

Whatever this "spirituality" thing is, I want some of what she's got.

After our visit, and many conversations later, bit by bit, I feel a place within me start to open to the possibility that Nancy is on to something... *whatever that something is, it needs to show itself to me soon.* I play the cassette tapes in my car, sometimes more than once. She's right; the services are very open-minded and educational. I learn a lot about life and kindness and acceptance and nonjudgment. I learn about new thought leaders and spiritual beliefs from all over the world. With every recording, I listen and search and hope that somewhere inside these tapes is the secret to how I can quiet my inner demons.

One tape stands out. This service revolves around the teachings of spiritual leader and medical doctor, Deepak Chopra, and his new book, *The Seven Spiritual Laws of Success*. The LEC minister encourages us to follow his suggestions of living a life within the flow of these laws.

The minister says that Dr. Chopra claims that we are not meant to struggle or to suffer. Struggling and suffering are internal signals that we are out of alignment with these laws. We can find our way back into alignment by getting quiet and calming our mind. When we do, we can tap into these seven laws that are meant to guide and support us. We are in alignment when we are at peace.

I have no idea what Deepak Chopra means by 'spiritual laws.' I have no idea what the minister means by being in or out of 'alignment.' But I do know about struggling and suffering. I sure want to be able to calm my mind and find that peace.

The minister goes on to quote Deepak as having said, "If we learned to love our enemies, there would be no more war." When I hear this, my entire body shudders as if this message is meant just for me. I replay the tape and listen to it again.

"If we learned to love our enemies, there would be no more war."

210

I wonder if this global concept could be internalized? Could I stop my own internal war, if I learned to love different or deeper?

I head out to Powell's Bookstore in downtown Portland to buy Deepak Chopra's book. The store is gigantic. I need to use the in-store map to guide me to the Red Room where the "spiritual, religious and self-help" sections are located. I am amazed there are so many books under the heading of "spirituality." Many are written on the topics Nancy has mentioned.

I had no idea spirituality was a thing, let alone so popular.

I find Deepak Chopra's name on the shelf and am surprised to see that he has his own section. I easily find the book because there are multiple copies of it. I'm even more relieved to see that it's a small book with a pretty cover.

When I dive into it, I find that the book is simply written, most likely for beginners such as me. Yet, I don't understand any of it. The concept is way over my head. I am disappointed, frustrated and confused. I had hoped for answers that would lead me to quiet my mind and I'm still right where I started. More frustrating is that the quote I was hoping to learn more about isn't from this book.

However, I have a strong feeling that the secret I've been looking for is hidden in that quote. I can feel it in my bones. The secret to stopping my internal war is to love. But this is confusing. I DO love! I love Scott, my son, my unborn baby, my dog, and so, so many others. The love the minister talked about in this quote must be different than the love I'm used to. It must be. Otherwise, I'd have been living in peace by now.

"If we learned to love our enemies, there would be no more war."

Chapter 6

THE FIFTH
MINOR STORM

In July of 1996, our second son Ryan is born. When I hold him in my arms, I am again overcome with maternal love. I had worried that I couldn't possibly love another child as much as I loved my first, but I was wrong. The love I have for this exquisite and beautiful child is just as powerful, just as spectacular, just as life-changing.

Could this intense love I feel be the love that will save me? Is this the love that the minister and Deepak Chopra talked about? Is the secret, the answer, found in genuinely and equally loving multiple people all at once? Maybe this ability…maybe this way of loving…is the love that can conquer all enemies.

How could it not be? It's enormous.

Although this love is intense and powerful, it doesn't bring any peace of mind.

Instead, Ryan's birth brings on a new level of anxiety. This deep love of family that I thought would pull me out of my darkness is taking me deeper into it.

I have so much more to lose now.

When I was 19, things were different. I was responsible for only me. Protecting just me seems minor compared to what and whom I must protect now. Two precious, innocent and priceless lives are now my responsibility. Even though my husband is perfectly capable of protecting us, I don't want him to be in danger either.

I can sense Bob's tentacles. They are creeping closer and closer into my perfect life. He's tracking me down. He might not be here physically, yet, but he is coming. I can feel him. He's nearby. He'll be here soon. Every time I turn around, I expect to see him standing there, ready to lunge, ready to strike. I'm afraid that my family isn't safe. What if Bob finds me? What would he do to me? And…worse…what would he do to my family?

Their safety is up to me.

This responsibility is overwhelming. I feel more vulnerable and helpless than I ever have before. Fear and anxiety consume me.

I jump at every knock on the door. I answer my phone with caution. I check the lock on my bathroom window every night. I'm afraid that he will sneak into my kids' room when they're sleeping, while I'm sleeping, and I won't be able to save them.

Safety for my family becomes an obsession. Fear for our safety governs my routines. When I drive into our garage, I close the garage door before I get out of the car. I wait inside my vehicle until I determine that no one has followed me in. Then…I unlock Eric and Ryan from their car seats, rush them inside and lock the house door behind me. I check under the beds and Ryan's crib, behind the shower curtain, inside closets, to make sure no one is hiding—to make sure Bob isn't there.

Eric doesn't have to ask me to check for monsters. I'm already doing it.

When I get a whiff of cigarettes I go into a tailspin and must leave the area. The smell of alcohol nauseates me. Every noise, every bump in the night wakes me up. I lay there shaking…waiting…waiting for another sound. I can't justify that it's just the house settling, or the dog chasing her ball. I can't pretend that it is nothing.

Because…once upon a time it wasn't NOTHING. It was Bob.

My nightmares are even more constant. They always begin with me screaming…that scream I never want to hear come out of me again. Yet, it's alive inside of me and won't let me sleep.

As hard as I try, I have trouble keeping all of this from Scott. Things have been wonderful, but now my nightmares are infiltrating our relationship. It's starting to affect all over again my ability to be intimate. I feel compelled to share some of my awkwardness, sensitivities and discomforts. I want him to know it has to do with my memories and not with him. I want him to know that cuddling is fine, his body warm, his smell heavenly. But with the resurgence of the memories, the panic resurfaces when I feel his breath on my neck…when he pulls my shirt over my head, when he caresses my body. I go into defensive mode and I feel my body shut down.

I try to push away the fear, without pushing away from him. I try to be present with his love and not with the memory of a monster. He is constantly patient, understanding, and tolerant. He treats me with kindness and deep respect. He shows me so much sympathy that I can't help but feel deeply loved and cared for by him.

"I'm not *him*," Scott assures me.

But still.....

My tension rises to an all-time high. I lose weight that I can't afford to lose. I break out in acne. I'm diagnosed with Irritable Bowel Syndrome (IBS). I don't sleep long or well. I am miserable. Darkness oozes out of me and I swear I infect everyone I encounter.

I am short-tempered with Eric, exhausted with Ryan. They deserve a mother who is kind and loving, patient and generous.

They deserve a mother who isn't bat shit crazy!

There are moments when I fear my craziness might harm them. I fantasize how my family would be better off without me. Maybe it would be best that I leave...just walk away, before it's too late...before I cause serious harm.

But...this is even crazier thinking.

I don't want to leave my family. They are my *everything*. I love them.

But...I'm reaching a breaking point.

I'm not sure what will happen to my beloved family when I fall to pieces. I'm trying to hold myself together. I'm doing the best I can. I'm trying to keep up a good front.

But...I'm out of control.

I'm losing my mind.

Chapter 7

THE SIXTH
MINOR STORM

I try to live life as if there is nothing creeping up on me or inside of me or around me. I go about my days trying my best to not let my craziness seep out. I take care of my nieces and raise my boys and train my dog. I mimic what it looks like to be a good mother, wife and aunt. I clean the house, cook meals, run errands and anything else that is required from me. For the most part, I'm successful.

Then one day something extraordinary happens. In October of 1996, I need to make a road trip to some county offices out in the country. Choosing a day when I'm not watching the girls, I load the boys into their car seats and toss their travel bag on the floor behind the driver's seat. The bag is filled with snacks, juice boxes, diapers, wipes, prescription medicines, toys, my flip cell phone, my purse and changes of clothes for the kids.

When we arrive at our destination, I unload the boys, grab my purse out of the bigger bag and lock the car. The passenger door on the driver's side doesn't automatically lock, but since my hands are full with Ryan in his portable car seat, I ignore it and head inside.

The line is long; the wait is longer. Eric gets bored, which winds him up. Frustration rises inside of me because I left the snacks and toys in the car—*what was I thinking?* I can't leave or I'll lose my place in line. I warn him to behave, but that makes him cranky. My nerves are stretched, my patience thin, I'm on edge already. To keep him from having a public temper tantrum, I let him wander around the room while I do my best to keep an eye on him.

When I finally get to the front of the line, I call Eric to me. He shows up with a pile of forms he's "filled out" and hands them to the lady at the counter. She isn't amused or pleased, but I don't care.

I'm about ready to have my own public temper tantrum.

Loading the boys back into the car, we head home. The autumn day is exquisite with orange leaves blowing across the country road. Up ahead, signs advertise a pumpkin farm. I ask Eric if he'd like to pick out a pumpkin. He squeals, "Yes!"

We find a spot in the gravel parking lot in front of the barn. After unbuckling Eric, I yell at him to wait but he races inside without me. I rush to the other side of the car and struggle to get Ryan's car seat separated from its base. Thank goodness, he's asleep. I stumble into the barn looking for Eric. I find him on top of a pile of large pumpkins.

"This one, Mommy! I want this one!"

"Eric, get down from there!"

My yelling wakes Ryan up and he starts to cry. Needing to find something to distract Eric and a quiet spot to feed Ryan, I spot a counter with free cider and cookies. I'm not a fan of filling my already hyper boy with sugar, but I again left the snacks in the car. I show Eric the cookies and pour him some cider. I do the same for me. Then we go sit down in a quiet, private corner so I can breastfeed Ryan.

As soon as Eric is done, he's back on top of the pile of pumpkins. He's pulling at the stem of a larger one.

"This one's mine. It's giant!"

I place Ryan's carrier on the floor, grab Eric off the pile, then heave his pumpkin into a nearby cart. He runs around the pile and picks pumpkins for Ryan, his dad and one for me. I load the other pumpkins into the cart, place Ryan's car seat on top, grab Eric's hand and head to the front to pay. I am even more exhausted and cranky and now filled with sugar and cider.

Yuck.

I wheel the wobbly cart and its contents across the gravel parking lot. When we get out to the car, something isn't right. The two passenger doors are open. How is this possible? Did someone break into my car?

Or, did I forget to close them?

I'm confused and concerned that I could have been so absentminded. I'm even more frightened by the possibility that someone might have been rummaging around in my car.

I snap Ryan into the base of his seat and close that door. I go around and buckle Eric into his toddler seat and shut his door. Next to our car is an older man sitting in his. I tap on his window.

"Excuse me, sir. Have you been here for a while? Were my car doors open when you got here?"

"Yep, they be open the entire time we be here."

Oh God, could I have really been that careless?

This is potentially awful—am I losing it even more than I thought? Have I become so distracted that I'm capable of leaving the car doors open? I jump into the car and drive toward the highway. I try to remember if I shut the doors or not. No matter how hard I try, I can't remember what I did or didn't do.

I am seriously losing my mind.

As we approach the highway entrance, Eric spots a McDonald's sign and begs to stop. I'm too tired and hungry to argue. I park the car in front of the restaurant, gather the boys, *deliberately* close the doors and push the automatic lock button. All the doors lock except for the left passenger one. Since I can see the car from inside the restaurant, I don't worry about it. We order, eat at record speed because we're starving, and get back into the car.

We enter the highway and head east toward Portland...toward home. I push the play button on the CD player and Raffi's song "Baby Beluga" fills the car with catchy, fun lyrics. Eric and I hum and sing along as he bounces to the music. I can see Ryan's arms reaching for his dangling toys. This is good. The children are happy. Eric will be asleep in no time. Ryan is content. I take in a deep relaxing breath and allow the music to cheer me up as well.

I stop singing when up ahead I notice a dog on the right side of the highway. He's walking along the grassy shoulder. I slow down the car and put on the emergency lights to warn the cars coming up behind me. I keep my eyes glued to the dog—begging him to stay off the highway.

As I drive closer, I get a better look. He's a black and white dog, a Border Collie, and is sniffing at something in the grass. He looks up at me, makes eye contact, looks back down at the item on the ground and back at me. A wave of déjà vu comes over me, making my body shudder. I push it away.

When I'm about to pass him, he looks at me again and then back at the thing in the grass—as if he's telling me to look, so I do. Then I see it. That *thing* the dog is sniffing is black and looks just like my boys' travel bag. I gasp, reach behind my seat and feel nothing. The bag is gone.

The bag is gone!

How did my bag get there, ahead of me, on the side of this road?

By now, I'm past the dog.

In my rearview mirror, I see him crossing the two lanes of eastbound traffic. I'm in a panic, both for the dog's safety and to get back to the bag before someone else finds it. I take the next exit, cross over the highway and get back on heading west. Up ahead, I can see that the dog made it safely into the median. As I get closer, he runs in front of my car, across the highway, up the side hill and disappears into the brush.

I take the exit where we ate at McDonald's, cross over the highway again and get back on the eastbound side of the highway. When I get to the spot where I saw the dog sniffing the bag, I pull over. I put the car into park, put on my emergency lights and warn Eric to stay put or be grounded for life. I jump out and run to the black bag. Sure enough, it's mine! The boys' clothes and toys are strewn all over the place. I gather everything and put them back into the bag. The prescription bottles are empty, the snacks and the juice boxes are missing. Fortunately, my cell phone is still in the side pocket.

I'm confused and shocked. This makes no sense. How is this even possible? How did my bag get here? When was it taken out of my car? The bag could have been stolen at the county offices—*my back-passenger door didn't lock*, at the pumpkin farm—*maybe that's why my doors were open*, or at McDonald's—*but I could see my car from inside the building*. I never would have found that bag again had it not been for the black and white dog.

As we drive off, Eric is full of questions about the dog, the bag, how did the bag get there, who stole it, his pumpkins, the face he'll carve in it, maybe he'll take Ryan's instead, or not, since his pumpkin is the biggest and the best. I'm listening, but not really…my head is too full of my own set of questions. What just happened? How did this happen? What are the odds? What are the odds that a dog would be on the side of road, sniffing at my bag, at the exact moment that I'm driving by? It's as if he were placed there JUST to guide me.

This feels almost otherworldly, mystical…*magical*.

This feels like…*something spiritual*….

Spiritual?

I flip open my cell phone and call my aunt Nancy to tell her about this crazy, yet magical dog. I want to find out if this is like one of her "spiritual type" experiences she's talked to me about. She tells me that it's most likely a sign or a message from the angels, God, the Universe, whatever I want to call it. They communicate through signs—messages—trying to tell us something, to guide us, to point us in a new direction. The fun comes with questioning the event, figuring out the mystery, then deciphering the message. Understanding the message will reveal the guidance.

Signs? Messages from the angels, God, the Universe? Really?

How do I figure out a message from the angels or God? I don't understand...but Nancy promises it's part of the fun. So...I try.... First, I question the mystery...why was the dog there? It can't be about finding the bag. There wasn't anything of value in it, except my phone. So...if not the bag, then the dog. I think of the dog and again feel a wave of déjà vu come over me. Something about the dog.... The dog was guiding me to look, to look at the bag, but if not the bag...then am I meant to look at something else? What *else*?

Then I think of the magic of the moment.

I can really use some magic right now.

I wish I could keep some of that magic with me because, as I get closer and closer to home, I feel myself sinking deeper and deeper back into the desperation and anxiety that have become so dominant in my life. I pound the steering wheel in frustration.

So much for finding a message....

As I drive, the noise in my head becomes deafening and overwhelming. My thoughts bounce from the magic to the nightmares. Magic and nightmares. Back and forth. I was so distracted today that my bag was stolen out of my car and I didn't even notice. My life feels as if more than a travel bag has been stolen...it feels like something in me has gone missing.

Yet...because of that dog, I found the bag.

What has this dog triggered in me?

Maybe the dog and the sign *are* about magic! Maybe this magic can help me find what's been stolen from me? Can it help me find my sanity? Can it glue back together the broken pieces of my life? Can it help me get rid of the demons that are chasing me?

Because...I can't continue like this.

I must find a way to stop this erratic and psychotic behavior.

I must find a way to get through this.

Was the dog there to guide me toward the magic?

I must find the magic.

Chapter 8

THE SEVENTH
MINOR STORM

I stumble through the next few months, struggling to hold my life together. I had hoped that magic would appear...*like the dog did*...and make everything better. But it doesn't. It doesn't arrive, or show itself, or if it does, I'm too distracted to see it. My erratic and psychotic thoughts and behavior keep the memories and nightmares coming. Fast and furious they attack like demons on the hunt. My health is rapidly declining. I spend more time screaming and yelling at the kids than I do smiling and laughing with them.

I'm miserable...and it's contagious.

Then one morning, in the shower, two words flash into my mind: Face. It.

Face it?

I'm not sure where this idea came from, but it might make sense... *maybe this is the answer.* Maybe I need to face my past. Maybe I need to force myself to look back—to dive, jump, plunge into the deep end of this pool of darkness. To face the memory of Bob. To face the demons that haunt me.

Perhaps I need to fall into the abyss of my fear and hope that I make it through to the other side.

I don't want to do this. But, it's getting to the point that I feel I don't have a choice. Something must give before my body and mind give up.

This scares the shit out of me. What if I do this...and I sink more into the darkness or get stuck inside of the abyss, or never make it out...? But something deep inside of me is pushing me to do this. It is telling me that this is the way.

I've never done anything like this before. I don't know where to begin. So, I decide to take it one step at time and be organized and methodical. I make a list of everything that makes up the story of the attack—the good and the bad. I list it, not by priority, but by chronological order. I feel somewhat in control this way.

...at least in control of something.

As I sit with my paper and pen in hand, I force myself to think back to every significant moment and event around that time. My mind begins to wander around the memories of the things I did to distract and prevent Bob from raping me. *How did I know how to do this?* It's a question others have asked me for many years. I never could answer them. It's a question, though, that I never really asked myself. I'd like to know the answer. Sitting with this question, really asking myself...spurs a memory from years before the attack. I'm a young teenager, reading a magazine...*Cosmopolitan.* I'm on a ski trip...with my dad. And as if by *magic*...the entire scene appears.

My father and his then girlfriend, Sarah, took us four kids on a ski vacation to Mount Bachelor in Bend, Oregon. I was infatuated with Sarah. She was beautiful, smart and owned two clothing boutiques. She brought with her a stack of fashion magazines.

It's because of Sarah that I became passionate about retail merchandising.

One night, after everyone went to bed, I looked through the stack. In that pile, I found *Cosmopolitan.* I had never seen this magazine before. The sexy woman posing on the cover and the quizzes about sex piqued my interest. I snuck that magazine inside my sleeping bag and with a flashlight, read it cover-to-cover. Inside that magazine, I read an article about how to protect myself from a rapist.

I snap out of the scene with a sudden compulsion to find that magazine. I need to see that article again. I want to compare what the author said to what I did the night I outsmarted Bob.

Is this how I survived?

I wonder if Portland's library keeps copies of magazines in their archives—especially ones with quizzes that have you rate your lover's skills in bed.

I'm willing to find out.

On Scott's day off, I mention that I have some research to do at the downtown library to see if I can find an article I once read in a magazine. I don't go into detail and he doesn't ask. I figure I'll fill him in when and if I find something. He's glad to watch the kids so I can visit the library and begin my search.

When I get there, I ask the librarian if she has any copies of *Cosmopolitan*—issues that go as far back as 1975 up to 1977. I'm planning on looking through the winter and spring issues that would have been published during that ski season.

A few minutes later she returns with a metal box, about the size of a shoebox, and directs me to the microfiche readers.

I start with January 1975. I place the film on the reader and turn the machine on. I position the lens over the first negative and a picture of the cover is projected on the screen. I read the headlines and then the table of contents. Nothing jumps off the page at me. I do the same with the February and March issues. I find nothing.

In April's edition, next to the cover picture of braless Farrah Fawcett wearing a flowered blouse unbuttoned down to her navel, is a featured article titled: "What They Don't Tell You About Rape" by Ann Roiphe. I write down the code: 178:225-27. Not sure if this is the article, I keep searching.

I jump forward to November then December of 1975 and find nothing having to do with rape, until I get to January of 1976. On the cover, next to the picture of model Patti Hansen, who is wearing a low-cut yellow jumpsuit without a bra, are the words: "How to Say No to a Rapist (and Survive)" by Frederic Storaska. Seeing it sends a wave of recognition through my body. I write down the code: 180:122.

I ask the librarian if I can look at both issues. When she brings them out to me, I compare them side by side.

It's the January 1976 issue—I know, I just know, know, know it.

I pick up the magazine, and a wave comes over me that almost knocks me down. I feel a crazy sensation of time collapsing upon itself... upon me. I am 14 and 34 years old at the same time, both holding this magazine. Flipping through the pages, I search out the article. Then there it is...a frightening full-page drawing of a man grabbing a woman...followed by nine pages of small print.

Nine pages of lifesaving information.

My body is quicker to respond to finding this magazine than my mind is. Concerned I might physically collapse along with the time warp I'm in, I force self-control as I walk to the copy machine. I insert coins into the machine and nine copied pages later, I return the magazine to the librarian. Then with purpose, I walk step-by-step to my car.

Once alone, inside the security and privacy of my car, I take the time to really look at the article. The black and white pages seem to come to life in my hands. They carry an energy that seems familiar and yet… unfamiliar. It feels like a reunion of a very strange kind.

I can still feel time folding in upon itself. It's difficult to distinguish the difference between the 14-year-old child Cinda and the 34-year-old mother Cinda because they're both me, both here in the car, both remembering this article. But there is a difference and it is huge and it is blatant. The 14-year-old Cinda is innocent, naive and curious. The 34-year-old Cinda is scarred, battered and frightened.

As I read the article, the words blur and dance on the pages. They seem to be celebrating me reading them again. Or maybe it's just the tears that are welling up behind my eyes. I try to suppress my emotions. My eyes squint to focus on the pages.

The title, "How to Say No to a Rapist (and Survive)" is in large, bold letters. It is written by Frederic Storaska, the author who had written a book of the same title, published in 1975. Following the title is an introductory paragraph that warns the reader how using conventional wisdom during an attack just might get you killed. The author then goes into detail sharing ways in which one can prevent a rape from happening and how to keep from being badly injured. He offers five main lifesaving techniques.

I focus on the five key points Storaska advises for protecting oneself (*paraphrased*):

1. Stay as emotionally stable as you can. Storaska states that every attack consists of three components: the victim, the perpetrator and the location. By keeping calm, cool and collected you can become more aware of your surroundings and the personality and actions of the attacker. By being aware, you can spot clues and moments where you might be able to save yourself. If you are in emotional control, this will calm the rapist down and you will become the one in control. By remaining emotionally in control, you will be clearheaded enough to figure out what to do next.

2. The rapist will respond to your expectation. If you feel that the rapist has all the power—he will have all the power over you. Knowing that the attacker will rise to

meet your opinion of him, keep your fearful expectations at a minimum. Treat him with respect, as a "human being," if you can—he may respond respectfully in return. The opposite is true as well; if the rapist expects you to behave in a certain way, you probably will. They are usually master manipulators.

3. Do not be viewed as a threat. The attacker is most likely just as scared as you are. This makes him unpredictable. So, try to gain his confidence by letting him know you won't fight, or scream, or harm him. If he has a weapon, it is vital to gain his confidence. Once he is confident and/or trusts that you are not a threat to his safety, he will relax and potentially put his weapon down. This is when you can safely negotiate a way out.

4. Fake it until you can safely react. The rapist most likely planned this encounter, including the time, the location, his strategy and his victim. He feels he has the upper hand. Let the attacker believe he does, by giving the impression that you are going along with him. This may mean succumbing to his sexual advances, but by faking your acceptance of the situation, you will calm the rapist down. This will give *you* the upper hand and time to figure out how to respond next.

5. Be creative! Storaska gives permission for you to use your imagination and good judgment. Take everything you know about the attacker, the location and your own skills/abilities/limitations into account. Then improvise, make something up, use a distraction, do the unexpected. His confusion will allow you time to plan an escape.

Here they are…the words, the instructions. I can remember reading them now. I somehow remembered them that October night. They must have been stored somewhere deep inside my brain…and I accessed them just when I needed to.

How does this happen?

How is this possible?

How is it that at 14, I find this article…read it undercover and in secret…then, five years later…implement everything it said?

As I ask these questions, a notion, a probable answer…slowly occurs. It is so profound that I have trouble grasping it. Is it feasible that *something* or *someone* bigger and greater than I…was looking out for me?

Is this what Nancy, the LEC minister and Deepak Chopra were talking about—invisible forces that support, guide and love us? Did this invisible force guide me to find that article? Did this source love me enough to protect me—years before it was needed?

I know of God. I went to church growing up. But they didn't talk about this. Or if they did, I missed that day. So…what is this? Is this God? Is this the Universe? Is this an angel?

The thought of something bigger and greater looking out for me, guiding me, protecting me, loving me…it's almost too big to take in…too much to accept. Because this would mean…that I'm not alone? This would mean that I wasn't alone during the attack.

…*that I'm not alone…now.*

I hold the article to my chest and cry. I cry because this article is a link to that something…*that invisible something*…that loves me enough…to have thought my life was worth saving and getting this article into my hands before anything awful happened to me.

If my life *was* worth saving back then…then it must be worth saving now.

I cry for what seems like a lifetime, until a lifetime of overpowering emotion settles. When my vision clears, I place the article on the seat next to me and rest my right hand upon it. I read the author's name again, Frederic Storaska, and thank him for writing such an important book and this sexy magazine for publishing it.

"*Thank you, Frederic Storaska. Thank you,* Cosmopolitan. *Thank you, God, and invisible forces. I am forever in your debt,*" I whisper.

These words are spoken with such a depth of gratitude that it's as if I'm not the one saying them. It's as if a part of me I'm unfamiliar with is speaking…as if something is speaking for me.

It's a level of gratitude I've never experienced before.

"Thank you."

Chapter 9

THE EIGHTH
MINOR STORM

A few days later, I pull out my list and examine what I need to face next. The next item is just too enormous; the reality is just so scary that I consider skipping it. But something is pushing me forward—that *something* won't let me ignore it. Perhaps it's the same invisible force that guided me to the article both at 14 and again the other day. If so, this force is telling me that my sanity may depend on following through with my commitment to *face it*—before I am committed.

I must do this. I must make myself go back to the place where it all happened…to the place where a real demon changed everything about me. I must go back to that neighborhood and face this monster head on. I must stand in front of that house and force myself to see, feel, hear, and remember everything. I must walk around that neighborhood again and revisit the blue house on the corner.

I must force myself to see the events unfold and play out as if they're happening again—but this time through the eyes of the 34-year-old me. It is imperative that I convince myself that what happened then can't hurt me now.

I want to meet up with the 19-year-old me and witness her turmoil. I want to hold her hand. I want to assure her that I feel her pain and that she is not alone.

This isn't going to be emotionally or physically easy. I put it off for days, using the kids as an excuse. I don't want to take them with me. What if I freak out or cry or yell or go stone cold and quiet? I don't want them to witness anything that might scare them.

I want to and need to do this alone.

Then one night, an opportunity presents itself. Scott tells me he'd like us to visit his parents' farm the next day. I ask if he would mind taking the kids and leave me behind. I tell him that this would give me a chance to run errands without them. I don't want Scott to realize what I'm thinking of doing. I can't take the chance that he might talk me out of going.

That morning, I hand Scott the boys' travel bag filled with everything he needs, including bottles of breast milk for Ryan. He loads the boys up into our family car, the navy Jeep Cherokee and I wave them goodbye. I get to drive our other car. It is a racy, white, two-seat, Nissan 280ZX. Like the Jeep, it was a hand-me-down from my father. It's a fun car to drive and I'm even looking forward to zipping about the city in this powerful sports car.

When I sink into the driver's seat, which is formed to fit my body, the smell and feel of its red leather interior surround me. I strap the seat belt around my middle. My hands grasp the red leather-covered steering wheel. I start the engine; it purrs like a kitten. I rev it up and it roars like a lion. I am ready. I am ready for my drive into hell.

Here goes nothing. Let's do this, Cinda. Let's go fight some demons.

I crank up the music. I'm driving and shifting gears with determination, trying not to get lost in the fear that keeps trying to surface. I swallow it down and give myself a stomachache instead. I drum the steering wheel in rhythm with the bass that is booming through the stereo. The car takes the beating without issue.

I can do this. I can do this...pound, boom, pound, boom, pound.

As I get a few blocks away from my old house, I can feel my blood pressure rise. I turn the music down...and then off. I'm no longer pounding the steering wheel, but instead *tapping* it with every one of my fingers in a nervous pattern. The one-way streets guide me into the neighborhood. The blue house is coming up on the left. I pull over and sit there looking at the front of this multi-level house, forcing myself to remember any events that took place on this corner.

I visualize the young me at 19, and 19-year-old Cinda materializes on the corner as if by magic. The black and white dog comes running up to her.

That's right...the black and white dog...oh my God, I remember now what happened next....

I watch as young Cinda makes sure the dog is safe. Then she hears a man calling out the name "Cindy," the name she grew up with, the name she gave Bob.

I feel her panic. She's frozen. I'm frozen with her. I recite her inner pleadings.

Please, let me have heard it wrong. Please, please don't let it be Bob.

I *tap* the steering wheel in unison with the younger Cinda as she snaps the rubber band around her files. She's hoping that whoever was calling out will assume the snapping keeps her from hearing him. I'm hoping now that my *tapping* will help me un-hear it again too.

Tap, snap, tap, snap, tap, snap.

In this moment, my biggest fear is realized. I've opened the floodgates. By inviting 19-year-old Cinda back, I've invited the darkness back too. I'm engulfed in it. I'm swimming in it. If I'm not careful, I may drown in it.

The only way to save myself is to keep swimming.

I close my eyes to block out the blue house. But behind my lids, the events of 15 years ago still play on. The dog seems to be looking toward the voice, toward the second floor or attic of the house. The dog seems to want the 19-year-old Cinda to look. At 19, I was too afraid to look. I open my eyes and look now. I almost expect to see a face—Bob's face. Instead, I see a sign, a current-day sign, taped up in the second-floor window. It reads: *For Rent* with a phone number. I grab my notebook and write it down.

I can't believe it. If I call the landlord, will he remember Bob?

I put my car in gear and take a right up the one-way street. This takes me away from the house, which is a block behind me. As I drive the block, I pass the vegetable murals painted on the side of the small grocery store.

I turn right at the stop sign and pull over at the corner in front of the store. The historical sign sticks out from the front corner of the building. The same striped awnings cover its windows. Everything looks as I remember it. I get out of the car, walk past the blue freestanding mailbox and peek inside the front window. I remember when the younger me saw the composite drawing of Bob behind the counter. I can see younger Cinda struggling whether she should say anything to the clerk about her connection to it.

Observing me back then, but in real time now, causes the two timelines to blend together. I gasp when I feel 19-year-old Cinda's presence next to me. My memory has transported her out of the store and onto the street. I remember this moment back then.... I relive it now.....
Cinda has just walked around the man who was mailing a letter in the

mailbox. That man is watching her in the window's reflection. Right now, it's as if I can see him too, as clearly as I did years ago. But this time, I'm fully aware of who he is.

"Cinda, go to the bus now. Do not talk to this man," I whisper to her.

I walk with my younger self down the sidewalk to the bus stop. Together we watch the man's strange actions as he walks the corners of the intersection and then toward us. I warn her.

"Cinda, it's Bob! He knows who you are!"

I watch as she gets a whiff of his foul body odor and stale breath. I smell it with her and feel sick with the memory. She gets on the bus. I want to trip him as he gets on behind her. I want to scream at the bus driver to remember this guy.

As that bus leaves, in my mind's eye, another arrives. Young Cinda gets off. I see her glance at the opposite corner and I follow her line of sight. The image of my detective, disguised as a bum, materializes on the corner. I watch as he follows her home. I whisper into his ear.

"Thank you for keeping her, keeping me, safe."

The scenes vanish and I am back in present time. The trees in this neighborhood have grown since I was here last. They create a canopy of cold, damp darkness. I shiver in their shadow and hurry back to my car. I'm not sure if it's the trees or what's coming next that gives me the chills.

My house is coming next.

I drive down the two blocks, turn right, then right again, pull over and park. I'm here. I'm back. Back to the place that's been the cause of my torment. Here's where it all began.

But there's a problem.

The house is gone.

Instead, a large apartment complex, running the length of the block, parallel to the road and highway, towers above me. The only thing that remains is the tree on the corner. I remember this tree. This same tree shaded our kitchen and made it so dark. I get out of my car and touch the tree as a gesture of recognition.

Across the street is the brown house where Katie and I saw a man climb through its window and Katie pushed the panic button. It was the first and only time we used that button. Looking back toward the apartment complex, I'm surprised by my disappointment. I had come back, hoping to face the old house and the memories. I had come hoping to fight the demons that live there—that were birthed there.

Now that the house is gone, what am I supposed to do?

How can I confront you when you aren't even there?

I lean against the side of my parked car and picture the house that once stood here. *What did it look like?* I picture the broken step and remember Katie's mother twisting her ankle on it. The steps led up to the decrepit covered porch with its peeling paint. As I remember the house, 19-year-old Cinda materializes on the porch.

I close my eyes to hold on to the vision. I follow her into the house. I can see the inside through her eyes. There's the living room with the hole in the wall, the dark kitchen with torn linoleum. Around the corner is the door to the scary basement. Farther in front of her is the bathroom and then to the right...my bedroom.

Buffett comes running up to the younger Cinda. She picks him up. I feel her love for this cat and it makes me miss him now. Out of the bathroom comes the naked and confident 19-year-old Katie. I admire her all over again. She welcomes Cinda home with a smile, tells her the laundry is done and goes into her room. There were moments when I loved living here...with Katie and Buffett, but that was before....

I open my eyes. I am back to leaning on my car and looking up at the white apartment complex. Under the building is an open parking garage. It occurs to me that the house may no longer be here, but its basement floor still is.

I walk into the parking structure and circle around until I find the spot where the basement would have been. There are no cars parked at this end of the garage, and no people around either. I have complete privacy. I lean against the garage's wall as if it is the wall of the basement and close my eyes. I bring back the smell of the old basement—its mildew, its dankness. The same smell lingers in the floor of this garage. The smell helps to guide me back in time...the basement appears. I see the single light bulb dangling from the ceiling, a chain to turn it on. It illuminates the pile of abandoned clothes. *Who did they belong to?* The washer and dryer are running. Above me is the house. I hear younger Cinda and Katie's muffled voices. Standing in the basement again, I take in a deep breath and decide to launch into the work I came to do.

"*OK, here I go. It's time to confront the demons. Let's do this, Cinda.*"

I transport myself into my bedroom and see my bed and box spring set up on the floor. I stand at the foot of my bed, watching the younger Cinda sleep. The clock reads 3:00. Buffett hisses and then growls and I jump in anticipation of what is about to come. I try to warn her.

"Cinda, wake up, he's here."

Bob sneaks into her room and stands at the foot of the bed staring at the younger me sleeping. Every ounce of me wants to kick, hit and scratch this man. Instead, Buffett does it for me. The cat goes after Bob's ankles, hissing, clawing, biting and growling.

"Good kitty! Wake her up!"

The younger Cinda slowly wakes up, confused. She can't fathom why the landlord would send the fix-it guy so early. I feel it all with her. When the realization comes that she's not safe, my chest tightens in fear, as hers does too.

"Oh my, God! Here it comes. Here he comes!"

Bob lunges.

She screams.

I scream with her.

I am desperate to protect her, to protect her from what's coming. But there's nothing I can do. I am completely helpless. This is that moment when everything changes for her...for me.

I watch as my younger self tries to find ways to stay ahead of Bob's moves. She's going to need more ideas.

"Cinda, remember the Cosmopolitan *article!"*

Bob puts a pillow over her head. Her body slumps. She's being suffocated.

"You're not going to die. Cinda, you've got this."

Time flashes forward. I watch the clock change time. Hours pass like minutes.

Bob pulls Cinda's bathrobe over her head. She struggles, fighting for her life, until her body stops moving. I share her anguish...the lack of oxygen, the darkness, the awareness of imminent death...certain he will succeed in raping her.

I want to pull him off her. I want to yell and scream, "What gives you the right, you son-of-a-bitch!" Instead I whisper to her.

"Cinda, wait for him to change his position then throw him off."

She does—she sits up, pulls the bathrobe off and throws it at him. She's naked, naked in front of this demon. I feel the same coldness of the room that she is feeling. She has no shame. She's mad. I am too.

"You're about to do the unthinkable...but trust me, Cinda. You will be safe," I whisper to her with confidence.

That dreaded, unbelievable, repulsive moment when she, when I, invite him under the covers. I am helpless to help her...to support her.

This memory is awful…*awful!* I cry out in sympathy for the 19-year-old me. The cry is primal…a pained, agonized howl from the depth of my being.

"How? How did you get to be so brave?"

Then a loud sound startles us. It is the lovely sound of Buffett doing his ninja move in the mirror. I hear it. Cinda hears it. Bob hears it. He stops.

"Cinda, use that sound. Stop this madness!"

She does. He leaves!

I want to follow him and see where he goes. I want to push him down the broken steps so he'll break his neck. But I don't. I stay with Cinda as she puts the red bathrobe back on, backwards.

"Call the cops. They'll take good care of you."

I open my eyes and shake off the dreadfulness of that scene. I feel as if it has oozed out of the house and is now sitting in a puddle on the parking garage's floor. I move away from it, to another section of the garage and lean against it for support. There are more things I need to see, more demons to be revealed.

I close my eyes and visualize the policeman entering the house. She leaves with him to go identify a suspect.

Time fast forwards and the front door opens again. Cinda enters. It's a different scene, a different day. She goes through a pile of mail on the coffee table, finds the letter and opens it. I recall the confusion she is feeling. The phone rings and I warn her.

"Cinda, it's Bob, it's Bob! Get him off the phone and call for help!"

I open my eyes and bring myself back into the present moment. I am still in the parking garage. I have spent the last hour pulling demon after inner-demon, horrible memory after horrible memory, out of my psyche and into the space where I stand. The garage is full of them now—full of my inner darkness.

Perhaps my demons will remain in that dingy, dark and dank place where they belong.

This is a great time to leave.

I walk out from underneath the apartment complex and look up the steep street. The blue house is up on the corner. The vacant lot that separated the two houses is half the size it used to be and is now a gravel parking lot. A retaining wall has been built up to level out the once-slanted lot. I step up the wall and onto the gravel.

I remember the paw prints in the snow, the ones I thought Buffett had made. I conjure them up and retrace them. They lead me to the backside of the blue house. I walk up to the makeshift plywood door. The hole in the lower corner that I feared Buffett had crawled into is still there!

I have an urge to lift the lock and open the latch like I did once before. Young Cinda appears next to me. I witness her opening the door and walking under the house. I groan in disapproval. I know… the thought of losing Buffett is fueling her bravery. But I know what, who, is coming next.

"Cinda, please don't go in. Buffett isn't there."

A door above us opens. We both look up and see a man.

"Cinda, it's Bob! Get out of here, NOW!"

She recognizes his hair, panics and turns to run away.

"Cinda! Hurry! Shut the door. Lock it! Lock him in."

She does just that and races back to her friends who are waiting for her. Cinda jumps into her car and leads the convoy away—away from this nightmare—away from Bob.

As she drives away, I come back to the present moment and find myself still standing at the blue plywood door. The padlock is there, looped through the latch, locked.

Locked—just as I left it years ago.

Locked—just as I locked away those awful two months.

I thought I had permanently locked it all behind me. But here I am, forcing myself to face it all again. I take in a deep breath, holding in the onslaught of emotions demanding to be released. I struggle to walk to my car. When I reach it, I get in, lock the door, turn on the engine, crank up the heat, lean over the steering wheel and let the screaming and the tears come.

I put on my seatbelt and feel the security that comes with the sound of the click. I put my car into gear and pull out into traffic. Just as I watched the younger me leave, it's now time for me to leave too. I stop at the sign and look at the blue house, wondering whatever happened to Bob. Did he live there? Did he live in the brown house across the street? Does he still live in this neighborhood? Did he attack or harm other women? Did those clothes belong to him? Was he an old tenant of our house? Did he have a key? Could he have been our landlord? Did he ever get arrested? Is he still alive? I prefer to believe he is dead—*yep, dead.*

Questions that never got answered....

A honk brings me back to reality. I wave an apology to the car behind me and move through the intersection.

As I drive away, I think about everything. I think about why I came...I came here to find and face the demons at the place they reside. I think about what I hoped for...I hoped that facing the demons would cause them to remain where they belong, and stop haunting me. I think about reliving and experiencing all the horror and terror and fear again.

I can't believe I faced my biggest fear. I did it. I hope it worked! I hope I never see the demons again.

Please! Leave me alone!

I am so very tired...tired, exhausted, drained....and eager...eager to get home...home to the sound of laughing boys and a husband who loves me.

Home...to a house without demons.

I hope....

Chapter 10

THE NINTH MINOR STORM

I arrive back home to what I hope will be a "new tomorrow," the bringing in of a "new dawn," the "first day of the rest of my life." I am desperate to experience every cliché about positive change I can think of.

A few days go by and I feel great.

I recite the positive affirmations out loud. I recite them to myself in the mirror, in the car, as I walk around the house picking up toys. I stop reciting them long enough to bark orders at the dog, scream at the kids, argue with my husband.

...I haven't changed....

I had hoped things would be different...they're not, I'm not. I go back to the list I made of chronological events to see what else I came up with... what else might help me get back onto the sanity track. The next item listed is to find the detective who had been assigned to my case. Perhaps by seeing him again, by being in his presence, I might feel that same sense of protection he gave me so long ago.

I've been with Katie. I've shared with Katie. I failed with Katie.

Yet the same desperation that drove me to share my memories with her is driving me now. I *need* to find my detective. I *need* to talk to him. I *need* to determine if he remembers me, the attack, anything about those two months of my life.

The problem is...I don't recall his name.

I call the Sexual Crimes Division of the Portland Police Bureau and explain to the woman on the phone what I'm trying to do. I give her my name and birthday. She transfers me to the only person from 1981 that still works in the department.

"I think I remember your case," he says in his gruff voice after I share some of my history. "It's not every day you hear about a young woman spending hours outsmarting a violent criminal. It was about that same time we started following a shady character that was making his rounds down Interstate 5. We called him the 'Gentleman Rapist' because he put pillowcases over his victims' heads, didn't use a weapon, and seldom beat them. After this creep raped a woman in her apartment, she grabbed a stun gun out of her nightstand and zapped him with it. That son of a bitch flew over the balcony of her loft and broke his back when he landed."

"Did he die?" I ask, shocked.

"No, but he got arrested. That was down in Eugene, I believe."

Was that Bob? Was this his fate?

I'm curious, but I have no desire to find out. I just want my detective.

A few days later, I receive two phone calls, both from the woman and the man I spoke to earlier. They give me the same information. The detective I'm looking for is Thom Redmond. Hearing his name instantly takes me back in time. That strange sensation of time collapsing upon itself floods me yet again. Memories of his face, his voice, the protectiveness he provided me, come flooding back. I call his office in the department where he now works.

"Thom Redmond," says the male voice on the line.

I take an anxious breath in, and talk on the exhale.

"Detective Redmond, my name is Cinda Stevens, now Lonsway. You were assigned to my case back in 1981."

"Yes, Cinda. What can I do for you?"

It's my detective. My Detective Redmond. I found him!

I remember. I remember him taking care of me, holding me up when I wanted to fall and keeping me steady when I was an unstable mess. I had hoped it would all come back once I knew his name, and it has.

What I didn't expect is the emotion.

His sincere tone of support, now asking how he can help, sets into motion a kaleidoscope of feelings I'm not prepared for. Emotions that I have hidden away for so long, are now bubbling up to the surface. I'm worried I won't get the words out. I share with him the history of my story. I share bits and pieces of our time together, hoping to spur his memory.

"Well…" I stall, struggling to keep myself under control, "…I don't suppose you remember me or that time, but I was hoping there might be a chance that I could meet with you. I won't take up much of your time."

"Sure, I can make that work. I could get you in for a few minutes next Tuesday around 10:00 in the morning. Will that work? I'll send for a copy of your file before we meet."

I agree. He informs me that the police department has moved since we last met and gives me the new address. He tells me to check in with the front receptionist. Someone will escort me to a private meeting room.

I hang up feeling anxious and relieved at the same time. I have a few days before we meet and I want to show up to our meeting fully prepared. I don't want to waste a minute of his busy schedule. Even though I'm a physical wreck, even though I'm an emotional mess, even though my psyche is shattered, I must hold myself together long enough to make a positive impression. I don't want to appear to be the same naive and scared teenager I was the last time we met. I want to be viewed, instead, as a practical and mature adult, a responsible mother and citizen—someone worthy of his time.

I type up a professional letter. I use bullet points with short yet descriptive sentences about each event that took place during those two months. I do this for his record as well as my own. I tell him, finally, about recognizing Bob in the blue house on the day we moved out. I apologize for not telling him before.

I include notes from my recent visit, informing him that the house is now gone. I print out a map of the neighborhood and highlight the areas of interest that go with each bullet point. I circle the blue house and write down the phone number I saw on the "For Rent" sign in case he wants to follow up. I slide the pages into a manila envelope and carefully print his name on the cover.

This isn't enough, though. What else can I do? He deserves more from me. When I left that house, I didn't give him any notice. I never thanked him. I never said goodbye. A wave of shame comes over me.

I need to make amends.

I want to bring him a peace offering of sorts. I want to take him a thank you gift. I want to thank him for being who he was to me back then and for meeting me again now.

The next day, I go on a mission to find the perfect yet unusual gift. I find what I'm looking for at The Real Mother Goose, a high-end artisan shop. I choose a stone-carved buffalo with an arrowhead and a piece of turquoise tied to its back. It is beautiful and it is perfect. The store clerk sets it inside a simple, cotton lined brown box and wraps a tan piece of raffia ribbon around it.

On Tuesday morning, I drop Eric off at preschool and with 8-month-old Ryan, I head to the Portland Police Bureau. With my boy on my hip,

I walk into a small lobby area. I give the receptionist, who sits behind a bulletproof panel, my name and Thom Redmond's.

Things are very different than before.

A uniformed officer comes into the waiting area and gives Ryan a teddy bear. Ryan squeals in delight and holds it close—*we name it Redmond.* He then escorts us into a small conference room. While I wait for Detective Redmond, I pull out the manila envelope, the gift and a baggie full of Cheerios to keep Ryan entertained.

When a man enters the room, I'm not sure if he's my detective or not. When he speaks, and shakes my hand, I'm 19 again, meeting him for the first time.

Here he is...my savior, my knight, my hero. My detective.

I tighten up my insides and hold physically strong. I want to appear as the adult I am now, but instead I fumble, I choke. I'm so choked up with memories of our time together that I struggle to talk. Nothing comes out but croaks. His face is kind, his demeanor patient, his ability to keep a professional distance and yet still be supportive and hold me up...it's all there.

He's all here...just as he had been all there so many years ago.

I look at him, embarrassed, struggling for words through my emotions. He helps me by changing the subject and talking to Ryan, giving me a chance to compose myself. It works. I'm able to tell him about my older child, Eric. He tells me that he now has two children of his own, a boy and a girl. I share the memory of the Halloween card his wife picked out for me. He smiles, but I'm not sure he remembers.

"So, what can I do for you, Cinda?"

"I expect that you don't remember me."

"Well, I had to read your file to recall, but your case was memorable. I'm sorry we never caught the guy."

"I'm not too worried about catching him for my sake. Seriously, I'm not. I worry and hope that he didn't rape other women. I'm not proud of the way I just left, but I can't fix that now." I shake off my guilt and continue, "But...the reason why I'm here...is that recently, it's all been coming back on me. I'm having a tough go of it and trying my best to get my life back on track. Part of that is revisiting the house and neighborhood and finding you again. It's all so strange, like a bad dream that doesn't end."

"That's to be expected, I suppose. Especially since there wasn't any closure for you."

I slide over the envelope. He reaches for it. But suddenly, for some strange reason, I don't want him to open it in front of me.

"You can open that after I leave. It's just some notes about my case that you may or may not find interesting. It's stuff that I've recently remembered. I'm not expecting you to do anything about it...I just wanted you to be able to read it—later." I hand him the small gift box, "But this, I'd like you to open now."

He unties the raffia ribbon, lifts the lid and looks at the carved buffalo. "This is beautiful...but I don't understand."

"There's a card inside describing the meaning," I point back at the box.

He reads the card out loud. *"The buffalo totem symbolizes good luck on the hunt. The arrowhead represents a swift and clean capture. Turquoise is a sacred stone for the Native Americans which they use for protection and healing."*

As he reads the significance of this *totem*, it occurs to me that I've just given him what someone might refer to as a "spiritual gift" and I didn't even realize it. This carved sculpture, arrowhead and the turquoise stone are symbols of Native American culture, their beliefs, their spirituality.

Aunt Nancy would be proud!

He looks touched, but still confused. I need to explain myself.

"Thom...Detective Redmond...," I take in a deep breath. "...I'm not sure if you're aware of the impact you had on my life back then. You came into my world at a time when I was scared. You helped me feel protected. I'll forever be grateful to you and for what you did for me and for how you made me feel so cared for. This is my thank you, to you. You're still hunting predators so I hope this will bring you good luck."

An expression flashes across his face. He hesitates.

"Cinda...I don't know what to say. I was just doing my job. We don't often get told such things—especially in ways like this. I'm not sure I deserve it."

He pauses, looks at the buffalo. His humility is heartwarming.

He has no idea the impact, the difference, he makes in people's lives.

"Unfortunately, no matter how hard we tried, we didn't catch the creep who harmed you. I'll always be sorry for that. I'll keep this buffalo with me and every time I look at it I'll think of you. And, maybe, hopefully, it will bring me better luck for others. Thank you."

Oh, my God, I get it!

I get it.

I get why I'm here. I thought I needed to see him in hopes he could do for me now what he did for me then. But, that's not it. This isn't about me right now. It's about someone else. It's as if the spirit of that buffalo and that arrowhead stone pierced my heart.

I'm meant to be here, with him, to give him this totem. I'm meant to be here to show him sincere gratitude for what he did for me. I'm meant to be here to get out of my self-centered pity-party and fear-induced psychosis and do something of kindness for someone else.

My heart is singing! This is a feeling I haven't felt for a very long time. I feel good! It feels as if the clouds might be parting and letting a ray of sunshine come through. The darkness that surrounds me might be a little less heavy and thick. The winds might be shifting!

I stand up to leave and ask if I can hug him. He puts his arms around both Ryan and me. The meeting didn't last long, but I leave feeling lighter and happier.

I feel a sense of hope.

I hope my life is coming back to me.

I hope my life is getting back to normal.

I hope I am getting back to normal.

Chapter 11

THE MAJOR STORM

I had been so optimistic when I reunited with Katie. I had been so optimistic that she, of all people, would relate to what I am going through. I had been so optimistic that she could help me clear up all the mess of my emotions and nightmares.

But...that's not what happened.

I had been so sure about facing the demons. I had been so sure that I could pull them out of the darkness and leave them behind. I had been so sure that my actions would force them to detach from me.

But...that's not what happened.

I had been so confident when I met with Detective Redmond. I had been so confident that he would provide the security and protection that he once did. I had been so confident that his wisdom and compassion could empower me again.

But...that's not what happened.

I am more lost than ever before....

A year after my visit with Detective Redmond, *a year of trying to hold myself together with the thinnest of delicate threads,* Scott gets a promotion and with that a raise. We look for a larger house and find a four-bedroom, two-story home on a quiet cul-de-sac in the suburbs of Portland. The moldings, wainscoting, lofty ceilings, along with its white walls, cabinets and counters make the brand-new place cheerful, charming and comfortable.

This move feels so right, so promising, so hopeful. It might be just what I need...to move out of the city...to move forward, to reclaim myself, my life, my sanity. After all, my marriage is wonderful, my boys are thriving and now we have this beautiful home in which to live and love. Everything should be perfect....

But...that's not what happens.

Instead, the burden...the heaviness of my past is too much to carry. I grow weaker every day. Then one day, something inside of me cracks under the weight of it.

I feel it. I can almost hear it...*a popping....*

Here it comes...I can't stop it...they...he, has found me....

Just as I locked the padlock on that blue door, I had shut and locked the door to my past. But now...the key that I had buried so long ago, so deep within, has been uncovered...uncovered and has found the tiny opening leading back to the memories, to the demons, to Bob. The protective barrier that I so stoically built up against them...the lock has been undone...the door has been opened. My body shakes with the sound of my internal lock snapping open.

I'm a goner.

I was so desperate to free myself of what haunts me that I thought my trip back to the neighborhood could cure me. But instead, it triggered... activated...this opening.

I thought that the demons dwelled where they came from.

But they *don't.*

They have been dwelling inside of *me.*

When I went back, I pulled them out of *me*—not out of our house, not out of the blue house, not out of the neighborhood—but out of me.

I thought they had been holding me hostage, holding my sanity for ransom. I *finally* realize that I have been their keeper, their warden. They are escaping now.

They are becoming more powerful than before. I can feel Bob taunting, tormenting, threatening me. He is not going to leave me alone.

I'm in even more danger.

I can sense the dark clouds of a storm hovering and it has nothing to do with the gray sky and rain outside. It is an internal storm of such magnitude that my emotions, my health, my sanity, are at risk.

I'm not sure how or if I can protect myself...my family.

Then...one night....

The storm hits.

While everyone is sleeping, I hear a loud noise, a thud, outside my window. I sit up in bed and listen. My dog Hannah is on alert; she heard it too. I hear it again. The bedrooms are on the second floor, so the noise had to have come from downstairs—from the windows right below me.

Someone's breaking in.

I look over at Scott. He's sound asleep. Not wanting to wake him, I jump out of bed and run down the hall to check on Eric and Ryan. Both boys are sleeping, *safe*, safe in their beds.

I call Hannah to my side. We creep down the stairs and into the living room. The front windows are shut, but one isn't locked. This makes no sense. I always make sure the windows are locked. So, why is this one unlocked? Someone must have climbed in through this window then shut it. That explains the noises I heard earlier. I panic.

Someone's inside the house.

Holding my breath, I sneak through the entire house, Hannah runs ahead—helping me search for an intruder we're positive is there. I'm ready to confront him. I'm ready to fight. I'm ready to defend my family.

Hannah is on a mission. She sniffs inside closets, behind couches, under tables. We find nothing unusual, nothing frightening, nothing threatening. I go back through the house, checking on the boys, on Scott. I triple check that each window and door is locked. I want to prevent whomever this is from an easy escape.

He's here, Bob's here, he found me...and now he's hiding.

How did Bob find me? He must have seen me when I went back to the neighborhood. He must have been spying on me again. He must have followed me home. Bob's here...here to finish what he started years ago. This time, he will do serious harm...harm to me...to my family.

I will catch him before he catches us.... I will beat him at his own game.

Shaded by the darkness of the living room, I sit...peeking outside from behind the curtains, watching the cul-de-sac. From here I can patrol the front of the house where he entered and the stairs to where my family is sleeping...unaware of their vulnerability.

I sit and I wait...and I wait...and I wait. I'm waiting to surprise him, when he comes out of hiding. I'm waiting to beat the shit out of him. I'm waiting to yell and scream and kick at the man who has tortured me for years.

The waiting is unending. The tension is unbearable. My entire body hurts with it. *But...I will outlast him.* I'm glued here until he shows himself. I will not leave. My family's safety depends on me staying right here.

I WILL NOT let you do this to me again. Not this time.

I wait.

I wait.

I have no idea how long I wait.

Hannah, once alert and looking out the window with me, is now sleeping at my feet.

Nothing.

Nothing else happens.

There are no more sounds. Everything is quiet. I hear no one inside. I see no one outside.

Where are you? Why don't you show yourself?

I remain glued to my chair. I have no choice. That *nothing* has my heart racing and I can't let it go. It wasn't *"nothing"* once upon a time. The fear that pulses through my body is nearly debilitating.

Flashes of that terrible night come at me like stabs of a knife, one after another after another. I can't breathe. They are too real. I want to scream. I want to scream at them to stop. I want to scream at the fear, at the tension, at the insanity. I want to scream at Bob to leave me alone and stay away. I swallow hard to suppress it. I try to calm myself down by breathing, but my breath comes in short, painful spurts. I can't get enough oxygen. I feel light headed. I'm going to pass out.

I hurt....

I'm tired....

I'm afraid....

I'm desperate....

I am losing my mind.

I am losing this battle.

I am defeated.

Let him come....

I give up.

Chapter 12

THE EYE OF
THE STORM

Defeated and exhausted, I force myself back upstairs. Hours have passed; an entire night has gone by. The sun is just starting to come out. I crawl into bed hoping that I can fall quickly asleep—hoping that sleep will ease the suffering, the pain.

Scott is gently snoring next to me. His heat is comforting to my aching body. I'm relieved my actions earlier didn't disturb him. I couldn't have dealt with him finding me in that state. I couldn't have faked it. I couldn't have taken care of him and his worry for me.

I can't even take care of me.

In total desperation, I weep. I'm so tired of everything. I'm tired of pretending to be strong, of pretending nothing is wrong, of pretending I'm not scared. I just can't protect my family and myself any longer. I can't fight it any more. I have nothing else that I can give, or do, or fix.

I give up.

I'm falling...falling into nothingness...falling beyond my sanity.... There is nothing more to cling to, hold on to, to grasp at, that can save me. The void is vast, the abyss is absolute, the emptiness is eternal. I'm spent beyond spent. I have no choice but to fall, to let go, to surrender... *to the demon.*

Come get me.

Silent tears run down my face and onto my pillow. I pray for an answer. I plead and beg to anyone or anything that might be listening to show me what I need to do. I think of the *Cosmopolitan* article and pray to that entity that guided me to find it back then to help me now.

God, help me. Please help me.

Fatigue takes over. I hope that I might be falling asleep. But it isn't sleep that's taking me over—it's the darkness, the demon.

He can have me.

I hear a voice. I hold my breath and freeze. Is he in my room? Am I imagining things? Am I losing my mind?

I beg for it to not be Bob. I beg for him to go away. I have no more energy. I can't bear to go through another freak-out. Not again.

Please, either take me or leave me alone. Just stop. Just stop torturing me.

I barely hear the words, but I hear enough.

"Love your enemy, Cinda. There you will find your peace."

"What? What did you say?"

The conversation is a silent one, taking place in my head, in my mind—the mind that I'm quickly losing.

"Love your enemy, Cinda. There you will find your peace."

The voice is gentle and clear. I feel a wave of warmth come over me. I'm in a daze of exhaustion, so I'm probably hearing things. But something inside of me is listening, is feeling, is hoping. I try to understand what those words have to do with me.

In a fog of semi-consciousness, I repeat the words to myself: *"Love your enemy. Love your enemy."*

I've heard these words before. *Where?* Deepak Chopra, the LEC minister? These remind me of the words I heard on the cassette tape. What do they mean? Why am I hearing them? What am I supposed to do with them?

Then I get it.

A wave of understanding flows through me. To stop this craziness inside of me...to find the peace that I seek...I must first find the love.

Lying in the darkness, my husband is still snoring beside me. Through my exhaustion, I work to gather enough energy, just enough, to do what I'm compelled to do.

My heart is racing. Focusing is beyond difficult. I must silence the noisiness of my mind and calm the anxiety running throughout my body. *Breathe.* I start by taking deep methodical breaths. I breathe in slow and deep, filling my abdomen, then expel the air with a long, gentle release.

IN and OUT…in, and out…. Calm down, Cinda…in and out…try to relax… breathe.

If I hold my breath a little bit between both breathing in and letting out, I quiet the internal noise and ease the tension even more. The more I focus on my breathing the more my nervous system turns itself down. I am alert now. Yet, I'm in a zone of clear calmness. I have never experienced anything like this before. My mind silences. My fear subsides.

It's almost blissful….

In this zone of clear calmness, I become the observer of my own body, as if from above. I'm watching my body breathe. I'm witnessing my serene state. This is so strange and so different, but I don't let myself think about it. I just watch my thoughts as they come and go. My body feels lighter... lighter...lighter. My stress is leaving, my anxiety lifting, my desperation dispersing. I don't dwell on it, I just witness it change and lighten and leave.

Is this the peace I'm seeking? Have I found it?

"Now the love," the voice says.

I don't know if it's my own voice or the voice I heard earlier. It doesn't matter. It's pure heaven.

Now the love.

I focus my awareness on my boys, on Scott, on my parents and my dog. I feel my body warm with the love I have for them. It is beautiful. This lightness and this love mix together. Yet, I'm not sure...if this is enough...if this is the love I'm supposed to be seeking. I probe deeper into the feelings of love and the experiences that have made me feel loved. I am so relaxed...so calm. I think I might fall asleep.

Is this it? Have I found it?

"Love your enemy Cinda. There you will find your peace."

An inner knowing comes to me. It's not the love of my family, or the love I've experienced...that's not the love I'm seeking. The love that I am to seek...is different.

I'm to love my enemy.

I'm to love the demon...to love Bob.

I don't cringe or worry or freak. I'm in such a tranquil state that I trust the advice. Something...*someone*...seems to be guiding me. I don't feel alone or unprotected. Therefore, I'm not afraid. Yet, I don't even think of being afraid or unafraid, I just *am*...here, right now, breathing my way into this state, surrendering to the guidance.

"Love your enemy. There you will find your peace."

I know what I need to do next. With my eyes closed and my body still, I call Bob to me. My mind is not the one speaking; it is silent. My heart...it feels as if my heart is the one calling out. Over and over, like a drum beating, I call his name.

"Bob...come to me. Bob, come to me. Bob, come to me."

Soon, in the center of the darkness, inside of my mind's eye, or perhaps inside my room—I'm not sure—a man appears. He's lit up as if a spotlight is shining on him. He looks around, confused and maybe even frightened. He squints into the brightness of the light and looks in my direction.

"Bob, do you know who I am? Do you remember me?"

I don't comprehend what's happening, I don't even try. My mind and my mouth are silent. Yet, I'm the one who is talking—it is my voice I hear. My eyes are not seeing; they are closed. Yet, my vision is clear. My body isn't responding either, for it's perfectly still, heavy as a leaded weight. Whatever this is, I don't understand, but it's occurring...almost without me. I don't judge it. I just let it take its course.

"Yes, yes, I know you. You're Cindy. Cindy, what am I doing here?"

Hearing him say my name doesn't send me into a tailspin of panic. I observe my non-reaction, but don't question it.

"Bob, there is something I need to tell you."

Moments before, I had filled myself with love. I can still feel the warmth and support of those who love me and whom I love. Inside my chest, I feel this love swirling and spinning. Momentum builds, and warmth spreads. This sensation grows and I can feel my upper body arch and arc as it expands in this current...this love. It is so powerful, so tremendous, so full of energy that it seems to lift my body off the bed.

When this incredible energy becomes too big to contain, it pulls out of my chest and hovers in front of me in the darkness. I can see it in my mind's eye. I reach out with my right arm. In my hand, I hold this energetic, glowing, fiery, ball of love. I can feel its life, its warmth.

This is a love so different...so powerful...so much bigger than any kind of love I have ever known. This is a love that is so vast it can be felt, touched and seen.

This is love of the purest, most sacred kind.

This puts me in a state of awe, but I don't think about it. I just feel it. I take in the beauty and magnificence of what I am witnessing. I'm not in control, and yet somehow I am. I'm watching and observing it all take place, yet my body and senses are responding. Words are spoken from me.

"Bob, I need you to hear me, to listen to me."

My tone is serious. He stops squirming and looks right at me.

"Bob, I want you to know...I want you to know...I love you."

Without thinking about what I'm doing, I throw the ball of energy, of love, of fire, right at him. I watch it fly. It resembles a comet sailing through the darkness that separates us. This meteor of pure love and sheer energy makes contact. It hits him right in the middle of his chest and enters his body. He shakes all over as light shoots out of his fingers, head and feet. The love-filled energy seems to spread to every dark corner inside of him, lighting him up...and then...disappears.

Bob collapses onto his knees. He's crying, sobbing.

"I'm so sorry, I'm so sorry," he weeps.

"Bob, I don't ever want to see you again."

"Cindy.... Thank you."

"Goodbye, Bob."

Everything goes black.

And Bob is gone.

Bob is gone.

I gasp for air. My eyes snap open. I'm back into the physical reality of my bedroom. I'm shocked by what I just experienced, by what I just said and did, by his reaction.

What? Was? That? What was that!

I look around my bedroom. No shadows are lurking in the corners. No Bob is standing at the end of my bed. My husband's snoring...sounds precious. Hannah's warm body lies between us. I breathe in her wonderful musky smell. My body feels light and airy, yet full of a new sensation... freedom.

Freedom...and peace.

I roll onto my side and hug my pillow tight. I internally inspect my body for any density or heaviness leftover from the demons, the demon. Where the darkness used to fill my insides...all I feel is lightness...a kind of emptiness. My body is empty...empty of the fear, the hate, the anxiety that filled up my insides and dominated my life.

They are gone...gone with Bob.

In their place is a new fullness. I'm filled with a sensation of...hope, *yes*...peace, *yes*...but there is something even better growing inside of me now. The feeling running through me...is beautiful...something I haven't felt in a very, very long time.

Joy.

Yes.

Something magical just happened. I feel different, altered, changed. I can't remember the last time I felt this serene. Sleep is coming, but before I drift off, I whisper to whomever or whatever guided me, *"Thank you."*

"You saved me."

The Calm After the Storm

It isn't long before I hear the pitter-patter of little feet running down the hall. I feel a jump followed by another as the entire bed shakes under my resting body. Bed covers are lifted as tiny bodies scramble underneath.

"Morning, Mommy. Morning, Daddy," says Eric.

"I'm in the middle," sings Ryan.

Morning has arrived already—glorious morning. However long I slept, I don't know...ten minutes, an hour, two...but I slept sounder and deeper and experienced more rest than I have for what seems...*well*...like a lifetime. I am awake now. I am awake and filled with joy.

I giggle and grab at my boys and slide them both in for a hug. Scott joins in the hug from his side of the bed. The boys squeal in delight with our tight family embrace. Hannah barks loudly while jumping on and off the bed.

I'm overawed by how good I feel.

Just a while ago, I had crawled into bed having given up all hope. I was convinced the demons and Bob had come for me. I surrendered to them. I surrendered my body, my mind and my soul to the darkness. But instead of losing to the madness that was consuming me, something magical, even mystical, came to my rescue. When I thought I was falling, something or *someone* caught me. Unseen forces understood what I couldn't see for myself...what was needed for me to mend emotionally. Their guidance saved my sanity...my life.

I sneak a peek at my right hand. It seems to be covered in a residual glow. I can still feel the energy of that ball. I'd been guided by the words, *"Love your enemy."* In a desperate need for the peace these words promised, I pulled from me the most profound love I have ever known.

The love for an enemy...the love that included an enemy...a love that included Bob.

I'm humbled to my core. Emotion fills up my insides and finds its way to my eyes.

"Mommy, are you crying?" asks Ryan.

I feel three sets of eyes on me. I laugh and say, "I'm just so in love with you, and you, and you."

I tickle each boy and squeeze my husband's shoulder. They laugh in response. The boys jump out of bed and race downstairs to watch cartoons and Hannah barks after them.

I love my life.

I love my life.

When was the last time I said that? I do love my life! I slide over to Scott and snuggle into his arms. He kisses me on the temple and I don't shudder or pull away.

The rest of the day is just as beautiful. I no longer feel anxious, afraid or out of control. All the scattered pieces of me seem to have been glued back together. I'm centered and more solid in my body. I feel as if I have been reformed and reborn into a new and improved version of myself.

I am changed.

I'm filled with hope, love, joy, and finally…the peace I've been craving. All my senses are alive. Everything appears more beautiful, smells more exquisite, tastes more delicious, feels more luxurious.

Everything has changed.

I'm not the same person, woman, wife, mother I was yesterday. The insanity has vanished and it didn't take me with it. My demons are gone and I believe they are gone forever. I am restored. I am whole. I am alive.

I've been touched and guided by grace

Grace…what else could I call it?

I can feel it.

This grace pulses through my body. When I woke up this morning, something else woke up with me…a connection to something far greater than I am.

Peace.

Peace is everything.

Peace is enough.

I don't try to understand the magic that took me over that night. I don't care about the *why* or the *how* I finally got to this place of beloved peace. To question it doesn't even occur to me.

I'm eager to live my life…to feel my life…to love my life again. I'm excited at the possibilities of what the new ME can and will do. I have plans and they are fueled by my newfound optimism.

I have blinders on.

Because…once again the quote: *"Life is what happens to us while we are making other plans,"* rears its pesky head.

I am not to take my healing for granted.

Life has other plans.

Part Three

THE AWAKENING

The Questions

Does a victim lose her victim sign, her victim status…or, if once a victim, is she always a victim? Does the trauma ever really release its grip? Do the nightmares stop? Are the demons, the memories, fully exorcised?

What does it mean to be healed? What is the effect of healing? What comes after healing?

These questions…I don't think to ask…because I believe that I'm complete in my recovery. I believe that I'm no longer a victim. I believe that my nightmares and the demons and Bob have vanished forever. Gone…the night I told Bob I loved him.

I'm cured.

I am.

I've moved on and I won't look back.

Ever.

I'm content with my life…and contentment is fabulous.

Until….

Until *life* decides that forgetting isn't true healing, that contentment is another form of hiding.

I believe I've been healed. And, that means I've put on blinders. I've closed my eyes and in a way fallen asleep to any other possibility or reality.

Until….

Life decides it is time for me to wake up—wake up to the understanding of the why and the how of my healing.

Unseen forces present themselves again and this time I listen, respond and follow the guidance without hesitation.

I'm guided on a mysterious, magical, mystical, journey that changes the trajectory of my life.

I'm guided on an exploration, an expedition, an excursion of a lifetime.

I'm guided to witness for myself that there is healing after violence…that can lead to victory.

There is hope after trauma…that can lead to truth.

I am awakened. I am awakened to embrace my calling, my destiny, my purpose.

This is the story of my awakening.

Chapter 1

MY CALLING

For the last 18 years my life has been filled with blissful chaos and sincere moments of happiness and finally…inner peace. Scott and I continue to live and love and raise our family in our beautiful home in the suburbs. I fill my days with volunteering in my sons' schools. I help to run a few non-profit organizations I care about. My nieces grow up and don't need my supervision anymore. Our beloved dog Hannah dies and we bury her ashes in our front yard. To share our love, we add to our family another Golden Retriever, Maggie, and two high maintenance cats.

Everything about my life…everything in me and around me is fearless, anxiety-less and shame-less.

And most importantly…demon-less.

The years before I was guided to do the sacred ritual of healing I experienced with Bob…were heavy years. The burden I carried wore me down and nearly took me out. So now…now, I feel like I float throughout my days. There is lightness in my heart, lightness in my walk, lightness in my talk. I no longer yell or rage or throw temper tantrums.

One day, my son Eric asks, "Mom, when did you stop yelling? You used to yell all the time."

Over the years, others have noticed the shift in me too. I don't have to think hard to remember when this shift happened, when I changed. *I know.*

I stopped yelling and started laughing the moment I told Bob I loved him.

There is nothing I lack or need or want. My life is full. I'm content. I'm healed.

Until….

One night, I'm startled awake by the sound of my name being called. The voice is clear and it is loud. I sit up in bed in a panic. Scott is still sleeping next to me. Maggie, in her bed on the floor, is awake and alert. She seems to have heard it too. But I see no one else in my room. I wait and listen. I swear I can hear a distant, soft knocking too. My heart is racing, my breath quickening. It's been years since a bump in the night has scared me.

This "bump" is different.

I hold my breath waiting for another sound, waiting to hear if my name will be called again. The knocking continues…I can even feel it. Wondering where it's coming from, I focus in on it. It isn't coming from the door to my bedroom. It isn't coming from the front door to my house. This sound…it seems to be coming from…*inside* of me. I glance at Maggie. Her head is down. She's resting. She's not worried.

Since I no longer allow fear to dictate my emotions, I lie back down too and try to calm myself. I close my eyes and center in on the sensation that is pulsating through me. The knocking has softened to a tapping and is now in pace with my heartbeat. I breathe with the rhythm. The tapping, my heart, my breath become slow and steady…slow and steady. A wave of peace comes over me.

I'm so calm that I almost fall back to sleep. I almost forget about my name being called. Suddenly, I become aware of a presence in my room. My eyes pop open, my heart starts to race again. I look around and see no one. I see no silhouette. I see no threat. But whatever *this* is that woke me up, that knocked on my heart, is here in my bedroom. I can feel its energy. I freeze…waiting…waiting for it to present itself to me. I hear my name again.

"Cinda. It is time."

The words are softly whispered. Yet they are as clear as if spoken by the man lying next to me. The words are backed by a peace that is so nurturing and strong that a wave of love fills my insides. I know this energy, this voice. *It is the voice that saved me.* I trust this voice, this invisible force…*with my life.*

So, I listen as it speaks again.

"It is time."

This message is backed by an expectation, a knowing that I understand without needing to be told. I take in a deep breath—the kind of breath one takes right before picking up a heavy load…*I'm tired of heavy loads.* The breath is filled with a realization, a comprehension… an apprehension. I let out a long sigh.…

It IS time.

On that magical night, years ago, this same voice, this energy, guided me through my mystical healing. All my fear and anxiety cleared in that moment. I had thought…I had hoped…that my recovery was complete.

But this presence is not going to let me rest. I'm not to take for granted the grace I was given. More is being asked of me. I'm not to deny it any longer.

I'm being awakened.

It is calling to me.

It is time.

"How?" I silently ask.

"Look for the signs."

Signs…messages…insights…. I've learned a thing or two about signs and symbols in the past few years. So, I understand what this means. This invisible force is suggesting that I go back in time to find the signs and decipher the messages that were there for me during the days around the attack—up to today.

This will be the second time I revisit my past. The first, when I was in my 30s and experiencing emotional trauma and physical distress, led to my ritual of healing. Now, I am being asked to go back again, but this time to observe from the unique perspective of knowing both the trauma and the healing.

I can do this.

I request that this energy guide and support me once more. I have faith that this invisible force will keep me emotionally and mentally safe as I revisit the horror of those two months. Perhaps there *is* more for me to understand about the violence of the attack, about the trauma I experienced, about the sacred ritual of love.

I will search out and decipher the signs. I will document what I find. Then…I will share my story.

I'm awake. I've heard the calling. I'm answering it.

I say, *"Yes."*

Yes!

Chapter 2

MY SOCIAL CHANGE

I've said "Yes" to the voice that awakened me. I've made a commitment to look for the signs that were present before, during and after the attack. I've made a commitment to revisit my painful past. I've made a commitment to document and then share what I find. Where do I begin? Where do I look? How do I remember what I've tried so hard to forget?

Looking back over the last 18 years I see why I'm being asked to do this now. It is as if I've been prepared for this journey. From the time my children were young to the present, I've taken up the hobby of writing. I've written children's stories. I've messed around with potential novels. I've expanded my spiritual beliefs, education and understanding. I've become deeply interested in angels, archangels and guardian angels. I've become passionate about the environment. And I've even mastered social media.

My mastery of social media reaches its tipping point back in May of 2010. My care and concern for the environment is escalated when videos of an oil leak in the Gulf of Mexico fill up my news feed. I watch in disgust as hundreds of thousands of gallons of oil spew into the bottom of the ocean. I watch in agonized disgust as sea life and animals get drenched in life-threatening poison. I watch in total disgust as politicians and petroleum corporations refuse to take ownership.

I watch in complete *disgust* as no one seems to do anything to stop it! I'm sickened—*sickened.*

An underwater camera set up near the leak shows a constant stream of oil seeping into the gulf. I stare at the screen in horror. I'm horrified because what I see isn't oil—it's blood. I see our Mother Earth hemorrhaging...*dying.* The leaders—*our* leaders, the government—*our* government, and the oil tycoons' lack of concern or regard or attempt to save HER fuels a sense of urgency, a sense of activism in me that I've never felt before.

I scream at my computer screen, *"If SHE dies, we all die. Don't you bastards see that?"*

HER suffering apparently doesn't matter. SHE doesn't matter. I see a parallel...a parallel in how Mother Earth and women have been treated for eons with disgrace, disrespect and disregard.

The world needs to be made aware that actions matter...matter to our survival!

When any woman, any mother suffers, we all do.

Once a victim of a violent crime myself—I sympathize, I empathize with Mother Earth.

Years ago, I walked away from that locked blue door leaving a criminal behind it. I did nothing then. I won't do *that* again. I'm no longer a victim, and I can't watch as another is victimized, especially if it's our ultimate Mother.

When any woman, any mother, suffers, we all do.

For the first time in my life I am inspired into action for something greater than myself.

But what do I do? What can I do? I can't afford to fly down to Florida and help clean up the mess. I don't know how to stop the leak. I write my senators and representatives...but this doesn't feel like enough.

Every night when I go to bed, I hope for inspiration. Every night I chant the words, I feel the words, I fall asleep to the words branded in my thoughts. Every night I want to scream out so the world can hear them too!

"When any woman, any mother, suffers...we all do!"

Some nights these words keep me awake. They begin to create a life of their own...a rhythm...a pounding...that repeats over and over.

When any woman...pound, pound...any mother...pound, pound... suffers...pound...we all do.

The drumming is soft but strong.

One night, along with the drumming, I hear whispering. The whispering grows louder and louder.

"Do you feel it? Do you feel it?"

The single whisper combines with other voices...women's voices. I hear them. I feel them. They are coming to life. They are giving me a message. They are demanding...demanding that their message be given a voice. The message grows and expands until it's too big, too much for me to keep inside. I spring out of bed, rush downstairs and with determination to keep up, I write.

A few minutes later, I set the pen aside, pick up the paper and read. I read words that I don't remember writing. I read words that are so powerful they make me weep. I read the words of a thousand plus women coming together, roaring to save each other, their families and their planet. I read the message given to me from Mother Earth.

I title it "ROAR!"

The words have strength and power and a rhythm that is like nothing I've ever read. This short story is a parable, a poem, a declaration, a reclamation, a lesson for all of us. With their feet planted, grounded in the earth, the women declare, "NO MORE!" and "ENOUGH!" By the end of the story, the world shifts on its axis and turns toward the light and power of women. The lesson, the message is clear: *Because of the action of women, the world is changed for the better.* Then all becomes quiet, peace is restored and all is well.

I share "ROAR!" with an author friend of mine. He tells me through his tears that I need to share it, and share it now. Without another thought, I post it as a "note" on Facebook and within hours it gets shared across the globe...in days it goes viral. People from around the world ask if they can make "ROAR!" part of their rituals, part of their discussion groups, post it in their personal and professional blogs, turn it into a stage production. It even gets translated into different languages.

I'm asked to create a workshop around the essence of "ROAR!" and the energy of "NO MORE!" and "ENOUGH!" I'm invited to travel across the northwest as a professional facilitator and speaker. I'm even queried about hosting my own internet TV show titled, "ROAR!"

My tool for activism becomes my pen, my keyboard—a powerful yet peaceful way to make a difference. Whether it makes a difference in getting the oil leak plugged, the beaches cleaned, the animals treated and released, I don't know. But I do know that the message I received and shared resonates with others across the globe. I do know that women will not sit in silence anymore.

NO MORE!

A few months later, requests to write for a variety of online magazines and websites come my way. I contribute monthly articles and they get published. My professional life takes on a new course as words become my focus.

I continue to use social media to share and promote my writings, my inspirations, my activism through words. I make connections with people across the globe. My reality surpasses any dreams that I've had for myself.

Then in the fall of 2014, around the same time that that voice woke me up and gave me the message to write my story, I begin to feel a gentle spiritual nudge to make a "social" change. Every time I'm online—on a social media site—I hear a soft voice giving me a cryptic message.

"Like a Band-Aid, Cinda."

I sense that I'm being told to disconnect from social media and do it quickly—like one pulls a Band-Aid

But I have no desire to be disconnected. Why would I want to stop something that has brought me so much happiness and success?

I ignore the message.

But I can't ignore how I feel. Every time I turn on a social media site—a wave of nausea comes over me. My body is even telling me to listen. But instead, I swallow down the queasiness and keep scrolling.

Ignoring the message doesn't work.

I should know better. I should pay attention. I should listen. Something is being asked of me. I'm pretty sure it has to do with the commitment I made to look for the signs and write my story.

In December of 2014, I type out the following message on my page: *"Heads up to all those in my FB land, I am deactivating my account. I have a book or three to write and I have become painfully aware that I spend more time reading other people's words than writing my own. It is toooooo much of a distraction. My editor is waiting, Cinda"*

I leave this message up for 48 hours. The response and support from my friends and followers is tremendous. Two days later, with apprehension and a bit of dread, I click the mouse's arrow on the deactivation button. The screen goes blank and instantly the dread is replaced with freedom.

I swear I can hear a party of angels cheering me on.

Yet, I continue to procrastinate. I struggle with my writing. I struggle with inspiration. I struggle with motivation. I try to bargain with the voice to let me get back onto social media.

"If I'm not giving my community daily updates, how will they follow what I'm doing? How will I create anticipation for my project?" I ask.

"You will practice what you believe and know to be true," it silently responds.

"How will I promote my book once it's done? Wouldn't it be better and serve me more if I stayed on social media?"

"It will not be you that promotes your work. Others will do it for you."

The withdrawal from social media isn't the only thing that's slowing me down. Reliving my story isn't easy. It isn't fun. It isn't enjoyable. It's an uncomfortable and frightening ride. Journeying through time is consuming, both emotionally and physically. At times, I find myself avoiding it with a vengeance. Then with reluctance, I turn back to the keyboard and force out a sentence or two or three. Sometimes a chapter is written. Sometimes a chapter is thrown away. Most times I stare at the computer and fight with the voice.

For five months, I commit to adding a page or more a day. Then tragedy strikes. In the middle of 2015, in the middle of the book writing process, I lose my father to cancer. Grief stops me in my tracks. But it isn't just the grief that halts my progress. The pain I feel is in the realization that he won't be here. He won't be here to support me. He won't be here to encourage me. He won't be here to celebrate with me when I'm done. He's been part of every big event in my life. He won't be here for this one.

I'm heartsick.

After two months of not writing, the nudging returns. It's time to pick up my pen, to start clicking at those keys, to keep writing the story. I sit with my fingers ready, my heart aching and my mind completely blank.

What will it take to fill this void? What is missing?

With a gasp, I realize what's missing. What's missing isn't a *what*… it's a *who*. And it isn't just one *who*. It's two…two who's.

Thom Redmond and Katie.

Chapter 3

MY DETECTIVE

To do justice to this story.... To tell the truth as I remember it happening.... To travel back in time and revisit the horror of October and November of 1981.... If I'm to do this awful job of remembering.... I can't do it alone.

I want, I need, Thom Redmond's support.

Assuming he's retired, I do an online search. I find a detective with the same name, who, years earlier, left Portland. He now works for a small county sheriff's department.

I send an email inquiry: *"Hello, I am inquiring to see if your Sgt. Thom Redmond is the same detective that was on my case in Portland during the early 1980s. If so, Detective Redmond was assigned to me after a man broke into my home and attacked me. Thom was my savior. I was 19 then, now in my early 50s. I'm writing about my experience and would like to talk to him. Feel free to pass on my email or phone if your Thom Redmond is mine. Thank you, Cinda"*

In case it's not the same Thom Redmond, I also email the Portland Police Bureau.

Immediately I receive emails from both police departments. The standard generic replies state that due to the multiple requests they receive, they will not be able to respond for many days.

I'm disappointed.

But then, to my surprise, within minutes another email comes through from Portland, telling me that Thom Redmond has retired. They have forwarded my email to him. A few minutes later, my computer dings again. An email comes through from the county sheriff's office.

"Thank you for your message. I have forwarded your e-mail to Sgt. Redmond. He is on vacation until next Monday. Thank you, T."

I squeal in delight. I can't believe they responded so quickly.

I immediately type back: *"I so hope HE is the same Thom Redmond. Thank you very, very much. Sincerely and with gratitude, Cinda."*

"Yes, it is the same Thom Redmond...and, he's still awesome!"

A few minutes later, my cell phone rings. The number is unfamiliar.

"This is Cinda."

"Cinda, this is Thom Redmond. I hear you're trying to get a hold of me."

I laugh. I giggle. I'm embarrassed at the thought that he's receiving messages from all over the place…while on vacation. Yet, he calls.

I am talking to my detective again.

"Thom, thank you. Thank you for calling me back."

To help him remember me, I fill him in on a few minor details of our old case and the last time he and I met.

"I remember our last visit…but right now, my memory isn't so great. Most days I can't even remember what I had for lunch," he laughs.

I laugh too, because I can't stop smiling.

My detective!

"So, Cinda, what can I do for you?"

"I've decided to write about the incident and how I recovered. I wanted to reach out to you because you're a major part of my story. I'm hoping, if you don't mind, if I can ask you questions along the way? It's also important that I get your permission to write about you."

"Tell me more about your case. Let's see if it sparks some brain cells."

I tell him more.

"Oh, yes. I'm starting to remember now…the guy lived under a bridge…or so he told you. You gave me some updated information when we met last. I believe I followed through on it, but it didn't pan out."

"Yes! Yes. That's right."

He remembers!

"I have the gift you gave me from our last meeting. It's traveled and changed offices with me. It goes wherever I go. Currently, it's on my bookshelf in my office next to a statue my son gave me from China and a Matchbox toy of a Portland Police car."

"Really?"

"When people ask me about it, and they do, I try to do justice to the story. I tell them what the buffalo and the arrowhead stand for. That it was given to me as a thank you gift from a woman, even though I never caught her perpetrator."

He continues, "You know, Cinda, I've worked on multiple homicides. I have about an 88 percent success rate of catching those criminals. Every now and then, but very seldom, do I receive a thank you from the victim or his or her family. Nor do I expect one. I'm just doing my job. Those whom I've failed, like yourself, those sometimes haunt me. I'm frustrated I couldn't catch that creep for you. I still don't feel worthy of your gift, but it stays with me as a reminder. I thank you again."

"I was young and afraid and stupid, making it difficult for you to do your job back then. I don't blame you at all. I honestly believe that I could NOT have made it through those weeks without your support and protection. THAT is what mattered then and still matters now. I don't care about Bob anymore."

When we finish the phone call, I'm filled with enthusiasm to get back to my story. He's given me permission to write about him and to call or email with questions.

With Thom Redmond by my side again, I can do this. I can write my story.

My phone buzzes with a text. Thom Redmond has sent me a picture of the shelf in his office. Next to a Chinese lion statue and a Portland Police Matchbox car is the carved buffalo with an arrowhead and a turquoise stone on its back. My heart swells with gratitude. I make the picture my phone's screensaver.

Next. . .find Katie.

Chapter 4

MY ROOMMATE

I begin my search for Katie. Since I've lost her contact information, I do a search via Scott's social media account and find her. I send her a private message.

"Katie, this is actually Cinda. I'm no longer on FB, so I'm hijacking Scott's account to connect with you. I would love to see you! Currently, I'm writing a book about the attack back when you and I were living together. I've come to realize that I can't do this without you. I'm back in contact with my detective. He's tried to find my case file, but fears it's been shredded. So, all I have to go with are my snapshot memories. Your take on that night and the days that followed are important to me (just as your support and stability for me during that time was). We sure went through it together. I miss you my friend, hope you're well. Love, Cinda"

I give her my email and my phone number. I click send and cross my fingers that it reaches her sooner rather than later.

Within a day, my phone buzzes in my pocket. I have a text message from an unknown number.

"Hi Cinda, this is Katie. Of course, I would love to see you and help in any way with your recall of events and visit while you're writing. Let me call you later."

When we do talk, the sound of her voice triggers memories that come flooding back so fast I can hardly talk. Once I gather myself, I invite her to join me the following week at a cabin Scott and I own along the Columbia River.

"It's only a 45 minute drive from Portland. I'm taking that week, using it as a getaway, as a chance to focus on my writing. I'd love it if you could join me for a day!"

She agrees.

After hanging up the phone, I quickly write out an outline of all the mental snapshots I have that include her. What does she remember? Will she recall the events in the same way I do? My goal is to compare her version to mine. I want us to reconstruct together *that* night and the days that followed and be unanimous in our playback.

On the day of our meeting, I'm so eager I can hardly sit still. When she pulls into the driveway of the cabin, I race outside to meet her. I bounce with excitement and impatience as I wait for her to emerge from her car.

There she is, after all these years. Katie!

We hug and breathe each other in. She looks and sounds just like she did all those years ago. Time folds back upon itself. We are 53, 33 and 19 at the same time. I'm overcome with love for this woman, this mother, this girl, this friend who shares my history. I feel my heart expand around all of us…all we've been…all we've become.

She's here to help me. She's here to help me remember.

We sit down and make small talk, but time is precious. We only have a few hours to get through my list of questions and compare notes about our shared hell.

"Katie, I thought that I would start with my healing," I say as I take over the conversation. "It makes sense to start with the positive before we plow into the frightening. I don't want you to think that I've been wallowing in self-pity, victimhood or fear for all these years."

I pause to take in a breath and take in HER. Her look is patient, kind and supportive.

She hasn't changed.

I continue, "I'm not familiar with your religious or spiritual beliefs. So…in no way am I trying to push mine onto you. I just want to tell you what happened, exactly how it did. Then we can go backwards in time from there."

She nods in thoughtfulness and assures me that she's open to all ways. I tell her about my emotional state just prior to being guided into and through the sacred ritual. In detail, I share what took place and how it ended with me telling Bob I loved him.

When I'm through, I pause. I can see she's thinking deeply about something. I'm curious to know if she doesn't believe me, or may even be disgusted by what I did or said to Bob.

I mean…saying THAT to a man who tried to kill me IS crazy.

"Cinda, wow…that's an amazing story. I can't imagine…. But, before you go any further, on my way here, I was trying to remember everything I could about that house and the time around the attack. There is one thing that I need to ask you. Do you remember me being naked all the time? I mean, I was *nay-ked*. We lived in that house for weeks without any blinds! What was I thinking? Do you remember?"

"Yes, yes! That's one of the questions on my list. I hoped that I remembered it correctly."

"I mean…I'm not an exhibitionist. I never have been. I just feel more comfortable in my skin than I sometimes do in clothes. I still do!"

I giggle in delight. She laughs too. The seriousness is gone and we are like two 19-year-old girls again, innocent and silly. I'm so relieved that she remembers her nudity and the lack of blinds just as I do.

Her voice softens, "I just wonder…I wonder if it might have been different, if I had been more careful, would Bob have still broken into our house?"

I stop giggling. I stop smiling. She isn't laughing anymore. Her face is serious, thoughtful, worried.

"Oh, Katie…are you wondering if Bob broke into the house because of you? I don't believe THAT for a minute! I don't believe that things would've been different if you had walked around in a bathrobe! Remember how our house was perched high off the ground because of the steep hill it was built on? That basement underneath? Remember that large vacant field off to the side? Without blinds on our windows, yes, perhaps we were fish in a bowl, but if anyone, like Bob, wanted to peer inside, they had to work for it. You know…when I think back to our time together, I remember admiring you. I was so shy, so gangly and awkward. Your habit of walking around the house in complete naked confidence…well…that was awe-inspiring. Seriously."

"I appreciate that, but I'm not so sure I agree with you."

She looks at her lap, deep in thought. I give her time to process. This can't be easy for her…bringing up things from our shared and scary past. I can see that she is struggling to say what's on her mind. She starts speaking again in a soft voice.

"Another thing I remembered on the way here was when we met up again. I'm not sure if you will remember this like I do. You started talking about that night…the night of the attack. You were telling me about what Bob said to you. You told me that Bob said he'd come into the wrong room."

I nod. What happened afterwards is imprinted in my mind. Will she freeze like she did last time? I hold my breath.

"You leaned over, took my hands in yours, looked me in the eye and said, 'Aren't we lucky that didn't happen?'"

She looks right at me.

"Yes…I did say that…I do remember."

"I shut down on you. I put up a wall. What you said back then scared me. It scared me to my core and I couldn't talk about it anymore."

"Yeah, I regretted having said anything. I'm so sorry I scared you. But Katie, I really meant it then, and I mean it more now. We ARE so very lucky that he came into my room and not yours."

The emotions are so thick in the room I can hardly breathe. I lean forward, looking in her eyes, willing her to not be scared anymore.

"Katie...the reason I think Bob was meant to come into my room is because, in some strange way, I was prepared for it. When I was 14, I read an article in *Cosmopolitan* titled, 'How to Say No to a Rapist and Survive.' Somehow...that night...I used everything I had read. It saved my life. I was prepared. You weren't."

"Are you kidding me? I didn't know that! That's remarkable."

"I know...right? A few years ago, I remembered the article. I went to the library and actually found the magazine. I made copies of the article. It blew my mind when I held it again."

She nods her head in amazement, but has more to say.

"Do you remember my reaction when you first woke me up to tell me what happened? You knocked on my door. Word for word you said, 'Katie, wake up. I don't want you to panic, but a man broke into my room last night and tried to rape me. I'm OK, but the police are here. So, you might want to get up.'"

It's exactly what I remember saying to her.

"Then, when I realized what you were saying, I sat up in bed, totally freaked. I saw the policeman behind you. I remember his walkie-talkie being so loud and noisy. I started screaming and crying, almost out of control. And of course, I was naked!"

She tries to laugh. I try to laugh too, but it's not a laugh based on funny. Our laughter is coming from a place of awkwardness, of disbelief and of the crazy strangeness of the topic we are sharing. There is a hint of remembered fear too...as her question takes us temporarily back to that moment.

"Yes, I do remember your reaction. And...Katie...."

I stutter and hesitate to continue, but if I'm to write about this part in my story, I need her to hear it from me first.

"There is another reason...I believe...that it's lucky Bob broke into my room that night and not yours...it's...it's because when I screamed... *THAT*...is what set him off. That's when he attacked. That's when he became violent."

I pause...hoping she can digest what I'm trying to say. She slowly recites back what she's heard, trying to make sense of it.

"Because…if Bob had broken into my room that night…and I reacted the way I did when you woke me up…he may have…."

Katie's voice cracks. She's trying not to be emotional. But the realization that she's coming to is very real and very scary. It doesn't matter that it happened years ago. Right now, it feels like it happened yesterday. I hold my breath as I watch her. I fear that she might shut down again.

She doesn't.

Instead, she takes in a deep breath, looks at me and speaks with conviction.

"You asked, 'Aren't we lucky that that didn't happen?' I mean…who says that? Who says, 'Aren't we lucky that that didn't happen?' We weren't lucky. There is no 'we' in this luck you speak of, Cinda. There was no luck in Bob coming into your room that night. The luck is mine."

Katie can no longer hold back her tears. I grab a box of tissues and hand them to her. Emotion is welling up inside of me too, but tears don't flow from my eyes. I've been reliving that night for months now. I've had time to deal, she hasn't. The main emotion that's enveloping me is compassion. Compassion, gratitude and awe for this magnificent woman sitting in front of me.

We sit in silence, taking in the majestic, expansive view of the mighty Columbia River that is flowing past our front window. Nature calms us as we regroup. I can't believe the fortune and the coincidence. So far… Katie has been the one guiding our conversation. She has been the one bringing up the topics I was most worried about. She is the one being brave, being kind, being supportive.

She hasn't changed.

This meeting…it feels as if it's been taken over by magic. It feels as if Katie knew the questions before I asked them. All my concerns and insecurities about seeing her again and asking the tough questions are gone, floating away…down the river.

We spend a few more hours talking and sharing. We laugh, we remember and I take notes. When it's time for her to leave, we hug goodbye. I do my best to express how much I appreciate her visit, her time, her friendship and her permission to include her in my story.

With Katie's support, I'm ready to move forward…headed back in time.

I am ready to ride the current.

Like the river in front of me….

The flow is in motion.

Chapter 5

HOUSE OF SIGNS

I stand at the gate of our cabin and wave goodbye as Katie drives away. My love for her is immense, my gratitude even greater. I now have more information and, with that, more confidence to move forward with my writing. I walk back into the cabin, pour myself a glass of wine and raise the glass in toast to the magic that made this meeting happen.

Inspired to get to work, I grab a blank sheet of paper and draw out the floor plan of the house we rented, including the furniture. Even though it's a one-dimensional drawing, the house springs to life under my pen.

I sketch the tiled corner—that odd corner where a wood stove once sat. As I draw the hole in the wall where its stove pipe would have gone, I swear I can feel a breeze as if I'm standing right in front of it again. The breeze increases and swirls around me—like a portal, a vortex from that time period, beckoning me to take a closer look.

The image of the floor plan shifts as the memory of the actual house takes over in my vision. Instead of looking down at a piece of paper, I'm looking down upon the real house, back then, as if I've been transported back in time. Younger Katie materializes. She's standing in the kitchen, pouring iced tea into a pitcher. The younger me is helping her cut up cheese and placing crackers onto a round tray. *This is the day our mothers are coming to see the house!* Buffet, the gray tabby, is doing a ninja type move against his reflection in the full-length mirror.

Using this strange ability to view my past life from my current life reminds me of going back to visit the neighborhood in my 30s. I had to physically visit the place back then. Now I can view my life from this unique perspective. I was frightened and broken then...but not now. Now, the scenes develop through the eyes of a woman who has survived.

I've been told to look for signs, messages and insights that may have been present during that time. THIS is how I will look for them, from this perspective, from above, through this portal to the past.

Were there signs in our house?

Hovering over my drawing of the floor plan, I allow myself to be sucked deeper into the vortex, drifting above the house, searching for signs. Not sure what to be looking for, I ask for help.

"OK, you told me to look for signs. I'm looking. Show me."

I see them!

Like popcorn, signs pop up one by one and show themselves to me. There's 19-year-old Katie standing on the decrepit front porch with 19-year-old me. We're waiting for our mothers to arrive. Katie asks, "Any sign of them yet?"

How interesting to be looking for signs and hear this question being asked.

Another scene is illuminated. Katie tries to warn her mom about the broken step. Her mother trips on it and responds: "Well goodness, that's dangerous!"

Was this a sign, warning us of the danger in that house?

Bits of the house get lit up, as if by little spotlights. The house itself seems to be warning younger Katie and Cinda to be aware, to take notice, to pay attention. The spotlights first direct me to the outside of the house. The front step is falling apart, the paint on the deck is peeling. Then, they move inside and light up the hole in the wall, the torn linoleum, the dark and dank basement, the unsettling pile of clothes left behind.

Signs.

They are all are signs. Signs—that warn us the landlord doesn't care about his property. Signs—that he won't care about his tenants— *about us.*

I watch Katie push against the door and lock the deadbolt. The front door won't stay shut unless it's locked. I laugh now... *it's so obvious!* This sign, this metaphor screams that our house is not secure. This metaphor screams, "You MUST lock your door!" and that includes locking all the windows, *especially the one in the bathroom.* We missed the metaphor then, but I see it now.

Cars drive around our block in an endless line. I can smell the exhaust and hear the grinding gears all over again. All that dust and dirt and noise stirred up by the traffic can't possibly be healthy—physically, emotionally or energetically. I feel out of balance and out of sorts with the memory.

When young Cinda takes a bite of cheese, I taste the bitterness with her. But the exhaust isn't all that's causing the cheese to taste sour. Her body knows something isn't right. Her nerves and her stomach are trying to warn her. I'm aware now of how my body communicates with me, but didn't know to listen to it then.

Jimmy Buffett's song, "The Great Filling Station Holdup," blasts from the record player. I hum along with youthful Cinda as Jimmy sings the melody about wishing he was somewhere else, drinking a beer and about the holdup that cost him two long years.

Then, I really hear the lyrics and gasp. Could those words in Jimmy Buffett's song be a warning? Could they be telling Cinda that she should be somewhere other than where she is? Is it a premonition of a potential holdup coming? Because I know now that a *holdup* IS going to happen. It lasts three hours and will become an emotional prison, a trauma that will last her a lifetime.

Another scene gets illuminated. Cinda's mother is whispering to Katie's mom, "I don't like this. Not one bit, I don't. I just don't like the feeling of this place at all."

There it is. The biggest, most blatant sign and message....

Cinda purposely ignores her mother's comment, not recognizing the importance of the message. Instead of addressing the uneasiness her mother feels, Cinda raises her chin, sets her jaw tight and doesn't budge. I am angered by my younger self's stubbornness and want to reach down and flick her on the head, to tell her to pay attention. Her mother's uneasiness is a sign. Yet, I am also sympathetic...Cinda doesn't understand, she doesn't know about signs.

If Cinda had listened...everything might have been different.

An interesting thought occurs to me...just as I'm hovering above our house now...did our guardian angels do the same back then? Having studied angels, I imagine they do hover above...sending signs and messages to protect and warn us.

I can almost hear them saying, *"Here, hopefully they will see this...nope.... OK, maybe they will listen to this...nope. Maybe this will grab their attention...well, that didn't work either. Let's try the mother...surely the daughter will listen to her mother."*

I whisper to the invisible guardian angels who must have been throwing signs to Cinda and Katie, trying to grab their attention, *"Thank you for trying. They just didn't know."*

I know now.

Chapter 6

SIGNS AND STUPIDITY

Viewing my past from this multidimensional perspective is an awesome trick. I'm having a blast! Each day, I'm curious about what signs will get illuminated, what messages will be heard, what symbols will present themselves.

Today, I'm concentrating on my friendship with Katie. The two of us interacted and joked and shared our mutual space with ease. We acted and felt as if we were mature, smart and invincible adults. Instead, we were young, naive and vulnerable kids. With that came a touch of stupidity. In our young minds, there was nothing to fear. The idea that danger could lurk just outside and in the shadows...didn't even dawn on us.

I allow myself to again be sucked back into the vortex of time. In her bedroom, Cinda grabs a box of tacks and starts to hang up sheets over her windows. Despite how much she wants to appear confident, mature and brave on the outside, on the inside she's painfully shy, awkward and insecure. Her bare windows make her feel apprehensive. Her apprehension is telling her, warning her, to take care and protect herself. Without understanding why, she responds to that feeling. I wish I could reach through time and demand that she does it for the rest of the house too.

I imagine the angels saying, "Well, she got part of the message. Maybe there's still hope."

Looking down at Katie's bedroom, I see that there is nothing covering her windows. This doesn't bother her, and therefore it doesn't bother Cinda either. Katie has a free spirit which is backed by a solid and practical side. Everything she says and does makes sense. She has an uncanny ability to take charge and Cinda lets her. Cinda trusts Katie's opinions because she trusts Katie.

Katie isn't concerned about the uncovered, naked windows in her bedroom or the living room. Nor is she concerned about her own nakedness. Therefore, Cinda convinces herself of the same.

Perhaps Cinda trusted Katie more than she trusted herself.

I relive with young Cinda the many times people tell them to put blinds up. The first warning comes from Scott when Cinda catches someone looking through the window while they are on the phone talking. When she screams, Scott yells at her to close her blinds—*which don't exist.* Bob attacks the next day. Other warnings come from the policeman who arrives right after Cinda called, her detective who scolds both girls, and then her father who insists on getting the windows covered. Finally, blinds get hung.

This message, which was important enough to be given by multiple people, was a sign. They disregard it.

If they had listened...?

I can now understand the symbolism in the word "blinds." They were *blind* to the danger and unknowingly allowed a predator to monitor them.

There is symbolism in the word "naked" too. They had naked windows, Katie ran around naked. Cinda buried her head in the sand of denial and pretended the emperor had clothes. The word symbolizes just how bare, exposed, visible and vulnerable they really were.

As I focus on this time when Bob spies on young Cinda, I see that this itself is a sign. This sign is warning Katie and Cinda that they are in *potential* danger without being in actual danger. This warning is the same as an alarm of an impending tornado being sounded, but they do not run for cover, or cover up their windows. Katie and Cinda continue swimming innocently and stupidly around in the fishbowl of their house. All the while, a stalking predator is outside monitoring the right time to pounce.

Katie and Cinda didn't recognize the threat. They ignored the warning, and missed an opportunity to protect themselves. If they had been smart, they would have called the police. The prowler would have seen that they aren't people to mess with.

Instead, the girls do nothing. The stalking predator can see that they are easy prey.

I see it all now...a series of three events, three signs that progressively get more serious. The events are set up and designed to warn and save Cinda and Katie. The first sign—Cinda's mother's intuitive feeling of the house—is meant to grab her attention. Since that doesn't work, a second sign—Bob peeking in the window—is meant to trigger the girls into action. But the girls don't respond to this warning. A third sign—people urging them put up window blinds—is meant to protect them from Bob's spying. Because they still don't recognize the danger, or pay attention to the three signs, the devastating event happens—Bob attacks.

The signs were there. The girls were stupid. They ignored those warnings. Paying attention to them would have made things different... *very, very different.*

I won't ignore them again.

Chapter 7

SIGNS OF INSTINCT

Another day, another sign. I'm anxious to see what I learn from my past today. I've mastered traveling back in time by closing my eyes to visualize the scene I want to focus on. I sit in front of my computer, close my eyes and transport myself to the dark October night when 19-year-old Cinda is walking home from the bus. This is *the* night and I want to see if there are any warnings or signs.

As Cinda walks, she feels the chill of Halloween in the air. Here, in the warmth of my present moment, I wrap my arms around my body—sharing the cold. Something other than the weather is causing her uneasiness. Her unease is getting triggered by her senses...*almost animalistic*...instinctual. Cinda's instinct is generating a warning that something isn't right—something is potentially threatening. The chill she feels is generated by fear—her fear is visceral, an attempt to caution her that danger is nearby...*a lion crouched and hiding*. Her instinct is telling her body to run for safety.

Instinct is nature's way of helping animals survive. Cinda's primal instinct is sending out sensors, catching a feeling of energy in the air that's different. Her instinct may even discern the slightest smell traveling on a breeze, or hear a distant sound that isn't normal. A warning should be registering in her brain. Her body should be activated into action. Unfortunately, Cinda has never learned to interpret her instinct's warnings.

I yell at her through time, begging her to listen.

"The lion is coming!"

From this multidimensional perspective, I search the neighborhood for Bob in the bushes, along the sidewalks, the streets. He's well hidden, but I know he's there.

Cinda rushes toward the safety of the house. But once safely inside, she ignores her senses, her instinct, leaving both her and Katie vulnerable.

I move my vision forward into the night when Bob enters Cinda's room. The 34-year-old Cinda is there too. When Bob lunges and Cinda screams, we all three scream together. The scream is primal. Her instinct has emerged.

Survival is all that counts. In an instant, with no time to think, Cinda turns into the animal that she is. My body is alive with it, both right now and back then. All her senses are awakened. She feels the pressure of Bob's hands over her face. She tastes blood from her cut cheeks. She can't breathe. Her primitive need to survive goes into overdrive, preparing her to fight.

Watching this take place and feeling it again is difficult, painful and frightening. I struggle with my emotions now, just as the younger Cinda struggles under the weight of Bob's hands. I feel as if I'm being pinned, trapped and smothered all over again. My current day instinct for survival is kicking in. My heart is racing, my breath is coming in gasps, my stomach muscles are tightening. But instead of preparing me to fight, like it's doing for Cinda in the setting below, it's prepping me to run...run away from this writing, from this remembering, from this horror.

I bring myself back to the present space...willing the memory to fade, to loosen its grasp on me. I shake my arms, breathe deeply, and then decide to stand up and run in place...*perhaps this will release the need to really run away.*

Could running away be a pattern of mine? Since I'm writing about instinct and fight or flight...it's worth exploring. I search for examples during those two months when I did flee, instead of remaining and fighting. It doesn't take long to find some.

An example is found when Cinda sees the dog in front of the blue house. She is too afraid to respond when the dog urges her to look up and see who's calling her name. She pretends she doesn't hear and quickly leaves for the bus.

Another example is when Bob follows Cinda onto the bus headed downtown. Her instinct tells her not to go to work but to The Galleria. She races off the bus and hides in the candy store.

On the day they are moving out, after following the cat's paw prints and seeing Bob, she runs away from the blue house. She flees again when she drives away in a panic. Cinda chooses not to tell Katie, Perry or Scott who are helping her move. She doesn't even think to call her detective. All she can think of is to get away from the neighborhood...*and the memories...* leaving them all...far, far behind her.

Throughout the two-month ordeal, when Cinda depends on her instinct, options for survival are generated. This causes her to make fast, impulsive, reactive choices. Relying on her instinct gives her tunnel vision, where she can see, feel, sense what is needed in that moment…fight, run, hide… She makes choices, *perhaps some choices are better than others.* Regardless of how impulsive and naive Cinda's responses are, she survives…her instinct helps save her.

No matter how real and painful these past memories feel now…I cannot let my instinct dictate or control my present circumstances….

My body and my mind seem to not know the difference in the timelines.

My body and mind need to realize that I am currently not in danger, that I am safe, that all is well.

My instinct needs to back off and let me face these fearful memories.

My instinct needs to release its grip.

My instinct needs to allow me to keep moving forward—to follow the river of my memories—to move forward in this exploration of my past.

Forward!

Chapter 8

SIGNS OF INTUITION

I'm not having fun anymore...*this sucks*. The memories are too real. My body isn't responding well to the negative energy this brings up. I can't risk the trauma returning. Concerned that this might be emotionally, mentally and physically harmful, I talk myself off the ledge and back onto the floor of real-time reality. After all, it's *just* a memory...an awful memory that can't touch me now—*I. AM. SAFE.*

Determined to keep moving forward, I take in a deep breath, hold it and jump once again into the pool of my memories. I swim back to the night Bob attacks. Cinda is pinned under the pressure of his hands but has stopped fighting, stopped struggling. She is no longer a frightened animal trying to survive. Something has shifted within her. *Something changes her....*

To understand this change, this shift, I connect with Cinda's emotions to sense with her as it happens. I feel it. It is subtle, smooth and silent, but there *is* an internal shift. Something other than Cinda's instinct is surfacing— part of her, yet separate. *Something* begins to guide her to behave in unusual and unexpected ways.

I know now what has surfaced.

It's her intuition!

Her intuition takes control away from her primal instinct. The transition is flawless. She barely realizes it's happening, except that her panic eases. She calms down and everything slows down. Although fear is still present, this calmness allows space for a different plan to be formulated. She's almost logical about it and makes a mental assessment of the situation— she can't breathe...she needs to get Bob off...she can't scream or fight or he'll respond with more violence. Her intuition silently brings her the answers she is seeking. She responds by following the thoughts and ideas that come to her.

"Tap on his hands. Distract him. Talk about the braces, the rubber bands. Offer coffee, steak. Give him a name.... Memorize what he looks like.... Invite him into bed...."

Cinda's animalistic instinct, which triggered her into action, is still present. I can feel it keeping her alert and hyper-focused. But her life is dependent on listening and following her intuition.

The two systems, instinct and intuition, are working together.

Cinda faces the biggest, most terrifying challenge of her life and because of her instinct and her intuition, she handles it. She survives it.

I am in awe of her, of the 19-year-old me. Intuition or not, I am blown away by her bravery, her courage, her smarts, her level-headed thinking. Days after, years after, she carries that bravery and stoicism out into the world. But as quickly as I feel pride, it is replaced with heartache. My heart bleeds for her too. Inside, she remains a frightened, lonely child—*for she was just a child.*

Writing this last paragraph, I feel a spiritual, intuitional, nudging, probing, almost an elbowing to view 19-year-old Cinda with a fresh set of eyes.

"Do you see how alone she is? Alone. . .in her agony." my intuition silently asks.

Alone? Cinda has the best roommate in the world, an amazing detective, police are everywhere, parents and a boyfriend who call, check in, visit. My intuition is suggesting that that isn't enough—that she is very much alone.

Slowly, I begin to see it…understand it…get it. I comprehend what my intuition wants me to recognize. It's bigger and more awful than being alone….

Isolation.

The attack leaves Cinda…*isolated.*

The violence of that night happened to *her.* She is the only one who knows what really happened, what it really felt like, what she really experienced. No matter in what detail she shares, there is no one, anywhere, who can or will ever truly know what is in *her* head, *her* body, *her* memories…*her nightmares.* Throughout the years that follow, she internally suffers...*alone.*

Alone. Lonely. Isolated.

I know.

I know...*now.*

She does not need to carry the burden of that night all by herself… *not anymore.*

My intuition encourages me to look even deeper—deeper into myself, into Cinda. What appears...breaks my heart even more…. I thought the 19-year-old Cinda was gone, all grown up, now living within and part of my 50-something-year-old self. I thought she was just someone I knew, someone I was, a long time ago. I thought she was someone to be observed and written about but that she no longer mattered, not today.

I thought that after the ritual of healing Cinda went through, that she was, I was, fully and completely restored. But that healing was meant for and occurred for the 34-year-old Cinda, curing her PTSD. My intuition tells me that I have forgotten to repair the younger one, the younger me.

The purpose of this process is now clear. I'm to bring 19-year-old Cinda back to life, to give her a voice. I am meant to relive the past with her, for her...for the sole and soul purpose of seeing, hearing, understanding and respecting what she went through. Her story, her truth, will be—*must be*—shared, told and heard by me, by my family, by others. For she does matter.

My intuition says that it is time to heal 19-year-old Cinda.

It is time to heal all of me.

Chapter 9

SIGNS FROM CHESS

Sitting down to write again, I want to keep in mind the voice and needs of younger Cinda. I want to make sure that her story...that she...is honored. I want her to feel and trust that she is no longer alone. Using this multidimensional trick of being in both the present and the past simultaneously, I work on bringing the 19-year-old me back to life by witnessing what is happening.

In a strange way, I feel like a god in my own life. I feel like a god looking down, watching a chess game being played. The chessboard is unfolding below me, the pieces are getting lined up. I can see both sides of the checkerboard. Cinda is a key player, a player in a game she didn't choose to play. Her pieces are white. She is playing a devious and skilled opponent. Bob's pieces are black. The game is a battle—a battle between the white queen and the black king—light versus dark. In this dangerous, frightening game, her very life is at stake.

With this chess analogy in mind, I rewind my mental movie back to the beginning. Bob moves the first pawn when he peeks into Cinda's window. Her pawn moves when she sees him, but is captured when she and Katie do nothing. Bob moves another pawn when he follows Cinda home that October night. Her pawn is captured when she hides in her house.

Each movement of Bob's chess pieces is a signal, a warning that an evil game is at play. Each move is a sign, a chance, for Cinda to respond. Each move is an opportunity for her to plan a strategic countermove. Unfortunately, Cinda is blind to this game. She is not aware that a strategy is needed to win, to stay safe. The queen remains in the center of the back row, oblivious to what is happening around her. She sees nothing. She knows nothing. She does nothing.

The game continues. Pieces from both sides are moved. Cinda's pawns are captured. The queen is exposed, allowing Bob to make the boldest move of all. He enters Cinda's home, the white queen's territory.

Cinda's rook, Buffet, moves in to protect and sound an alarm. Bob captures her rook when he shuts the cat out of the room. She finally wakes up to the danger. Her first response isn't very queenly—she screams. The black king moves in for the capture.

Her quick-thinking tricks her opponent. Bob lets his guard down. He loses his pawns as she distracts him with offers of coffee, tea, steak. He loses his rooks and his knights when he tells her of his escape plan, that he lives under a bridge, that he's a Vietnam veteran, when he agrees to be called Bob. He gains his momentum back by getting her to tell him her name, where she works. She holds her ground and memorizes his appearance.

With every lunge, every attempt at suffocation, and the final attempt at strangulation, he gains a stronger position, a stronger hold. He's about to win the game. Cinda risks a move that will save the queen…or entrap her. Her bold move stalls Bob long enough for her other rook, Buffett again, to come into play. The game goes into a draw, a stalemate. Bob forfeits when he runs away.

But…the match isn't over.

The next game is set up. This time Cinda makes the first move with her pawn, when she calls the police. Her knight pieces move to surround and protect her when the detective and other police officers show up. Divine interventions, angelic support, are the queen's bishops. The black king cannot get to her. He tries, he intimidates, he spies, he follows, but he never again attacks. The white queen's team is strong.

Cinda is strong. Cinda proves to be emotionally and intellectually smart—smarter and stronger than she thought she'd ever have to be. She appears to have beaten her opponent at his own game.

I, on the other hand, know different. I know that Cinda is living in constant fear and insecurity. Her strength is a disguise, a front, a lie that she shows the world. She knows the truth…the game.

The black king almost won the first game.

The queen was almost captured in the second game.

The match goes on….

Chapter 10

SIGNS AND STRATEGIES

I stop writing and think about this concept, this analogy of a chess game. In chess, each player comes to the gameboard with a preplanned strategy of how they expect to win. The players plan moves and countermoves two or three turns in advance, depending on their opponent's tactic. If I take this game analogy and incorporate it into the event of the attack, could it have been possible that prearranged strategies were given to me ahead of time? Could they have included both defensive and offensive moves?

I think of 14-year-old Cinda reading the 1976 *Cosmopolitan* article, "How to Say No to a Rapist (and Survive)." I can see the importance of that moment...this article must be a predestined offensive strategy for Cinda, the white queen, to use to survive Bob's, the black king's, attack. Although she doesn't remember having read the article five years prior, she utilizes all the information she had read and it saves her life.

For fun, I search online, find and order a copy of the magazine on eBay. I scan the article again. Author Frederic Storaska advises the *Cosmopolitan* reader to stay as emotionally stable as you can. Treat the perpetrator with respect, as you would treat another "human being." Do not be viewed as a threat. Fake it until you can safely react. And be creative, use your imagination and good judgment.

Fast forward from 1976 to 1981. Cinda's at the orthodontist. He's cementing brackets to her back teeth. To correct her bite, every night she's required to wear six rubber bands connecting her upper and lower jaw.

Since I'm looking for predestined events, I know now the role these braces will play months later during the night of the attack. They tear into Cinda's cheeks. The pain and the taste of blood become a distraction. This distraction cuts into her frantic thoughts and her panic, bringing clarity and giving her time to plan a countermove.

I scroll forward through the mental video of my memories, searching for another predetermined strategy. Pausing at a scene, I chuckle...*of course*. Katie. When Cinda meets Katie, it seems so random. *But it isn't...*. They move to Portland together, they live through the attack together. Katie becomes *that* girl, that woman, that friend. She is Cinda's confidant, the saner person between them, the grounding agent of Cinda's soul, the backbone to her reality. Katie helps Cinda make it through to the other side...*to where I am now....*

So...I can tell my story.

This is strange...looking for events that seem prearranged. I almost miss one because it seems unimportant and trivial. Cinda's getting ready for bed. She forgoes wearing her usual pajama bottoms and T-shirt for the floor length, red sweatshirt-style bathrobe. The significance is that she has never worn this to bed before.

Even though Bob will use the robe as a weapon to strangle her, it will save her. Pajamas would have been difficult to remove, causing a commotion. Resisting would have meant more violence. Instead, she's able to remove the robe in one fluid motion, surprising and confusing Bob. His confusion causes him to stall and gives her time to strategize what move to make next. She may appear to be naked and vulnerable, but this moment gives Cinda the upper hand. She gains control.

The conversation I had with my aunt Nancy is forever imprinted on my heart and in my thoughts. She used her trauma to become an advocate and help victims of sexual assault and then help to train the Portland Police in rape victim sensitivity. I believe that her effort, her training, her experience, is the reason the police treated me with such respect and dignity.

The more I look back, the more I see, the more I am convinced that there *are* predestined, predetermined, prearranged events that take place prior to Bob entering Cinda's room that night. These events prepare, support and protect Cinda before, during and after the attack.

If this is true…then would it be safe to surmise that perhaps everything may have been arranged in advance—by some higher, mystical, invisible power? If so…there must be a purpose, a reason, an intention….

Could the purpose be…that the attack is predetermined, meant to happen…to me…because I am the one meant to speak of it?

Could the reason be…that I experience PTSD in order to arrive at the place of surrender leading to healing…because this healing is meant to be shared?

Could the intention be…that I am being asked to write this story…because I'm being asked to be the messenger?

At this point, I'm not sure I can answer these questions. But the possibility has my emotions swinging on a pendulum between being nauseated and intrigued, frightened and thrilled, confused and enlightened. Perhaps…the more I dive into these questions, the clearer the answers will become.

I'm starting to believe that the answer is…

Yes.

Chapter 11

SIGNS OF ANGELS

I'm fascinated and awed by what is getting revealed. Writing is fun again, every day scraping back the layers and finding the concealed treasures of my past. I had no idea there were so many hidden meanings, signs, set up to help me along the way. A two-part theme makes itself visible: protection and support. Prearranged or not...Cinda is protected and supported—*over and over and over.*

Protection is evident when Cinda is sitting naked and vulnerable in front of Bob. She's at his mercy. She's out of options and knows it. So, when he crawls across the bed like the predator that he is, she has no choice but to give him the impression that she's succumbing to his advances. She invites him under the covers. Something deep inside trusts that she will be safe. Her faith, fed by her intuition, guides her to take a risk—she's protected.

When the policeman shows up, needed protection arrives, so needed that he at first appears oversized. This continues as other officers come to help. Each officer...a knight in shining blue armor. Each officer... dedicated to apprehending and arresting Bob. Each officer...committed to protecting the young women.

My current study of angels helps me understand the role they played in protecting Cinda and Katie. Archangel Michael, or St. Michael, is known as the protector of God's children. He is also the angel of justice and strength and the patron saint for police officers. Those who can see him say his aura is blue and that he carries a sword. This may be one of the reasons why police officers' uniforms are traditionally blue.

Curious if other archangels might have played a role in my protection, I search for other potential encounters and find one when Cinda meets with Janet Frances.

Janet Frances's connection to an angel isn't surprising; she glows like one. Archangel Jophiel represents the beauty of God. This angel helps in resurrecting things that may be forgotten due to trauma, insecurities or fear, bringing them to the surface to be resolved. This amazing angel takes negative feelings and events and transforms them into the positive and lovely. She is surrounded in a bright pink or a golden yellow aura. I have no doubt Archangel Jophiel influenced Janet's gifts.

This influence continues years later, when I see Janet on TV and the memories are triggered of that horrendous night in 1981. Archangel Jophiel seems to be reaching out to me through Janet to help me look at the negative and guide me to transform it into the positive. Unfortunately, I resist the help and my PTSD is triggered, but eventually, it all leads toward my healing.

In another setting, I see the young man, wearing a pink apron, in the candy store where Cinda is hiding. He comes to her rescue. Archangel Ariel, the lioness of God, offers courage when fear overcomes the senses and bravery is needed. She's surrounded by a soft pink aura, resembling the man's pink apron. Ariel may have influenced this young man to offer courage and support to Cinda in that frightening moment.

Next, Cinda is walking to the bus after work. Her tension grows as she tries to avoid a pack of teenagers being rude and bullying people on the street. One of the punks leaves his pack and steps into her path. His actions are meant to threaten her, but she's tired of being scared and of being intimidated. She glares at him. He glares back. When their eyes connect, she is frozen in place. His eyes are the most astonishing green she has ever seen. Magic seems to happen for both in that shared moment. She's filled with a sense of peace and he backs down. He apologizes and she's given a chance to stick up for herself.

In the realm of angels, Archangel Raphael is known as the angel of healing. He presents himself by emanating the most magnificent green. This scenario seems to be created just for the sake of helping Cinda overcome her lack of confidence and feelings of unworthiness. The young man helps heal a part of her that felt invisible. When those eyes connect to hers, they seem to see into her. A sacred moment is shared between them.

Even now, I can still see and feel the impact of those green eyes.

Angels, especially archangels, are part of each person's support team. They sometimes work through others to offer emotional and/or physical assistance when needed. Being aware of this support makes me feel blessed by these magnificent beings.

I AM Blessed.

Chapter 12

SIGNS FROM ANIMALS

Learning and witnessing how angels may have worked through and with others to get messages and signs to Cinda and Katie brings joy to my heart. I have learned how isolated and alone Cinda felt in her fear and suffering, but knowing now that these loved-based entities were with her—*then, now and always*—brings me peace of mind.

I've felt like a god watching a chess game being played below me. The angels must look down and view things just as I am now during this writing process. I've seen the signs and messages that were delivered through music lyrics, through people's comments, through people being influenced by angels and now I'm looking at the animals. Angels can use animals to help get their messages across. My studying has taught me about spirit animals too. Spirit animals are like guardian angels but in animal form.

Angels use animals to reach Cinda multiple times. Buffett! Buffett— that wild and funny pest of a cat, that cat who hates men—isn't even Cinda's pet. Yet he tries his best to protect and warn her when Bob first enters her room. Later, at the exact and perfect time, Buffett makes a noisy ruckus, giving Cinda an opportunity to trick Bob into leaving.

What would have happened if there had been no Buffett?

Another bit of animal magic presents itself with the cat tracks in the snow, leading to the blue house. Buffett didn't make them and no other cats ran loose in the neighborhood. Yet *something* made those tracks, and those tracks lead Cinda to see Bob one final time. Had she known about signs, she could have seen this as a message, an opportunity, to have Bob finally caught.

The black and white Border Collie! This dog appears several times. The first visit is when he tries to get Cinda to look up at the window in the blue house...*to see Bob.* After Cinda tells her detective and he asks around the neighborhood, she finds out that no one has heard of or

305

seen the dog before. That dog appeared to exist only to help Cinda in that moment.

Years later, she has another incredible, magical encounter with a black and white Border Collie. This one leads 32-year-old Cinda to her stolen bag on the side of the highway. During this time, Cinda is in the beginning stages of PTSD and is trying to hold her life together. She is also learning about spirituality from her aunt Nancy. What makes this dog so incredible is that as soon as she recovers her bag, he seems to disappear. This is the first time she is aware of a potential sign…a message. This opens her mind and her heart to the possibility of magic and that maybe…there is something out there that is supporting her. It is as if the dog is telling her to slow down...not just the car, but her life too...slow down, Cinda, and look....

Then, two years later, when Cinda returns to the old neighborhood to fight her demons, she remembers the strange dog whose name might have been Cindy. She visualizes the scene in front of the blue house and the black and white dog appears. He motions her to look up—this time she does. Instead of seeing Bob, she sees a "For Rent" sign with a phone number.

The angels use Cinda's puppy Hannah to attract Katie to Cinda's side when both women are picking up kids at school. This is the first time Cinda brings the puppy to school. Both women have been at the school at the same time, multiple times, without seeing one another. The angels know Katie's love for dogs. The angels know Cinda is in the beginning stages of PTSD and work to reconnect the women.

Buffett, the Border Collie and Hannah are prime examples of signs and messages getting delivered by spirit animals and angels. Each one does its best to reach Cinda and give her guidance and support. But at 19, fear and ignorance keep Cinda from being able to receive their guidance. In her 30s, her personal struggle to keep herself sane and in one piece keeps her from being open enough to understand and receive the help.

Yet, these beautiful and magical forces keep figuring out different ways to get through.

They never give up.

Chapter 13

SIGNS AND IRONY

Noticing all these signs, recognizing the involvement of angels and animals, figuring out their messages and meaning...it's like solving a mystery years later. There is great reward and internal cheering as I celebrate each realization. There is also a humbling...followed by touches of embarrassment because...*if I only knew then what I know now....* I knew so little back then.... The things I'm finding and learning...*it could have changed everything....*

In looking for the signs, they present themselves in a variety of ways and...the list keeps growing.

As I'm remembering and then writing what comes to me...I find myself thinking of the word irony. This is interesting...why irony? Irony...when a word or expression means something completely opposite of its intended definition. There must be a reason that I'm contemplating this word. This is a sign that I need to look for irony within my story.

I find it.

The panic button.

The key word: panic. The fact that the device is called a *panic* button and not a "security" button or a "safety" button is the irony I'm looking for. Something that is meant to be a source of security for Katie and Cinda actually has the opposite effect. The irony, the contrast between the button's purpose and its effect on the girls tells me that this is a sign I need to look at.

This panic button is a huge source of stress and distress for Cinda and Katie. That panic button triggers a lot of emotion in Cinda...in me, still to this day. It's understandable. Detectives Redmond and Cooper believe that Bob will return. They install the panic button as a source of protection for the girls. They hang it next to Cinda's bed, but they do not put one in Katie's room. It is obvious to the detectives and the girls that Bob is after Cinda.

The button is a constant reminder of why there *is* reason for their panic. The button scares them because if they need to push it, it will be because something worth panicking about *is* happening. This petrifies them. They can't grasp that this button is *not* meant to scare them. It is meant to make them feel secure. It is meant to help the police capture Bob if he returns. It is meant to empower the girls.

Since they can't embrace the purpose of the button, they are given an opportunity to test it when they are not in any actual danger. The test comes after Cinda sees a man climb through the neighbor's window. This bizarre occurrence happens just a couple days after Bob claimed to have climbed through *their* window. After a quick bout of panic, Katie pushes the button. The police respond quickly. This reassures the girls that the button works, that they *are* protected, that they *are* safer with it installed.

There is no need to panic.

Chapter 14

SIGNS AND METAPHORS

Finding the signs is now a game of its own. Each day, I look forward to discovering what I'll learn from the hidden messages I find buried in Cinda's denial, her fear, even in her stress. Sometimes a message isn't obvious, even after it is unearthed from Cinda's psyche. Sometimes the message is buried deep inside and it takes a metaphor to reveal the message's meaning. The sign must be picked apart, spelled out and broken down into pieces, into metaphors, to be deciphered and understood.

A simple metaphor I find, is the snow that covers the ground on the day Cinda and Katie move out. The early November snow gives the neighborhood the illusion of peace and beauty. Cinda notices and is aware of the illusion. Her awareness that things feel, look, even seem different tells me that this is a sign, perhaps a metaphor worth deciphering.

When Cinda returns to the house, it's as if the snow precedes her return to ensure she continues to feel the peace and serenity she has been experiencing while living at her grandparents' home. The snow also represents how Cinda is covering up her trauma and not addressing it. Like the light blanket of snow, she is starting to cover up, layer by layer, the events and trauma that she has gone through.

When Cinda runs away from the neighborhood, vowing to never return, she covers up her feelings with this same illusion. She buries the key and locks up the memories...way under the *fluff* of her future, like the *fluff* of the snow. If she had been brave enough to allow the truth to *melt* away her emotional protection—*like the footprints that melted away the snow*—she might not have lost all those years to suffering.

Then there are complicated signs and metaphors that require in-depth deciphering. The more random the event, the more likely a metaphor. I search out events that don't seem to be related to anything surrounding them, or ones that stand out as having potential significance. Cinda experiences two such events on the same day.

Cinda is downtown, walking to the bus after work. A random homeless man spits on her foot. She is disgusted, angry and completely helpless and unable to clean up the mess. She reaches the bus stop irritated and angry. She can't find a place to sit and her frustration grows. She stands at the corner minding her own business when another random stranger approaches her. She scowls at him. The man tells her, "Someone as beautiful as you shouldn't be frowning." Her first response is to be pissed and insulted. Then something shifts in her. This guy is genuine and kind. He sincerely wants her to smile. She does and her mood shifts. She gets on the bus and despite the grossness in her shoe, her mood lightens as she heads home.

To decipher the metaphor, I first compare key words related to these two events to what is happening during this time: There's the attack… Bob, who claims he's homeless and the homeless guy who spit…Cinda's feelings of helplessness both from the attack and being spit on…there's nothing to clean up the spit or what's happened in her life…she's asked to accept kindness from a stranger, while she is shown kindness from the police and her detective…Cinda is told she's beautiful despite her feelings of the opposite...she's told to smile, in spite of her victimhood….

I decipher the metaphor to learn the lesson. It reads like a message: *"Cinda, what this homeless man did, be it Bob or the one who spit on you, is awful. You feel helpless without any way to clean yourself up or fix the problem. Since you can't change what they've done, feeling like a victim isn't helping. Despite how you feel, you are still a beautiful person. You can still smile. The only solution is for you to keep moving forward."*

If Cinda had been looking for the metaphors in random events, these two encounters could have offered her comfort.

I feel it now for both of us.

Chapter 15

SIGNS OF TRUTH

Signs, signs...everywhere are signs.... Today, I'm on a mission to find serial signs that lead up to and connect my past to now. The idea or concept of signs coming in a series intrigues me. Miniature signs, appearing as coincidences, when laid out side by side, create one giant sign—one very important sign—one truth-telling sign—a sign not to be missed. Since I've learned that I was a master at missing signs...is there a series of signs that could have led to one giant sign? Did I turn my back and ignore them?

I decide to start with an event that still has me pondering.... Was it a sign leading up to a bigger more important message? A policeman refers to the attack on Cinda as an "attempted burglary." His casual comment demoralizes her heart and messes with her head. She's worried that the police don't take her or what happened to her, seriously. She's worried that they might not believe her. She's worried that her feelings of unworthiness are justified.

During that time, she feels the personal stigma of being a victim, a personal stigma that a victim is someone of lesser value—*a stigma that some carry throughout their lives.* This random comment triggers in her a need to ensure that she is not devalued.

When she brings it up with her detective, he helps her see the truth. His answer, and the respect with which he reassures her, changes her understanding of the police's perception. He helps her see that she *is* a person of value, worthy of protection. Detective Redmond helps Cinda remove the stigma and embrace his and the police's help.

In this moment, her sense of being a victim diminishes. She realizes that she doesn't need to carry that 'victim' sign any longer.

This might be the first time in her life, in my life, that she experiences what it means to be empowered.

This random comment, from a random police officer, on a random night, gets Cinda to seek out the truth. The police officer's misguided comment...leads Cinda on a quest for answers. This leads me on a current day quest for answers too. I email Detective Redmond to get more clarity on the term "attempted burglary." His email back shakes me to the core:

"I suspect the officer who responded with 'recent attempted burglary' was avoiding saying 'attempted rape' in deference to the ordeal and trauma you experienced, but technically if apprehended the suspect would have been charged with burglary, assault, kidnapping, attempted rape and attempted murder. And you're correct in knowing that there was never any doubt in anyone's minds that what you reported was entirely true. We responded with any and all resources. Unfortunately, we weren't successful. As for the burglary, whenever you enter a residence unlawfully, with the intent to commit a crime while there, you commit Burglary 1. Have a great week, Sgt. Thom Redmond"

The shock I receive from reading the list of Bob's crimes freezes me on the spot. My body shakes, my breath quickens, my heart races. My body tells me that there is something more to this that I'm missing. My body wants me to understand this better. This email, this list, forces me to acknowledge, years later, that the crimes Bob committed didn't just feel scary, they *were* scary. They were extreme, real and dangerous.

I am furious at Cinda, *at me.* How could she have been in such denial that it took 33 years to get this? How could she have not known? I pound my forehead with my palm. I pace around my office. I'm determined, determined, to look back over those two months and learn for myself what Cinda refuses to see. I am determined to see Bob for what he really is. He isn't just a "normal" bad dream or nightmare or a scary dude on a dark Halloweenish night, or a fucking awful memory. Bob is a serious, serial, psychotic criminal.

I beg the angels to give me a clue, show me something that Cinda has missed...something that warns Cinda of the real danger she is in. Then, just as fast as I ask for help, a vision begins to appear...mini signs...a series of events leading to one huge message. I play the scenes over, again and again. Then, bit-by-bit, piece-by-piece, the puzzle begins to put itself together.

One morning, Cinda takes a different route to the bus stop, past the grocery store. She sees a man at the mailbox and walks around him. He sees her and responds as if they're acquainted. She peeks into the store's window looking for the composite drawing of Bob. At the same time, that man is looking at her. His face is reflected in the window.

I can see the sign: *Cinda taking a different route is no accident or coincidence. In doing so, she catches Bob mailing a letter. She also sees his reflection in the window. She's meant to witness both. Bob is right there and she ignores him.* I shiver at the coincidence and her obliviousness.

While Cinda waits for the bus, she notices this odd man circling around the intersection near the store. He then approaches her at the stop. When she gets a whiff of his awful breath and body odor, she finally realizes who he is. He follows her onto the bus. She leads him to a different location other than her work and successfully diverts him by hiding in a candy store.

Bob, realizing that Cinda doesn't recognize him, makes him assume it's safe to approach her at the bus stop. But once she smells him, she knows. She now knows what he looks like in daylight. This is not in his favor. He follows her. Thank God, she loses him.

She tells her detective and a sting operation to capture Bob is planned for the next day.

Even though the sting operation fails, the events cause Cinda to seek help and increased police security is sent to the neighborhood.

A few days later, Cinda receives a letter from a childhood friend, Ron. As she's reading it, the phone rings. The caller identifies himself as Ron, which she thinks is a crazy coincidence since she has the letter in her hand. Then, the guy asks if she found *the* letter on the coffee table. She instantly knows that this guy isn't Ron. It's Bob. In case he's watching her, she pantomimes another call coming in and hangs up on him.

This is where I get confused. All these years, I have pondered how did Bob know about Ron and the letter?

Cinda and Katie surmise that Bob must have a key. He must have been watching the house to know that Katie had gathered the mail and left. Then he must have gone inside, snooped through the mail, seen the letter and maybe even read it. He waited until Cinda was home alone before he called. He asks about the letter he saw in the pile.

It is not until I am writing this...trying to decipher this scene, trying to break it down and piece it back together, that I finally realize what I am missing.

The letter, which Cinda thinks is from her friend Ron, isn't from Ron. The letter is from Bob! Cinda assumes the letter is from her friend, all these years I have believed this, because he is the only person she knows with that name. Why does Bob use the name Ron? Perhaps that's his real name or he forgot what name Cinda called him.

Signs are mystical, mysterious creatures, especially when they work together. One sign after the other, one coincidence after another, trying to grab Cinda's attention...trying to give her a message...trying to warn her. But she doesn't read them. She has blinders on. Her denial is strong, hoping her life will go back to normal. Cinda is counting on Bob being captured. She can't fathom that this is happening and how it came to be. She can't fathom that Bob would come back and finish what he started.

She can't fathom the magnitude of the danger she and Katie are in.

I thought the scariest part of this story was when Bob attacked and tried to suffocate and strangle Cinda. I thought the foulest part of this story was when she invited him into her bed and he caresses her body. I thought the weirdest part of this story was when she tried to identify the suspect. But it's not.

The scariest, foulest, weirdest part of the story is that Bob is everywhere.

Bob. Is. Everywhere!

Bob is surrounding Cinda, Katie, their home. They have nowhere to hide. Bob has infiltrated every part of their lives...of their safety. He is not about to let up.

He's watching and spying on Cinda. He's mapped out where she lives, her routines, where she catches the bus. He's followed her downtown. He's sent her a letter. He's called her on the phone. He's been inside their house...*multiple times.* He has a key.

He will not let Cinda go.

His agenda is serious. His intention is ominous.

Bob's intent is to do harm, serious harm. He isn't done. He isn't finished. He will return.

A new chess game is being played. Bob's strategy is frightening. His pieces are surrounding her. The black king is setting up the board for the climax, the capture, the checkmate.

If he does capture the queen, he wins the match.

The white queen is in danger...her kingdom threatened. Cinda forfeits the game when she runs away.

Thank God, she did.

Chapter 16

SIGNS FROM SUFFERING

This writing process…is a major process. I just learned how close Cinda came to being killed…*thank God, she ran away when she did.* The denial Cinda hid behind misguided her throughout time, up to the present…up to where I sit right now. Her protective shell, which has been mine, is cracking, crumbling, falling away. Breaking down Cinda's truth has left me feeling exposed and raw.

She is here sitting next to me…her head on my shoulder…her arms around my waist. We hold each other as our emotions blend. She's suffered through so much…shame, embarrassment, humiliation. I've been humbled by the awareness of what she's gone through and how far she has come.

Together we have ventured into her life. Together we have relived what happened to her. Together we have analyzed the signs she missed. She has become my tour guide, my wayseer, my teacher. As she learns, I grow. As she finally accepts the past, I expand into my future.

These insights into young Cinda's life are so valuable. I thought I was meant to share what happened, so others may learn from her, from my, experience. I didn't realize that this process *is* intended to reintroduce her to me. She *is* to be heard, seen and understood. I'm honored to be her witness and now her scribe. I am grateful for her company. I am blessed by her insight. I hope she finally feels validated…*she deserves it.*

Today, I focus my attention toward those emotional and painful years when a brutal, psychological storm begins to brew around and within Cinda. For five years, after she marries and has children, minor storms pile on top of one another, building momentum until they almost sink her into the depth of darkness and despair. This isn't a frightening ride like the one before it. This is a roller-coaster of internal turmoil and trauma. This is a ride into hell.

I want to understand this period in Cinda's life. I want to see if there are signs, signs that could have helped guide her through these painful years. I want to know if God, the angels, her animal guides cared as much for 30-something Cinda as they did for the 19-year-old Cinda.

The five years of turmoil play out below me.

She gives birth to Eric, causing her to feel vulnerable…she sees Janet Frances on TV, the memories come flying back…she is reacquainted with Katie, but Katie shuts her out…she gives birth to Ryan, which activates more fear and need to protect her family…she faces her past head on by visiting the old neighborhood, but instead of leaving the demons there, they seem to follow her home…she is convinced that Bob *did* follow her home…she reaches the point of no return, her sanity barely there…she surrenders to the darkness.

After years of dealing, why did the memories suddenly get triggered? Why did they even *need* to get triggered? Why couldn't Cinda continue to live out her years in denial?

There must be a reason….

With each emotional and traumatic incident, the 30-something Cinda goes deeper into denial. Just as the 19-year-old did, she resists the stronghold the memories have on her. But…with every flashback…with every attempt at denial…with every shield of resistance she puts up, the opposite happens. The memories grab her, they choke her, they shake her. The more she fights, the bigger and more powerful the memories' grip becomes. She feels as if she is losing the battle, losing her mind, losing her grasp on life.

Could there be a purpose to these traumatic events?

I hear a whispering in my ear.

"Yes…each episode was designed to help you."

"Really? Why?" I ask back.

"How did your body feel?"

I think before I answer. I think about how I felt the weeks following the attack, and then the years after. My body hurt…it shivered with the tension…my muscles cramped and spasmed…my breath hard to come by…my stomach nauseous…my intestines shut down or sped up…my sleep patterns restless...my skin covered in acne. I lost weight. I was anxious. I was controlling. I was filled with rage.

"How long could your body have kept going?"

"Not much longer," I answer.

"Unresolved trauma causes many serious illnesses."

I have learned that my body knows, before my mind does, when something isn't right. My body seems to have an intelligence all its own. My body acts like a Geiger counter warning me when the toxins—chemical or emotional, are too high. These days, I try to listen...but back then... Cinda didn't realize that her body was trying to signal her.

The whispering continues....

"Suffering is designed for guidance, not for pain."

Really?

Suffering is designed for guidance, not for pain...?

If I am to believe this...then...that would mean...that each incident Cinda went through had been for her own good. Then...that would mean...when Cinda suffers, each episode of suffering is a sign that she is heading in the wrong direction. Could the purpose be *not* to drive her crazy, but instead to drive her toward healing? Instead of running from her memories, is she meant to stop, turn and let them catch up? Is she meant to intentionally walk into the storm instead of avoiding it?

Her suffering isn't meant to *be* the cause for her pain.

Her suffering is meant to shepherd her toward what she is avoiding. Her suffering is meant to guide her toward the ultimate result which is peace, tranquility and sanity. *Like a Border Collie shepherding his flock, a sheep gets nipped when it roams off the guided path.*

Cinda's suffering, her body's ailments, the painful events...are all signs nipping at her ankles, barking warnings at her, circling around her...all trying to get her to face what happened. But, since she doesn't know about signs, she can't read what they want from her. Instead, she takes the signs as personal attacks, reasons for her torment and torture, justifiable victimhood.

The minor storms are a series of signs, all playing out with a purpose. She ignores all of them. They build up and create a major storm...meant to steer her back to shore, not further out to sea where she's drifting. But in her mind, shore is where the pain resides...and needs to be avoided. What she can't see is that her avoidance is the *cause*...the cause of the dark clouds and violent seas. The more she fights the memories, denies them, avoids them...the more they grow, the more frightening they become, the more powerful they are.

Her acceptance is the *solution*...solution to her pain and suffering. Her acceptance will steer her to the calm, clear sky and peaceful, still water she is seeking. Her acceptance comes when she can look at the past and ask, *"What do you want me to see, know, learn from you?"* Everything will calm, her fear will subside, the power those memories have over her will diminish.

When the major storm hits, Cinda feels she has lost all hope. She cries into her pillow begging for help. She gives up and surrenders to the demons and their leader, Bob.

But, instead of the devil showing up, God does.

"Love your enemy, Cinda. There you will find your peace."

She is guided through a profound and life-changing ritual that leads to her ultimate healing.

Instead of the devil showing up...God does....

Does this mean...when Cinda was running away from her suffering, from the demons, from Bob...she was running from God, the angels, the signs?

Yes.

Suffering is designed for guidance, not for pain.

Chapter 17

SIGNS OF COMPASSION

The lessons keep coming. Like the minor storms of Cinda's trauma, my current day learning piles on top of me and the wisdom it brings with it is profound. To understand the power and purpose of suffering…changes everything. Suffering becomes an option—which means, if I don't resist it, if I work on accepting what is the root cause of it…if I surrender to it and allow myself to learn and listen to its messages…the suffering will ease, leave and I can heal…*from anything.*

After Cinda surrenders and follows the guidance which tells her to love Bob, she is released from her suffering. She wakes up feeling like a different and new person, because she is. Her suffering was so great that she doesn't care how or why that profound experience worked. She just cares that it did work. Without stopping to think about it, or analyze it or understand it, she moves forward in her new and cured psyche, in her new and healthy body, in her new and recovered life.

She finds the peace she has been seeking.

She moves forward as a reborn, renewed and reformed woman. The Cinda that survived the attack and the scary days that followed escaped with her life. The Cinda that experienced intense inner suffering and PTSD was guided through a profound healing. That Cinda is now well and resting and writing.…

From 1998 to 2000, I live in the blissfulness of inner peace…the peace that I longed for and found. My life is beautiful. I am content. I yell less.

I laugh more. I sleep better. I've gained back the weight I couldn't afford to lose. The IBS is magically cured. I experience joy in the little things and well up with emotion during sentimental moments—and there are lots of them.

I spend my days volunteering in the boys' school and have embraced my role as a PTA mom. The strongest level of stress I experience is what to serve my family for dinner. This stress is minor compared to what used to race through my mind, my body, my psyche.

When a new millennium arrives, I welcome in the new world—a world which doesn't collapse under the pressure of change. We made it to 2000!

A new millennium, a new life, a new perspective doesn't mean all is forgotten. There are other plans for me. My hiatus is over.

In 2003 signs from my past begin to present themselves again. I'm taken by surprise…I had hoped I was done. This time, the signs are gentle. They show themselves in the way of coincidences, serendipity and synchronicity. My experience has taught me to not ignore them. I am compelled to pay attention.

In December of that year, a sign, a huge sign, grabs my attention. After I put my boys to bed, make some popcorn and pour myself a glass of wine, I turn on the TV to keep me company until Scott gets home. The channel surfing comes to a stop on a news program. They're airing the trial of the Green River killer.

This monster, having killed over 49 women, had been haunting the Pacific Northwest for over 10 years. He has been sentenced to life in prison without parole. To avoid the death penalty, he has agreed to tell the police who else he murdered and where he buried them.

The killer is dressed in a white jail shirt over an orange jumpsuit. He's handcuffed at his wrists and ankles. He sits in silence at a table next to his lawyer. As the camera focuses on the criminal's face, I can't help but compare this man to Bob. It isn't Bob, it doesn't look like him, but it could have been.

I haven't a clue how many women Bob violated before or after me. I haven't a clue if he ever got caught, ever went to trial, ever got thrown into jail. I haven't a clue whether he's dead or alive, homeless living under a bridge, or in that blue house on the corner.

I'm surprised and disappointed in myself for thinking of Bob and that night again. I shake the thoughts off.

That part of your life is over so let it be, Cinda. Let it be.

The reporter's voice on the TV brings me back to the scene on the screen. The courtroom is filled with people—angry, emotional people. The camera jumps from the judge, to the killer, to the crowd, as the reporter tells us what is taking place in front of him. The judge is allowing the crowd, filled with the families of murder victims, an opportunity to tell this killer what they think of him before he's sent away.

Family members stand in a line, waiting for their turn. The tension in the air is palpable. If looks could kill, this man would be dead on the spot. One by one, grief-stricken parents and/or siblings sob into the microphone. Each person, finally able to tell this man how he's ruined their lives by stealing the life of their loved one. They call him evil, selfish, a coward. Many are full of rage and yell obscenities. Some even growl at him when they are done. One grieving woman tells him through her seething hatred that she hopes he rots slowly, in a tortuous, fiery hell, and that his death is long and painful.

The judge allows it all.

Simultaneously, as the family members spew their raw emotions of anger, grief and damnation toward this violent criminal, the reporter is whispering what's happening, the judge is nodding and encouraging them to continue, and the Green River killer...smirks.

The reporter can't help but be appalled at the killer's behavior. Even the judge comments on how callous the murderer's expressions seem. The emotions of the victims' families reach a tipping point. They begin to chastise him from their seats, until the judge gets control of the courtroom again.

I, too, am appalled by the Green River killer's attitude. I wonder what I would do if I were in that courtroom and my beloved had been killed by this madman. I fantasize about what my statement might be. I wonder what I would say to Bob if he were sitting at the table in that courtroom, and I was surrounded by his other victims.

But then I remember...I remember that I had already spoken to Bob. I had already told him what I felt. I didn't tell him I hated him. I didn't damn him to a fiery hell. I told the man who tried to rape and kill me...that I loved him.

For the first time, I realize how truly bizarre and unconventional that action was. I'm also awed by it. I'm humbled by it. I can hear the words again: *"Love your enemy, Cinda. There you will find your peace."* A wave of peace flows over me. I look at the courtroom with a new set of eyes.

I can't imagine these hate-filled family members telling the Green River killer they love him. To even consider such a thought is crazy. After all, the families are gathered and bonded together in their hatred of this man.

Yet…here it is…I cannot deny the sensation of peace I'm experiencing and they are not. Something very important is brewing up inside of me. I can feel it percolating. I just can't place it, or give it a name, but it is powerful.

Then it hits me. This knowing….it fills me and it is strong. I'm in a frenzy about it. I get what is really happening in this courtroom!

These people, these poor people, they don't.

I scream at them through the television screen.

"Stop! Stop! You're giving him the power! Power over you!"

The camera is focusing on the killer's face. He's still smirking. He's emotionally unmoved by any of their statements. The crowd is furious. But, I can read exactly what is going on in his head.

Can't anyone else see it?

His smirk IS the look of power. He has all the power in that courtroom. He's already tortured, raped and killed their loved ones. Now, they're letting him know that his actions have caused them a lifetime of suffering. He has tortured them as well. The cliché: *killing two birds with one stone* comes to mind. Even though he got caught and is sentenced to jail for life, in his mind, he's still won.

Thinking of the night when Bob assaulted me, I had to learn on the spot how to read and determine who had the upper hand—him or me. If Bob had the power, I figured out a way to steer the power back into my favor. The easiest and quickest way to regain control was to use distractions. I had to keep him thinking and questioning what I might do next. Whatever I did, it had to be unexpected.

Listening now to the victims' families and watching the smirking killer, I question:

What is the purpose of this exercise? How can this be helpful or beneficial?

Once upon a time, I too would have welcomed the opportunity to yell at Bob, to wish him to rot in hell for ruining the sanity of my life. I didn't realize until right now that my healing also opened the door for another emotion…an emotion that's unfamiliar to me…unfamiliar, that is, to be directed toward a serial rapist and a killer.

Compassion.

With this new perception, I look at the killer through the eyes of compassion. I watch his expression closely. I set the bowl of popcorn aside so I can lean into the vision on the TV screen while I pull from the back of my mind the vision that is beginning to form. I can see something different than what the reporter wants us to pay attention to.

Behind this killer's eyes, he looks exhausted. I can read his exhaustion like a book. His smirk is the expression he wants the world to see, but really, it's saying something quite different.

His exhaustion is saying: *"Tell me something new. Tell me something I haven't heard all my life. You may feel you're being unique in your hatred, but you're not. I've heard it all before."*

In that moment, I am overwhelmed with compassion for this man. I want to weep with it.

Bob and this Green River killer have something of importance in common…something ominous and dreadful. The vision that was developing in the back of my mind is now front and center and clear.

I see an innocent child, born into this world with the necessity of being nurtured and loved. But that doesn't happen. Someone or some event destroys that innocence in him. He grows up feeling hated, being ridiculed, beaten and abused throughout his younger years. He begins to believe that he's a despicable, loathsome person—unworthy of love and kindness and compassion—and worthy of all the abuse. In response, he treats others with the same hatred and loathing he feels about himself. *"Why not? What is there to lose? You hate me, I hate me, I hate you,"* he might say to himself to justify his actions.

The cycle of destruction of self and others is awful, and awfully sad. Bob and this killer on the TV destroy what is good, in hope that they will feel something better. Instead they feel nothing. They feel no remorse, no guilt. This lack of emotion or empathy for someone else is misunderstood by their psyches as power.

They feel powerful because they feel nothing.

I am awed by this vision and the wisdom that comes with it. I question it, *"Is it real? Is it true?"*

And I hear the answer, *"Yes, Cinda. It's real. They're victims too."*

Bringing my attention back to the TV, back to the courtroom, the families continue to take their turns speaking and spewing hatred. A man approaches the microphone. He is introduced as Robert Rule, the father of one of the victims, Linda Rule. He looks like Santa Claus with his long white hair and beard—a big man wearing a white shirt, a striped tie and rainbow suspenders. This man is different. He is calm. He takes a deep breath and looks straight into the prisoner's eyes. His speech is slow, deliberate and with purpose.

"Mr. Ridgeway," his low fatherly voice shakes with emotion, "There are people here that hate you. I'm not one of them. You've made it difficult to live up to what I believe…and that is what God has said to do…and that is to forgive. You. Are. Forgiven. Sir."

There it is! The unexpected!

Everyone in the courtroom gasps. The camera zooms in on the killer's face. The Green River killer's face crumbles. His emotionless demeanor disappears. This Santa Claus man has just taken away his power. The violent man breaks down in tears. A bit later, his tears continue to flow when assigned his punishment. He apologizes for his actions. For the first time, he shows remorse.

While witnessing this beautiful man forgive the violent one, I wonder if maybe…in the victim's actions of forgiveness…if more than just the victim is freed? Perhaps…whatever guided me to tell Bob I loved him, also freed Bob of his torment?

Perhaps…this sign, this synchronicity of being at the right place at the right time, happened so I could *physically* witness the transaction of a victim's forgiveness. So I could understand the power and importance of compassion, even for a killer. When I told Bob I loved him, I may not have used the words *I forgive you*, but I did follow God's instructions, just as Robert Rule did.

I now have a physical example and proof of what my ritual looked like.

What I did, what Robert Rule did, is important, if not mandatory in the healing process.

I know now...that loving your enemy is more than a human connection.

It's a God connection.

Chapter 18

SIGNS OF HEALING

The profound revelation I have during the Green River killer trial opens the floodgates to my spirituality. I dive into learning as much as I can about forgiveness, compassion, love, healing, and anything else that seems to call to me. Throughout the following years, I connect with many spiritual teachers and absorb information from their different paths and beliefs. I attend multiple classes, seminars, retreats and meet multiple like-minded people—people who are as curious as I am.

Every time I learn something new, my mind and heart expand even more. My knowledge grows, *yes*, but so does my faith and my love and my gratitude for that invisible force that has been with me from the beginning. It is an endless stream of beauty and grace.

My greatest education and joy come from reading, and my collection of books is vast. My bookshelves are overflowing and piles under my nightstand topple over. Every book is a member of my family, my community, my heart.

My obsession with books reaches a tipping point one night in 2005. My husband and I are sitting in bed, both reading. He interrupts the silence by blurting out his opinion of my preoccupation.

"Dang, Cinda. You act like you're studying for a test."

I laugh, seeing it through his eyes. I'm in the middle of reading a spiritual/self-help book. I am underlining important information with a ballpoint pen. I've highlighted noteworthy quotes with a yellow highlighter. In pink, I've highlighted beautiful, meaningful information. In green highlights, are paragraphs that contain concepts that I find confusing and need to learn about more. There are sticky notes along the edge of the pages; each contains a comment too big to write in the margins. My book looks like a colorful porcupine.

"In a way, I am," I tell him, still laughing around the pen in my mouth. "What I'm really doing is trying to take in all of the teachings of this author."

"Well," he says, not impressed, "It seems to me that reading should be fun. Maybe you should lighten up and enjoy the book instead of trying to master it."

I think about that word *master*. I like that word—*a lot*. Yes, this feels as if I'm trying to master something. I want to master and learn and absorb and grow and excel and evolve in all ways possible. Scott thinks I'm obsessed. I feel I'm not any more obsessed than any student who's studying their passion. This passion has a stronghold on me and nothing will slow down the momentum to expand my spiritual knowledge and awareness.

A few weeks later, another book reveals itself to me in a beautiful, magical way. I'm in the Red Room of Powell's Bookstore. Not sure what I'm after, I ask for a sign. This has worked for me in the past and I am usually guided to the right book. I slowly walk down an aisle filled with stories about my current fixation, mythology—Greek, Roman, Celtic, modern day.

Something catches my eye. The spine on a book seems to be glowing. The book is black, so for it to reflect light seems strange. The title reads, *The Power of Myth*.

Sign received.

I take it home and with my highlighters, sticky notes and pen ready, I dig in.

The Power of Myth is a transcript of an interview of Joseph Campbell, an expert in mythology, conducted by journalist Bill Moyers. In this book, Campbell shares his knowledge about the common thread of mythology he has found in multiple cultures, religions and beliefs around the world. Every one of them, he says, has a higher power, a Source, a God they pray to, do ritual for and offer gratitude to. He believes that, in fact, they derive from the same myth and lead to the same God. Thus, not one belief is better or different or more correct or more right than another.

I devour this book. There is such freedom in this information because it removes all judgment and separateness between people of different cultures and religions. As much as I love this book, it isn't until deep in the middle I find the reason I was guided to buy it. Joseph Campbell is sharing a random story about a personal synchronicity. He is talking about the power of signs that come from coincidences and the great things we can learn if we are aware of them.

The story is sweet and funny but somewhat uninteresting. Yet, what happens next takes me by surprise. The words and page reflect a light...bright enough that it blinds me. I close my eyes to protect them. But even then, the light expands inside of my skull. The sensation is so unexpected that I need to sit and wait for the light to calm. I open my eyes and as my sight adjusts...I swear I can see a giant glowing finger pointing to the page.

I follow the guidance and reread the chapter. I reread it a third time.

Joseph Campbell, to make his point clear and pull all the synchronistic pieces of his story together, quotes a Bible verse: *"For God has consigned all men to disobedience, that he may show his mercy to all."* Campbell describes the meaning as: *"You cannot be so disobedient that God's mercy will not be able to follow you, so give Him a chance."*

He then quotes Martin Luther: *"Sin bravely, and see how much of God's mercy you can invoke."* Campbell translates this to mean: *"The great sinner is the great awakener of God to compassion."*

Campbell states that no matter what anyone's actions or crimes may have been...they will always be viewed as worthy of this powerful, all-encompassing love. God, Source, doesn't condemn or judge...only humans do.

I let the words digest...the wisdom sinks in...as the message, the sign, presents itself. The insight I'm being shown settles deep inside of me... consuming me. My equilibrium becomes unsteady as the information is assimilated.

I hear a soft whisper.

"Here it is, Cinda. The answer you have been seeking."

The answer to a question...a question I hadn't even known I was asking.

Why did my healing work?

Slowly...slowly...it comes to me.

"For God has consigned all men to disobedience, that he may show his mercy to all."

A complete understanding arrives. Source, God, this invisible higher power, loves ALL. This energy loves everyone and shows mercy to all men, women and children. But some of these people have lost their way. They have forgotten. They have forgotten that they are worthy of this Divine love. They suffer because they feel separate from this love... alone and powerless. This causes them to harm and hurt others—creating suffering that is equal to their own.

As a parent, my love for each of my children is deep and powerful and unending. Regardless of their behavior, positive or negative, I still love them. I may not approve of what they've done, but my devotion to them is just as strong as before they misbehaved. This is what a good parent does—they separate the behavior from the child.

How could God be any different?

I will never, nor could I, love one child more than the other. They are both loved equally. God will never love one of us children more than another. We are *all* equal in the eyes of God.

In other words.... This higher power loves Bob as much as it loves me, regardless—*regardless*—of Bob's intent to harm or hurt me.

"The great sinner is the great awakener of God to compassion."

The *great sinner*—Bob.

The great sin—his attack on me.

The *great awakener*—Bob, the great awakener of me, to my spirituality—of me, to my capacity to love my enemy.

Of God to compassion—God's compassion for Bob, who has lost his way—God's compassion for me, for experiencing suffering at the hands of Bob—my compassion for Bob, as a victim himself.

Divine love represents a love greater than any other love there is. It is the love of family, yes. It is the love we have for God, yes. But is *also* and *must* include the love for an enemy.

The night of my healing, I expressed this love...this Divine love to my enemy, to Bob.

So, why did my healing work?

The answer starts in my misunderstanding of my healing. For all these years, I assumed I was guided through the ritual because Source saw me as the victim, the wounded child—the one who needed to be nurtured and cared for and fussed over. I assumed that I was the only one who needed help...that this higher power worked with me, to reach Bob—so *I* would be healed.

But...I wasn't the only victim needing healing in my room that night. Bob also needed to know he was worthy of being healed, of experiencing God's love.

I saw it when Robert Rule said the words of forgiveness and broke down a killer into tears. I saw it when I told Bob I loved him and brought him to his knees.

I know now why I am NOT to take my healing lightly or for granted. Although this story is mine, it goes beyond me, it goes beyond the resolution of my suffering. This goes beyond me and reaches out to all women and men and children who have been hurt and have suffered because of the pain caused by another.

This healing…also reaches out to those who have caused the pain, the torment and the sorrow. This healing reaches out and holds the hands and the hearts of both the victim and the violator.

The healing worked because it touched both Bob *and* me. The ritual worked because it released the grip, the unhealthy connection that we had on one another. I felt that I, the victim, was only worthy of God's love and that Bob, the violator, was unworthy of it. These identities and labels don't serve either of us because they aren't real…*they are false*. When this ritual is done with love, for love, guided by God's love…both parties are equally loved and honored by God. AND…when the connection is severed, both are set free and healed.

Free.

Chapter 19

SIGNS OF PSYCHIC CONNECTIONS

If...in my ritual...both Bob and I are healed by Divine love and this love sets us free by separating us...what held us together? Could there have been an actual connection, a connector, between us?

I wonder...when a person is violated, attacked, harmed by another, are the two, victim and violator, attached in some energetic way? And if so...could this attachment last forever? When I think back to the years before the healing took place, I could feel Bob's presence; it felt like a haunting, like he was haunting me, as if his tentacles could reach through time and find me. After the healing...I no longer felt his presence. Perhaps a severing of some kind happened between us.

Had Bob and I been energetically connected?

Based on all the learning and reading I've been doing, the spiritual practitioners and authors would tell me, "Yes, there are invisible connections that exist between people." The harmful connections are referred to as psychic cords, suction cords, energetic attachments and energetic nets. These invisible connections are made when negative, compulsive thoughts and/or events happen between two people. Once these invisible connections are made, personal energy is exchanged between both parties.

This would explain why during those years, Bob dominates my quiet moments. With every anxious, angry and fearful thought I have, I unconsciously send out waves of energy which find him and attach. Once attached, our personal energy is transferred through these invisible cords. As disturbing as this information is, it helps make sense out of what I experienced.

When I went through the ritual of healing, I called Bob's spirit to me. He energetically stood in my room talking to me. Could this have been possible because of the connection we shared through one of these psychic cords?

I visualize that night...Cinda can't visibly see the cord, but she senses and feels it—because she senses and feels Bob. When she throws that ball of Divine love at him, it travels along a line that carries it straight to his heart. As it flies between them, it resembles a comet with a tail. Could that "tail" be the cord, the connection between them? Could that ball of energy, traveling along the cord, sever it...permanently?

Looking back to the Green River killer trial, I see how these psychic attachments can ruin lives. The victims' family members, without realizing it, are psychically attached to the killer through their anger, hate and fear. These negative emotions travel through these cords and feed his anger and hatred. They, in return, absorb his lower, darker energy. Their lives are impacted with considerable negativity.

When Robert Rule speaks his magical words of forgiveness to the Green River killer, he creates the same energetic effects as I did with Bob. His soul sends out Divine love to the killer's soul through the invisible cord that attaches them both. The love connection is made, the attachment is severed and both are freed.

The Green River killer's reaction shows me that he feels the power of Divine love...*perhaps for the first time in his life.*

The profound power of Divine love is a beautiful recipe for recovery, the most powerful medicine...because I believe it heals in both directions. It is more than the power of forgiveness. It is the next level of spiritual understanding, growth and healing.

But can it work for others?

The angels provide a perfect opportunity for me to test this theory. A dear friend, Tammy, confides in me that she's feeling haunted by her deceased stepfather. This man molested her as a young child. She hates him so much that she has nicknamed him *step-monster.*

I share with her my story. I tell her of the concept of invisible psychic cords and the ritual of Divine love I did with Bob.

"Tammy, if I'm right...you may still be psychically attached to him. Perhaps he is haunting you because he can't 'move on' until you sever this connection. You can't be free of him either, until you disconnect. The way it worked for me...I used this cord, this connection to call him to me.

Then I partnered with God to send Divine love to him. After I told Bob I loved him, I found the peace and bliss I was craving."

Tammy sits in front of me, looking conflicted. She has hated this man for so long, how can she possibly tell him she loves him? But she hears the truth in my statement and is willing to have me guide her. I begin by having her visualize this hurtful, awful man as an innocent child. Tammy's a wonderful mother, so this is easy. She sees this precious child being mistreated by those who should have loved him and, instead of making him feel safe, cause him harm. Tears of empathy run down her face.

"Cinda, I can feel him here next to me, right now. But I'm not afraid of him. I feel sorry for him."

A window inside her heart that has been shut and guarded for so long has just allowed the light to filter in. I can see it on her face. Instead of poised for battle, her head is tilted in kindness. Her slight smile tells me she is no longer afraid or filled with hate. Compassion is now her dominant emotion.

She opens her eyes, wipes away the tears and shakes her head back and forth.

"I can't tell him I love him. It's just too hard. But maybe what I experienced will be enough."

We hug goodbye. I hope for her sake that compassion will be enough. *It isn't.*

Two days later, she calls me to say, "Cinda, you won't believe this! Yesterday...I was driving down the highway and my dead stepfather's face appeared on the other side of the windshield! Clear as day, there he was looking right at me. It scared the crap out of me. I'm lucky I didn't crash. I yelled at him to go away and leave me alone."

She pauses to take in a breath and continues, "Then...a song on the radio caught my attention. Cher's techno song 'A Different Kind of Love Song' came on loud and clear. You've heard it, right? She sings about universal truths...that we're the light that travels through everyone...we are part of each other...it's a higher place we're from. Well, in that moment, it felt like Cher, or God, was trying to tell me something. So, I listened. I realized that it's a *different* kind of love you were talking about. It's a different kind of love I needed to pass on to my stepfather. Not *my* human kind of love, but a higher kind of love."

I hold my breath.

Will it work for her too?

"I looked right at him, through that windshield, and I told him…I told him I was sad. I was sad that as a child he wasn't loved the way he should have been. But, as I child, I deserved to be safe, nurtured and cared for inside of my own home. He had no right to treat me the way he did and take away my childhood."

Her voice cracks with emotion.

I still haven't taken a breath.

"Cinda. I did it. I said: 'Stepdad—*by the way, I can't seem to call him step-monster anymore*—even though I have hated you for what you did to me, I don't hate you anymore. I love you. My soul to yours, I love you. And, I don't ever want to see you again.'"

I let out my breath. "And…?"

"I felt a wave of the most powerful love come over me. Then the bastard left. Oh, my God! It's over! It's over! He's gone for good! I can feel it, he's gone!"

I can hear the jubilation in her voice. I am feeling it too.

"Cinda, it works!"

It works!

Chapter 20

SIGNS OF EVOLUTION

Knowing that my personal experience might help others gives me a newfound purpose. This causes me to dive deeper into my spiritual healing studies. Scott thought I was consumed before…now, I'm deeply committed. The more I explore, the more I expand, the more my spirit evolves. I settle into a personal and sacred relationship with the Divine.

During another trip to Powell's Bookstore in 2008, in search of the next book to add to my collection, to add to my inner education, to add to my husband's irritation, a beautiful orange, red and yellow covered book calls me over. The title reads, *A New Earth: Awakening to Your Life's Purpose* by Eckhart Tolle. When I pick it up, I swear it seems to have a heartbeat that beats in connection to mine. But, since I feel I've found my purpose, I have no interest and put it back on the shelf. Instead, I buy a book on the myth of King Arthur, my current fixation.

I should know by now. I should recognize the signs by now. I shouldn't ignore what is right in front of me. Coincidence plays its game with me when the very next day Oprah announces her newest book club read. She looks directly into the camera, holds up Eckhart Tolle's *A New Earth*, and says: "This book will change your life!"

I race back to Powell's, buy the book and with all my study supplies ready, jump right in.

The first chapter is complicated and makes no sense. I reread it because Oprah has promised inspiration. I keep rereading, underlining, highlighting and trusting inspiration will find its way to me, but it doesn't. Despite my frustration, my intuition is telling me that this book *is* important. I just need to make sense of it. I need to *master* it. I create an ongoing list of questions—questions I hope will get answered by the end of the book.

Otherwise, I'm selling this book back to Powell's.

Oprah seems to read my mind—perhaps others in her book club are feeling the same way—because a few days later she makes an announcement on her TV show. She and Eckhart Tolle have created a 10-week online course to help the reader understand the concepts of the book. This will be the first of its kind, the largest worldwide online classroom ever. Eckhart will be taking and answering questions. I'm so relieved that I run to my computer, type out my questions and send them to the designated email address.

Maybe my questions will get answered by the author himself.

A follow up email arrives, requesting a phone conversation. A producer with HARPO calls and tells me that Oprah has selected one of my questions.

A week later, a production crew of one man comes to my house and sets me up with a laptop, a camera and a microphone. After a few days of practice runs, the moment arrives. My in-house producer connects me with an online HARPO producer and I'm Skyped into the classroom with Oprah and Eckhart. I get to ask my question. I get to meet and talk to Oprah and Eckhart.

Oprah welcomes me, "Well, I see Cinda from Oregon has been waiting to talk to us. Hi, Cinda from Oregon. What is your question?"

I make small talk and say something I hope they will find humorous. They both laugh. I laugh. I can't believe this is happening.

This. Is. Amazing!

"I want to ask a question…and I believe that the way Eckhart answers this question might just be the catalyst for change that we need in order to save our planet and ourselves."

I'm surprised by what I say. I had researched my question repeatedly. I did not expect to say this. It's as if something or someone is making this statement and speaking through me. I am aware enough to know that this must be important. I need to pay close attention.

I ask my question: "On pages 20 and 21 in the book, you talk about—in an ever-changing environment, a species needs to either adapt or they will die…. You go on to say, and I quote, '…humanity is now faced with a stark choice: Evolve or Die.' When you say, 'Evolve or Die,' do you mean that literally, and it sounds like you might, or do you mean that metaphorically, which I hope you mean?"

My voice cracks. My emotions show. I'm dreading his answer… *it scares me.*

In many spiritual practices, the metaphor of death is used to teach or illustrate cycles in life, endings that lead to new beginnings. Does Eckhart Tolle mean this kind of metaphorical death? Or…does he mean it literally? Are we humans headed toward extinction?

As a mother, this is a frightening thought.

Eckhart's answer is long and complicated. But, I've been reading his book…I've grown accustomed to his style. He tells me that many people believe that who they see in the mirror is who they really are. But, he says, this is not accurate. Our consciousness, our inner spirit, is who we really are. Even if our humanness dies off, our consciousness will live on forever. There is no death, only the transformation of form. In other words, if my body dies, my spirit lives on forever. If my children die, their spirit lives on in a different form.

Humans may go extinct, but our spirits will not.

His answer is: YES.

Yes. If we don't evolve, we will die.

He then says, in a voice overflowing with compassion and tenderness directed to me, "So there's nothing to be scared of…. The fact that we are here tonight should give us hope and confidence that humanity is going to make it…. There is an enormous awakening happening on the planet—I do feel more confident now…."

Eckhart has HOPE.

In this instant, the instant Eckhart answers my question, I make a bigger commitment to my personal journey. Just as his book title promises, I *have* awakened to my life's purpose. That purpose is to spiritually evolve and help others do the same.

When the webcast finishes, I can't wait to hear what my family and friends thought about the show. When my husband shows up, he has a pained look on his face.

"Cinda, our computer didn't connect to the show. We didn't see you."

I look at the producer just as his phone rings. He tells us that the entire system, worldwide, crashed. When 70,000-plus people logged onto the show at the same time, the system couldn't handle it and it shut down. No one, anywhere, could see the first episode.

The irony is not lost.

The sign is huge…a huge worldwide sign.

Eckhart Tolle wrote *A New Earth* to help us become aware of the conflict between our egos and our inner spirit. The number of egos attached to a show of this magnitude and undertaking had to be hundreds deep.

Hundreds of people from the publishing house, to HARPO Productions, to Skype and the internet company, to the participants and our families, and even Oprah—all our egos were counting on the webcast succeeding.

And it fails.

How can a show based on the awareness of our ego succeed when every ego involved (except for Eckhart Tolle, the ego-slayer) is attached to the outcome? It was a beautiful, tender slap on our universal hand.

Wake up. Become Aware. Evolve.

As I continue to read *A New Earth* and participate in the following webcasts, all of which are recorded, including the first one, I learn more about the ego and its control. Eckhart Tolle teaches that the ego and the spirit cannot coexist at the same time. Either I am awake, aware and conscious—living with Spirit, or I am asleep, unaware and unconscious—living an ego-driven life.

Since I am committed to evolving spiritually, understanding my ego's patterns is imperative. She/me/it rearing its mighty head causes me to behave in an unconscious and unacceptable manner.

I look at the time around those two months in 1981. I see the determination of the 19-year-old me. She is stubborn, wants it her way, and ignores anyone's advice, even her mother's concern. Her denial, her hiding, her keeping parts of the story's truth to herself...all are her ego's need to control her through stubbornness and through fear.

Fear is ego's mighty weapon of control.

After beating Bob at his own game, she feels pride and boasts, "If I can do that, I can do anything!" She uses this mantra to convince herself she's no longer afraid. But it doesn't work. It never works or succeeds when the ego is in control.

The ego is never, ever satisfied.

The struggle Cinda experiences with PTSD is her inner spirit screaming for her to wake up...to wake up and stop being a victim... to ease the pain and suffering. But her ego prevents this because...if she listens to her spirit...the door to Spirit will open...and her ego will lose its grip.

Playing the role of a victim is the ego's way to show it's in charge.

I can also see when Cinda's ego is not in control. During those horrific three hours of the attack, when intuition takes over, her ego is required to take a backseat...and this saves her life. With Cinda's intuition in control, ego's fear gets set aside and she's open to receive guidance from a higher power.

Years later, when Cinda collapses in bed and surrenders to the demons, she stops struggling and denying her pain. In this place of surrender, ego loses its grip and Spirit again rises to help. Her ego backs down. Healing follows.

If the ego is present, intuition isn't. If intuition is present, ego isn't.

After my healing, my ego tries to gain control again. My spiritual growth is slowed down when my ego puts me back to sleep in another kind of hiding and denial—contentment.

The book, *A New Earth,* wakes me up to another level of spiritual understanding and awareness. This awareness is powerful. This awareness tells me when my ego is inflamed and once I am aware, the ego's power is dissolved. This awareness tells me when someone else's ego is activated, and I can hold space for this awareness and not take things personally.

The more I become aware of my ego, the more I trust my connection to Source.

The more I trust my connection with Source…the more I choose to spiritually evolve.

The more I choose to spiritually evolve…the closer I am to Source.
I choose to evolve.

Chapter 21

SIGNS OF DIVINE LOVE

Tomorrow is a big day. Tomorrow I send out the first draft of this manuscript to my editor. Tomorrow, someone other than myself will know the truth of my story. I am both excited and apprehensive. It's been a long time coming.

I take a day off from writing to celebrate with a friend. We head to downtown Portland for dinner and cocktails. We park the car and walk the city blocks toward the old Meier & Frank building. This historical building is more than just an Oregon monument. This building holds memories of young Cinda—following her passion for retail, so eager, so naive, so vulnerable. Now a Macy's department store, a high-end hotel and two upscale restaurants and bars fill the space. We're going to eat in the restaurant where the older one of my nieces I used to nanny works.

On this warm summer night, the city is alive with people leaving work, shopping, sightseeing or heading to happy hour. As we approach a corner and wait for the light to change, I spy a pair of dirty, hairy, hobbit-like feet protruding from behind a blue U.S. mailbox. The filthy feet, sticking out from a pair of very clean, green pant legs, belong to a man whose face is covered by a green blanket...the deepest, densest, richest green I've ever seen. I have a sudden and unexplained yearning for the blanket.

When the light changes, we turn and cross the street. But something makes me look back. The man, who appears to be homeless, sits up and cuddles against the mailbox, using it as a head rest. He has no belongings, not a backpack, not a shopping cart...not a thing...

except *that* blanket. A wave of compassion for him floods over me as I walk away.

I can't let it rest…I'm intrigued by the strangeness of the situation. There is more to this…more than a homeless man…more than the contrast between dirty feet and clean pants…more than a wondrous blanket…and missing belongings. I ask my friend if she noticed that homeless man on the previous corner. She says, "What homeless man?" She didn't see him….

Deciphering signs is now a passion of mine. I'm experiencing a "full circle moment." In one instance, on one corner, my past and my present all converge. I'm headed to my old place of work. I'll be visiting my niece…whom I used to babysit. I just saw a homeless man, next to a mailbox, at an intersection…just like years ago. The spectacular green of this man's pants and blanket…remind me of the gorgeous green eyes of the young man who tried to bully me on these same Portland streets.

I'm also recognizing that there are no negative emotions. There is no residual fear creeping up, nor shame, nor threat. Instead, I feel compassion for the man and a bizarre and intense yearning for his blanket. My reaction is a relief…the green yearning represents healing…. I'm being given an opportunity to see and experience how far my healing has come since I began this writing project.

I'm also realizing that this "full-circle" moment has brought 19-year-old Cinda, 30-something Cinda and the Cinda I am now— together into one spot. Up to this point, I'd been working with each as a separate identity, but now the three "*shes*" have become one…*me.*

In bed that night, I lay with gratitude for having been given these signs, to help me appreciate this "full-circle" moment. The timing is perfect with my manuscript being sent off in the morning. This part of my journey is coming to an end, and it seems fitting to be visited by my past in this way.

I feel the angels celebrating my accomplishments.

I am done!!!

NOT!

Of course, *not.*

The minute I assume I have the answers...the minute I become too sure of myself...the minute I get too cocky—my ego takes control. I am humbled and reminded that there is still so much more to learn.

The journey never ends.

The lessons begin anew in the middle of that night. I'm wide awake. To distract and quiet my mind, I click play on the current Oprah and Deepak 21-day meditation. With my headset on, I lie back and listen.

Oprah comes on first and says, "Welcome and congratulations for making it this far. You have reached the end and we are proud of you. Let's now listen to what Deepak has to say."

I'm curious about what she means. This is only the sixth meditation in the series, not the last.

Then Deepak's beautiful, soothing voice speaks to me. He begins the same way, "Congratulations for making it this far. Your dedication is appreciated."

Something is different about this meditation. They are confused with which meditation they are talking about. But I don't dwell...I just settle into my bed and allow myself to be carried away by his voice. I begin to drift off...part sleep...part meditation.

I hear the words: "We tend to hold people away at an arm's length because of their differences. These differences scare us. We may feel that by doing this we keep our own self safe. But holding others away makes them feel separate, isolated, afraid, lonely, and potentially victimized. This can cause a negative response. This is the reason of many internal and external wars."

I visualize myself holding my arms straight forward, palms pushing another away from me.

I did this motion with Bob, when I tried to keep him away from me.

"With a slight turn of the arm, we go from holding them back, to embracing and welcoming them in. When we do this, we invite them into our family," Deepak's voice reaches deep into my spirit.

I did this with Bob too.

I shudder at the memory, but I am so deep into the meditative trance that the thought doesn't take root. It drifts off and away.

His sage advice continues, "When you come upon a homeless man, you do not need to fear him. Nor do you need to physically embrace him. Instead, energetically send him a message. Invite him into your spiritual family. His spirit will accept the invitation. He will no longer feel invisible and alone and forgotten. I promise you, he will forever be altered and changed."

Did he just mention a homeless man?

This doesn't seem like a generic meditation. This voice doesn't seem like Deepak's. This recording seems to be speaking directly to me.

Being in a meditative, trance-like state is bliss because I can observe my mind making these comparisons but the thoughts don't stay. I don't dwell. Instead, I'm fully and completely aware of my relaxed state, the thoughts drifting in and out and away. My mind goes into a deeper mode of shut down.

Although I'm relaxed, with my mind shut off, I observe a change happening within me. My heart races. A surge of energy fills up my insides, building and swirling within me. This sensation is not new… I've felt it before…during the ritual with Bob.

This energy…this sensation…is Divine love. It's back. It's beautiful. It's consuming me.

Why?

Once I shared this energy with Bob. Am I being asked to share this energy again?

If so…with whom?

Then, I understand. I understand what this meditation, what this trusted voice is trying to tell me. I AM meant to take this Divine love and share it, spread it and sow it into the hearts of others.

Last time, I called Bob's spirit to me.

This time, I'm to go to *them.*

As soon as I realize this, my spirit leaves my body. Dreaming or not, I don't know and don't question it when I find myself floating above my bed. I think of my family and instantly can see them sleeping below me. I switch my awareness to the neighborhood, and am flying over the cul-de-sac. Hovering over my city, my state and then over the American continent...I feel one with the stars, with the Universe, with God.

Energetically, I seek out the darkest corners—corners where the saddest, the loneliest and the most isolated people are hiding. I take this energy, this Divine love that has been building up inside of me and send it out...send it out as an energetic blanket of love and support, wrapping around each lost individual.

Then, like the meditation suggests, I open my arms and invite them in for an energetic embrace, my higher-spirit communicating with theirs. I invite every one of these forgotten and frightened souls into the oneness of this Divine and Universal hug—into the spiritual family. I tell them that they are part of my family, this family...we are all one with it—they no longer need to feel so isolated. They are not forgotten. They are loved.

I fly over other parts of the world, over war-torn continents. I repeat the ritual by directing this energy toward both the violent and victimized. Every angry, bitter, resentful soul is wrapped in this energetic blanket of peace. No matter their faith or lack thereof, their negative thoughts or fears, their crimes or destructions they have caused—I hold them—hold them until they calm—hold them until they can recognize this Divine and Universal love.

I'm not afraid of their darkness, of their hate, of their fear, of their anger or of their pain and suffering. There is no psychic attachment, no exchange of personal energy. There is only love. Love fills my energy field; it grows and expands. The more I give and share, the more I seem to have. I'm overflowing. There is more than enough room for all souls in this Divine energetic embrace.

The Divine, Universal Source, is working through me to embrace all humankind...all life...all beliefs and systems. I feel as big as this planet, as if I am one with God.

Perhaps I am.

I find myself floating back above my bed and then into my body. Sleep overcomes me. A couple hours later, I wake up, still filled with this expansive sensation of what I experienced.

It is a fabulous hangover.

What was *that?*

What did I experience?

I listen to the sixth meditation again. But what plays isn't the same one I heard last night. I play the fifth and then the newly released seventh meditation—but neither is it. I'm confused. I know I heard a prerecorded meditation, but it doesn't seem to exist.

What did I listen to? What guided me on that spectacular and magical journey? Was it a message? And why...every time...when I experience a profound spiritual moment, is it Deepak Chopra's words and/or voice that guide me?

Was this a Divine intervention?

Yesterday, a "full circle" moment showed me how far my healing has come. Last night, my healing expanded and raised my awareness to an entirely new level. My ritual with Bob, meant to heal me, the individual... potentially healed both of us. But this ritual last night has shown me that I can take this healing, utilizing the power of Divine love and heal a planet. It is and is meant to be larger than the individual, yet the individual is needed...the people are needed...needed to be used as a conduit for God's love to reach those in pain and suffering and those wanting to cause the pain.

If our planet is to heal...God needs our help. I will be of service, be that conduit, offer that help, offer that healing, work in partnership with the Divine.

I know now that my whole life—all the good, bad, ugly and beautiful—everything...has been preparing me for this understanding.

Everything.

This is my awakening.

This is where the evolution of my spirit has taken me.

This is the power of Divine love.

Just as it healed me...so it will heal the world.

Out of exclusion—into inclusion.

Out of difference—into oneness.

Out of separation—into unity.

This is my life's purpose.

This is the reason.

This is the intention.
This.
I know now.

I Know Now

Today I AM a mother, a wife, a daughter, a sister, an aunt, a friend, and now a writer and perhaps a spiritual healer and teacher. I have lived longer with the memory of the attack than without it. It is a part of who I am, but doesn't need to define who I am becoming. Yet, I cannot deny the impact and the power and the wisdom that came, and comes with it. The trauma and everything that followed are just parts of my recipe, additional ingredients that add to the depth and flavor of my essence, my life.

What intrigues me about this process...is that despite Bob never having been caught.... Or with so many questions still unanswered...I could heal. I can move throughout my life and into my future despite, or perhaps, in spite of having no traditional form of closure. I know now that closure isn't necessary.

As I complete this story, the 54-year-old Cinda of today can feel the bravery and stoicism of the 19-year-old Cinda. At such a young age, she is jolted into a nightmare that becomes her daily reality...a reality that she doesn't deserve, isn't prepared for and refuses to face. But she faces it anyway—head on. Despite her denial or lack of knowledge of the signs, they are there—preparing, supporting and protecting her. It has been an honor to tell her story, to finally give voice to her truth.

I have a huge amount of empathy for the 34-year-old Cinda. I can feel her agony and suffering as she fights to ignore the past, until it almost destroys her. When she throws that fiery ball of Divine love into Bob's heart, she, the white queen, wins the game and match. I am grateful that she finds her way back...back to sanity, back to her family, back to herself...back to me. I am forever grateful for the Divine ritual of love that guided her to be healed.

I'm awed by my younger selves and how each chooses to survive, each doing the best she can. I now honor all aspects of myself, my inner spirit, and the sacred relationship I have with the Divine. My spirit is in constant evolution.

I choose to evolve rather than die.

I know now that there is hope after violence...that can lead to victory. There is healing after trauma...that can lead to truth. It is an ongoing process. I am not alone on the journey. The signs keep coming and coming, and with them my faith and my intuition grow stronger. I know now the beauty in this Divine and higher power, which has been and always will be there, leading and guiding me.

I'm ready to move forward, ready to share, ready to live my life fully and completely. I'm ready to hold space for the energy of compassion that has led me to this beautiful place called peace—experienced as grace—felt as hope.

I'm hopeful that by sharing my story, my process, my journey, others who read my words may find their way to this vital inner peace as well.

For inner peace *is* possible, no matter the violence or the trauma or the grief that we bear.

There is always a way back to grace. Always...it comes through Divine love

Always.

The question remains: *If I knew then, what I know now, would I have done things differently?*

The answer is: *NO.*

I look at the current-day Cinda through an ever-widening lens. I'm excited by the Cinda I've become and the Cinda I've yet to meet. I know now that I will use my words to continue my work with Source. I'll help others awaken and evolve into their own relationship with this mighty, loving Divine force. All signs and the messages tell me this is so.

This is my purpose.

This is my destiny.

This is my truth.

I know now.

I can't help but wonder…when I'm 74, where will this journey have taken me?

What will the signs show me?

Where will the Divine lead me?

If I could only know now—what I will know then….

ACKNOWLEDGEMENTS

Writing this book, telling my story, traveling back into my past and bringing it forward to now…has been an incredible journey of self-discovery. The healing—*sometimes painful, most certainly heart-wrenching and opening, often exhilarating*—that came from this process was unexpected and took me by surprise. I will forever be grateful to that voice that woke me up and directed me onto this path of seeking out the signs through sacred insights. Saying YES! to this calling has changed me, changed my life…and the journey has just begun…*the story and the healing continue….*

There are many people I need to thank for making this book possible:

Kelli Lair at new72media/publishing. Knowing that my story, once finished, had a place to land and arms to fall into for safekeeping, made the journey far easier. I can't wait to see where we go together next. I love you, my soul friend.

Mary L. Holden, my editor, my friend; your dedication to your craft and to the 'word' made the edits painless. Your patience and belief in me and this story gave me the needed confidence to keep plodding along. More than just edits, it was your genuine tears and heartfelt counseling that guided me along this delicate, long and rough road. Thank you for your emotional and professional support. I've learned so much.

Mavis Nickels, my beloved friend through lifetimes, if it weren't for you…for your commitment, patience, love of me and belief in the purpose of this book…there wouldn't be one. I could not have done this without you. You held me accountable to my truth when I didn't want to remember. Then you held my hand—*and my heart*—as I dove into the darkness and pulled out treasure after treasure. The most valuable treasure I found…storytelling, story writing, story rewriting *and rewriting* with you. May we continue to share this treasure for years to come.

My beta readers, all dear friends, for your valuable input and support. If you didn't notice, all your suggestions are in here. To Shannon McElroy for your 'fresh eyes' perspective—thank you for catching the little stuff so my story reads bigger and better.

My family Scott, Eric and Ryan, I love you. Thank you for your patience and understanding as the last two years consumed my attention and my time. Scott, for your compassion, love and respect you've shown and continue to show me throughout our life together.

My extended family, related or not, alive today or not, I am so grateful: Linda Patterson, Kenneth Stevens, Bill and Frances Palmer, Nancy Palmer, Karen Lonsway, Sydney James, Margot James, Traci Page, Tom Nelson and to all who knew me when......

The archangels and guardian angels for never giving up on me.

To Bob...whoever you are and wherever you went...*may God bless you.*

ABOUT THE AUTHOR

Cinda Stevens Lonsway writes magazine articles, children's stories, novels, and nonfiction. Her blog is titled "Cinda's ROAR!" and is found on her website, www.CindaStevensLonsway.com. She is a spiritual advisor, workshop facilitator and speaker. Cinda is also a cofounder of new72media. Owner of a Golden Retriever and high maintenance cat, Cinda is devoted to Family, Nature, Spirit, Angels and Life. She lives in Portland, Oregon with her husband, and treasures visits with their two adult sons.

CPSIA information can be obtained
at www.ICGtesting.com
Printed in the USA
FFOW03n1749161117
43572816-42355FF